MODERN LEGAL STUDIES

PRODUCT LIABILITY

by

ALISTAIR M. CLARK LL.B., Ph.D.

Lecturer in Law, University of Strathclyde

LONDON
SWEET & MAXWELL
1989

Published in 1989 by
Sweet & Maxwell Limited of
South Quay Plaza, 183 Marsh Wall, London E14 9FT
Laserset by P.B. Computer Typesetting,
Pickering, N. Yorks.
Printed in Scotland
Reprinted 1990

British Library Cataloguing in Publication Data

Clark, Alistair M.
Product liability. — (Modern legal studies)
1. England. Products. Defects. Liability of
manufacturers & retailers. Law
I. Title   II. Series
344.2063'82

ISBN 0–421–38880–3

for
Jackie, Hannah and Alistair

PREFACE

This book comprises an attempt to analyse the central features of the new scheme of strict liability for loss caused by product defects which was introduced by Part 1 of the Consumer Protection Act 1987. The matters to be examined are: the meaning of "defect"; the meaning of "product" and the chain of liability; the role of warnings; recoverable and non-recoverable loss; the development risks defence; other defences and prescription and limitation. Other matters such as conflict of laws and criminal liability, are excluded from this discussion. The aim of the work is to assess the impact of the new rules both against the background of the various proposals for reform which had been mooted and in the light of the considerable American experience of product liability law.

Following upon an introduction to the new regime, each of the above elements will be analysed. There will be some consideration of the pre-existing legal position, and a discussion of the leading proposals for change. This is then followed by an examination of the appropriate provisions in the new legislation and then by an analysis of the American experience. Where necessary, this structure is not adhered to with excessive rigidity. Policy considerations affecting the working of the new rules are ventilated.

I wish to record my gratitude to Professor J. M. Thomson, who read the whole manuscript in draft, and offered many helpful suggestions, and to Mr. E. S. Young and Mr. W. J. Stewart, each of whom read and commented upon some of the work. My thanks are also due to the secretaries in the Law School at Strathclyde for assistance with the typing. Finally, I wish to thank my wife, son and daughter for their tolerance and support.

Alistair Clark
October 1988

CONTENTS

OTHER BOOKS IN THE SERIES

TABLE OF CASES

TABLE OF STATUTES

EEC DIRECTIVES

Chapter 1

INTRODUCTION TO THE NEW REGIME

After a lengthy and at times difficult gestation period, the debate on liability for defective products finally resulted in legislation on product liability in the form of Part I of the Consumer Protection Act 1987. Of the four major contributions to the debate made during the 1970s—the Strasbourg Convention[1]; the Report of the Scottish and English Law Commissions[2]; the Report of the Pearson Commission[3]; and the EEC Product Liability Directive[4]—the last achieved primacy. Adopted in July 1985, it required Member States to implement its provisions within three years. The idea behind the Directive, and the resulting legislation, is straightforward enough: to provide a system of strict liability, rather than liability based on fault, for certain types of harm caused by defective products. The new measure came into force on March 1, 1988, and will apply to products supplied from that date.

This chapter will provide a brief and general introduction to the new rules, prefaced by an examination of the history of this area of the law. It will also be convenient to set the new regime against the background of the pre-existing legal position, the major proposals for reform of product liability law, and, in general terms, the experience of product liability in the United States.

At the outset it must be stated that the description here offered is brief and in places rather rudimentary, the details being discussed more fully later, where appropriate to do so.

HISTORICAL INTRODUCTION

The pre-Donoghue position

It may be thought that product liability is purely a modern phenomenon, born in the heat of an industrial revolution which

---

[1] European Convention on Products Liability in Regard to Personal Injury and Death (DIR/Jur. (76)5).
[2] Cmnd. 6831 (1977).
[3] Cmnd. 7054 (1978).
[4] Later to become Council Directive of July 25, 1985 (85/374/EEC).

resulted in mass manufacture becoming common. While the subject has experienced rapid growth in comparatively modern times, its roots can be traced to Justinian's Digest.[5]

These roots possessed the key characteristics of the modern law: an imposition of liability upon those who supply products in the course of a business; and, a public policy basis, including the encouragement of higher standards of work. As far back as 1266 there was legislation in England imposing criminal liability for the supply of "corrupt" food.[6] However, failure to match the prevailing standards seems also to have grounded a civil remedy.[7] Although this remedy was initially exigible independently of contract against those who followed a common calling,[8] the barrier of privity of contract soon intervened to result in the supplier of goods having no liability to non-purchasers. From the nineteenth century, serious attacks on "the citadel of privity"[9] began to be mounted. In the early stages, as a precursor to recognition of a broad fault-based liability for loss caused by defects in products, English law created a distinction between goods which were inherently dangerous and those not so dangerous.

The beginnings of attempts by counsel to create this dichotomy, as a means of finding an exception from the general rule of non-liability, can be traced at least as far as *Dixon* v. *Bell*[10] where the owner of a loaded gun, who had sent a young servant to fetch the weapon, was liable for the injuries caused to the son of the plaintiff when she discharged the gun. However, no separate class of dangerous goods was introduced by the decision. Rather, Lord Ellenborough identified the weapon as having by lack of care been left in a state capable of doing mischief.[11] Thus, the case was taken to authorise the more limited proposition that liability would be imposed upon someone who carelessly permitted a dangerous article to fall into the hands of one who could not be entrusted with safe use of the article.

---

[5] See Tebbens, *International Product Liability, Sijthoff & Noordhoff, The Netherlands* (1980), pp. 2–3.

[6] Prosser, *The Assault upon the Citadel (Strict Liability to the Consumer)* 69 Yale L.J. (1960), 1099 at 1103.

[7] *Ibid.*

[8] Winfield, "The History of Negligence in the Law of Torts" (1926) 42 L.Q.R. 184.

[9] Prosser, *op. cit.*

[10] (1816) 5 M. & S. 198.

[11] *Ibid.* at 199.

The distinction again was rejected in a later case, *Langridge* v. *Levy*[12] where a defective gun had blown up in the hand of the plaintiff. Recovery in this case was permitted, but not on the basis that the gun was within a class of products dangerous in themselves. It seems that the court found there to have been conduct tantamount to fraud on the part of the defendant in stating the gun to have been safe in the knowledge that it was not. In addition, the requisite privity may have been established in that the immediate purchaser—the father of the plaintiff—could, it was thought by the court, effectively be treated as the plaintiff's agent. However, the court refused to recognise the category of inherently dangerous articles, for fear of creating potentially widespread liability. This case again authorises a limited exception—knowingly selling a dangerous item without warning the user.

These cases were swiftly followed by what has become famous as the classic exposition of the non-liability rule: *Winterbottom* v. *Wright*.[13] There, the plaintiff was injured and rendered lame when a coach broke down due to latent defects in its construction. The defendant, who was not the manufacturer of the coach, had contracted with the postmaster-general to provide the coach for the carriage of mail. A third party undertook to provide horses for the route to be travelled. The plaintiff was hired by this other party as driver of the coach. Rejecting the claim of the plaintiff, the court reasoned that the duty of the defendant, to keep the coach in good condition, was a contractual duty owed to the other contracting party—the postmaster-general—and not to the driver of the vehicle. In the words of Lord Abinger, if liability were to extend this far:

> "the most absurd and outrageous consequences, to which I can see no limit, would ensue."[14]

The decision in *Winterbottom* has been criticised as failing to properly examine the question of the existence of a duty of care.[15] However, in *Longmeid* v. *Holliday*[16] where the plaintiff was injured by a defective lamp, it was said of the circumstances in which persons not in privity might recover that:

---

[12] (1837) 2 M. & W. 519, affirmed (1838) 4 M. & W. 337.
[13] (1842) 10 M. & W. 109.
[14] *Ibid.* at 114.
[15] See dicta of Brett M.R. (as he then was; later Lord Esher) in *Heaven* v. *Pender* [1883] 11 Q.B.D. 503 at 510.
[16] (1851) 6 Ex. 761.

"And it may be the same when one delivers to another without notice an instrument by its nature dangerous, or under particular circumstances, as a loaded gun which he himself loaded, and that other person to whom it is delivered is injured thereby, or if he places it in a situation easily accessible to a third person, who sustains damage from it. A very strong case to that effect is *Dixon* v. *Bell*. But it would be going much too far to say that so much care is required in the ordinary intercourse of life between one individual and another, that, if a machine not in its nature dangerous—a carriage for instance—but which might become so by a latent defect entirely unknown, although discoverable by the exercise of ordinary care, should be lent or given by one person, even by the person who manufactured it, to another, the former should be answerable to the latter for a subsequent damage accruing by the use of it."[17]

Longmeid was taken along with dicta in other cases[18] to vouch the rule that liability will exist where things dangerous in themselves are supplied without warning of their true character, although on the facts, the lamp was not of this nature. However, in *George* v. *Skivington*,[19] a chemist who made up a hair shampoo was liable for injuries caused by the preparation to the wife of the buyer. No attempt was made to fit the hair wash into a category of inherently dangerous goods. The decision was much criticised, and was described in 1929 in a leading article on manufacturer's liability[20] as:

"if not overruled, at least discredited by constant adverse criticism."

By the time of *Heaven* v. *Pender*, in 1883[21] further recognition of a limited duty in respect of dangerous goods was apparent. The defendant dock owner, who had supplied staging and ropes, was held liable for injury caused to an employee (a ship painter) of a master painter who had contracted with the shipowner. The employee was injured when defective ropes, bearing the staging, snapped. The majority based their finding

---

[17] *Ibid. per* Parke B. at 767.
[18] See Bohlen, "Liability of Manufacturers to Persons Other Than Their Immediate Vendees" (1929) 45 L.Q.R. 343.
[19] (1869) L.R. 5 Exch. 1.
[20] Bohlen, *op. cit.* at 344.
[21] [1883] 11 Q.B.D. 503.

on the rather narrow ground that the defendant effectively had invited the painter to use the premises and appliances, whose dangerousness was a matter within the control of the dock owner. Of more enduring interest, however, is the much wider basis for liability posited by Brett M.R. (later Lord Esher). Identifying two different sets of circumstances in which earlier cases had found a duty of care to exist, Brett M.R., in an interesting piece of inductive reasoning, sought to state the wider principle which embraced both propositions:

> "Whenever one person supplies goods or machinery, or the like for the purpose of their being used by another person under such circumstances that everyone of ordinary sense would, if he thought, recognize at once that unless he used ordinary care and skill with regard to the condition of the thing supplied or the mode of supplying it, there will be a danger of injury to the person or property of him for whose use the thing is supplied, and who is to use it, a duty arises to use ordinary care and skill as to the condition or manner of supplying such thing."[22]

Brett M.R.'s view was, however, overly modern in its recognition of a duty of care to users or consumers. Accordingly, the pre-*Donoghue* state of the law could be summed up as involving a general principle, put thus by Lord Sumner in *Blacker* v. *Lake & Elliot*[23]:

> "The breach of the defendant's contract with A to use care and skill in and about the manufacture or repair of an article does not of itself give any cause of action to B when he is injured by reason of the article proving to be defective."

To this general rule of no liability, there were admitted two exceptions:

    (a) liability arising from articles dangerous in themselves; and

    (b) liability where the article is not in itself dangerous but is in fact dangerous, by reason of some defect or for any other reason, and this is known to the manufacturer.

This traditional approach was adopted by Lord Buckmaster, who delivered the leading dissent in *Donoghue* v. *Stevenson*.[24]

[22] *Ibid.* at 510.
[23] (1912) 106 L.T. 533.
[24] [1932] A.C. 562.

His Lordship was scathing both as to the decision in *George* v. *Skivington*, and as to the dicta of Brett M.R. in *Heaven* v. *Pender*:

> "So far, therefore, as the case of *George* v. *Skivington* (*supra*) and the dicta in *Heaven* v. *Pender* (*supra*) are concerned, it is, in my opinion, better that they should be buried so securely that their perturbed spirits shall no longer vex the law."[25]

However, in the leading speech of the majority, Lord Atkin was much influenced by the dicta in *Heaven* v. *Pender*, although he accepted that without the qualification that there must be sufficient proximity between the parties the dictum was too wide in its ambit. The decision in *George* v. *Skivington* was expressly approved, and the category of goods variously described as "inherently," "imminently" or "eminently" dangerous was characterised as unhelpful.

In Scots law, there was no clear recognition of a category of things dangerous in themselves, at least until a decision of the Second Division just three years prior to *Donoghue: Mullen* v. *Barr & Co.*[26] In this case, "indistinguishable from [*Donoghue* v. *Stevenson*] except that a mouse is not a snail"[27] an action of damages was brought on behalf of two children who had been injured as a result of consuming a bottle of ginger beer which contained the decaying remains of a mouse. The defenders were exculpated, and on the basis of a number of English authorities, including the cases discussed above, it was held that no duty was owed to the consumers of the ginger beer since the defenders neither knew that the contents of the bottle were dangerous, nor were they dealers in articles dangerous *per se*.

Lord Anderson, under reference to the words of Lord Abinger in *Winterbottom*, quoted above, said that,

> "...in a case like the present, where the goods of the defenders are widely distributed throughout Scotland, it would seem little short of outrageous to make them responsible to members of the public for the condition of the contents of every bottle which issues from their works. It is obvious that, if such responsibility attached to the defenders, they might be called on to meet claims of

---

[25] *Ibid.* at 576.
[26] 1929 S.C. 461.
[27] *Per* Lord Buckmaster in *Donoghue* v. *Stevenson* [1932] A.C. 562 at 578.

damages which they could not possibly investigate or answer."[28]

This "floodgates" fear much impressed Lord Buckmaster, who, in his dissent in *Donoghue*, stated:

"In agreeing, as I do, with the judgment of Lord Anderson, I desire to add that I find it hard to dissent from the emphatic nature of the language with which his judgment is clothed."[29]

At all events, any distinction as to existence of a duty of care as between inherently dangerous goods and other goods, ought not to have survived *Donoghue* v. *Stevenson*. There, Lord Atkin said:

"I regard the distinction as an unnatural one so far as it is used to serve as a logical differentiation by which to distinguish the existence or non-existence or a legal right."[30]

His Lordship agreed with the view of Scrutton L.J. in *Hodge & Sons* v. *Anglo-American Oil Co.*[31]:

"Personally, I do not understand the difference between a thing dangerous in itself, as poison, and a thing not dangerous as a class, but by negligent construction dangerous as a particular thing. The latter, if anything, seems the more dangerous of the two; it is a wolf in sheep's clothing instead of an obvious wolf."

Having enunciated his famous neighbourhood principle, Lord Atkin went on to find comfort in the knowledge that American law had reached a similar conclusion:

"It is always a satisfaction to an English lawyer to be able to test his application of fundamental principles of the common law by the development of the same doctrines by the lawyers of the courts of the United States. In that country I find that the law appears to be well established in the sense in which I have indicated. The snail had emerged from the ginger beer bottle in the United States before it appeared in Scotland, but there it brought a liability upon the manufacturer. I must not in this long judgment do more than refer to the illuminating judgment of Cardozo J. in

---

[28] 1929 S.C. 461 at 479.
[29] [1932] A.C. 562 at 578.
[30] *Ibid.* at 595.
[31] (1922) 12 Ll.L.Rep. 183.

MacPherson v. *Buick Motor Co.* in the New York Court of
Appeals, in which he states the principles of the law as I
should desire to state them. . . . "[32]

In this way, the law reached its broad proposition of a duty of
care being incumbent upon the manufacturer of products, and
the ideas of Lord Buckmaster and Lord Anderson gave way to
the new order ushered in by Lord Atkin and presaged, albeit in
rather wide terms, by Brett M.R. 50 or so years earlier.

The post-Donoghue position

The immediate choice open to a plaintiff claiming in respect
of loss caused by a defective product thus became whether to
found the claim in contract or in tort. Clearly, the former is
more attractive than the latter, in that questions of fault are, in
the former, irrelevant. But, for contractual liability to arise, the
victim will have to be a party to the contract.

If the claim is founded in contract then the seller will be liable
if the buyer can establish breach of one or other of the implied
terms of sections 12 to 15 of the Sale of Goods Act 1979. It is of
course possible that a contract claim will fall outside the Act
(for example where the seller does not sell in the course of a
business) and here the common law criterion will usually be
applied, but the vast majority of product liability cases, in
contract, fall within the 1979 Act. In the context of product
liability, claims for damages will commonly be based on section
14, and will often cover loss or damage other than to the
product itself, for example to the person of the plaintiff. The
measure of damage in such cases is that prescribed by section
53(2) and section 54 of the 1979 Act—the estimated loss directly
and naturally resulting in the ordinary course of events, from
the breach, including any special damages. Thus in *Grant* v.
Australian Knitting Mills Ltd.,[33] the buyer of woollen undergar-
ments who contracted dermatitis as a result of the presence of
an excess of free sulphites in the underwear, was able to recover
damages from the retailer, for breach of section 14 of the Act.

It has long been recognised that this liability in contract is
strict and consequently that proof of having taken reasonable
care will not afford protection to the seller. So, for example, in
Frost v. *Aylesbury Dairy Co.*,[34] damages were awarded to the

---

[32] [1932] A.C. 562 at 598.
[33] [1936] A.C. 85, P.C.
[34] [1905] 1 K.B. 608.

husband of a woman who died as a result of contracting typhoid fever from germs present in milk which she had purchased. It was no defence that the presence of the germs could not have been detected by the exercise of all due care. Dicta in more recent English cases reinforce this point: in *Henry Kendall and Sons* v. *William Lillico and Sons Ltd.*,[35] Lord Reid stated that section 14 covers defects

> "which are latent in the sense that even the utmost skill and judgment on the part of the seller would not have detected them";

In *Ashington Piggeries Ltd.* v. *Christopher Hill Ltd.*[36] liability was imposed, under section 14, for loss caused by the poisonous effect of herring meal on mink, despite the fact that:

> "in the then state of knowledge, scientific and commercial, no deliberate exercise of human skill or judgment could have prevented the meal from having its toxic effect on mink."

As is shown by cases such as *Vacwell Engineering Ltd.* v. *B.D.H. Chemicals Ltd.*,[37] the presence or absence of an adequate warning may be relevant to the question of merchantability or fitness for purpose. In that case, glass ampoules containing a chemical which combined explosively with water were unfit for their purpose when bearing a warning only of "harmful vapour."

There is, however, one major limitation on the availability of a contractual remedy—the principle that only the parties to the contract can acquire rights and duties under it. Thus, the buyer can sue the retailer but not the manufacturer. Further, a party other than the buyer (*e.g.* a donee) who suffers loss has no action in the absence of a collateral contract.

If a product liability claim is founded in tort then the injured party, to succeed, must prove negligence on the part of the manufacturer, retailer or other person responsible. In rudimentary terms, the plaintiff must establish that the defendant owed him a duty of care, was in breach of that duty, and that the breach caused the harm complained of.

Since *Donoghue* v. *Stevenson*[38] there has, of course, been no doubt about the existence of a duty of care in the situation

---

[35] [1969] 2 A.C. 31 at 84, H.L.
[36] [1972] A.C. 441 at 498, H.L.
[37] [1971] 1 Q.B. 88.
[38] Above, n. 24.

where goods are supplied by a manufacturer to a consumer. However, establishing breach of duty and causation can be rather difficult, since access to production processes and scientific expertise is often required. But it is not always necessary for the plaintiff to pinpoint a specific act of negligence, and fault can be inferred in respect of a defect in a product. Thus, in *Lockhart* v. *Barr*[39] the presence of phenol in a bottle of aerated water was sufficient to justify an inference of negligence on the part of the manufacturer. The presence of a manufacturing defect, as in the above cases, commonly gives rise to a presumption of negligence on the part of the producer, and in some cases the application of the maxim *res ipsa loquitur* can assist the plaintiff.[40] However, in many other instances proof of causation will be extremely difficult, for example, where it is argued that cigarettes have caused lung cancer, or that asbestos-related illness was caused by exposure to that substance, or that a vaccine has caused brain damage.[41]

Defences available in tort actions generally apply to product liability claims based on negligence. In all such cases proof of having taken due care will exculpate the defendant, marking a major distinction between claims arising *ex contractu* and those arising in tort. Satisfaction of the requirement to take due care depends upon a number of factors including the presence or absence of adequate warnings. Thus in *Vacwell Co. Ltd.* v. *B.D.H. Chemicals Ltd.*,[42] mentioned above, the words "harmful vapour" on glass ampoules containing boron tribromide did not give adequate warning of the explosive properties of the chemical on contact with water, and the manufacturers were held liable, in tort as well as in contract, for the extensive property damage and death of a visiting scientist, caused by an explosion.

Accordingly, if loss has been caused by a defective product bought by the injured party, liability is strict if visited upon the retailer, in contract. If someone other than the purchaser has suffered loss then negligence has to be proved, and the claim is normally against the manufacturer. This aspect of the contract/ tort dichotomy is quite arbitrary and can be capricious in operation.

---

[39] 1943 S.C.(H.L.) 1.
[40] See, *e.g. Grant* v. *Australian Knitting Mills Ltd.*, n. 33, above. This case was also of importance in showing that *Donoghue* v. *Stevenson* principles could extend beyond products intended for internal consumption.
[41] See, *e.g. Loveday* v. *Renton and The Wellcome Foundation, The Times*, March 31, 1988, C.A.
[42] Above, n. 37.

Proposals for reform

This capricious nature of the law on liability for defective products was illustrated by the Thalidomide tragedy, the victims of which had to rely on extra-legal payments of compensation. It was this disaster which proved to be the catalyst for the whole debate on product liability throughout Europe, causing a number of major inquiries into the subject to be mounted in the 1970s.

In November 1971 the Scottish and English Law Commissions were asked to investigate the law on liability for defective products. Then in 1972 the Prime Minister announced the setting up of the Royal Commission on Civil Liability and Compensation for Personal Injury, part of its brief being product liability. European institutions entered the debate in the same year, when the Hague Conference on Private International Law drafted a "Convention on the Law Applicable to Products Liability." Then, in 1976, the first EEC Draft Directive on product liability was presented by the European Commission to the Council of Ministers. After some 10 years of shuffling around the corridors of Brussels, the amended Directive[43] was adopted by the Council on July 25, 1985, and now forms the basis of the new product liability regime introduced by the Consumer Protection Act 1987. In January 1977, some months after the first draft of the Directive was promulgated, the Council of Europe adopted the Strasbourg Convention on Products Liability in Regard to Personal Injury and Death.

EEC Directive—a brief summary

The basis for liability under the Directive is given in Article 1:

"The producer shall be liable for damage caused by a defect in his product."

This strict liability is, however, subject to a number of defences including the centrally controversial "development risks" defence: Article 7(e) of the Directive states that a producer will not be liable if he proves that:

"the state of scientific and technical knowledge at the time when he put the product into circulation was not such as to enable the existence of the defect to be discovered."

[43] (85/374/EEC).

However, by Article 15, Member States are permitted to derogate from the Directive by excluding the development risks defence. None of the other proposals allowed this defence. The need for the presence of this defence is to be reviewed by the Council of Ministers in 1995.

Under the Directive, "product" means all moveables with the exception of primary agricultural products and game, although Member States have the option of not allowing this exception. Moveable property incorporated into another moveable or into immoveables is included.

"Producer" is defined as the producer of the finished product, the producer of any raw material or component, and any person who, by putting his name, trade mark or other distinguishing feature on the article represents himself as its producer. Importers into the EEC also figure in the chain of persons potentially liable. "Damage" includes damage to personal property, with a lower threshold of 500 ECU (European Currency Units), as well as personal injury. In this respect the Directive differs from the recommendations of the Law Commissions who felt that strict liability should not extend to property damage, and from those of the Pearson Commission, whose terms of reference were limited to personal injury and death.

Under the Directive, an article is defective when it does not provide for persons or property safety which a person is entitled to expect, taking into account all the circumstances including its presentation, the use to which it could reasonably be expected that the product would be put, and the time at which it was put into circulation. The intention of the latter part of the definition of "defective" is to take account of the age of the product rather than allow a defence based on the state-of-the-art at the time of manufacture.

A number of defences are provided, including: that the person proceeded against did not put the product into circulation; that the product was not defective when put into circulation; that the product was not manufactured for an "economic purpose" nor manufactured or distributed in the course of business; that the defect is due to compliance with mandatory regulations issued by the public authorities; in the case of component parts, that the defence is attributable to the design of the product in which the component has been fitted or to instructions given by the manufacturer of the product. It is also a partial or complete defence to show that the plaintiff's negligence contributed to his own loss.

The Directive contemplates a global limit on liability of at least 70 million European Units of Account (approximately £45m) but individual Member States may choose whether to include this provision. Actions have to be commenced within three years of the injured person becoming aware of the damage, the defect and the identity of the producer.

The Directive provides for a 10-year time limit on the producer's liability, commencing from the date when the product was put into circulation, as well as the three-year limitation period for the commencement of actions.

All of the proposals for reform listed above recommended a similar scheme of strict liability for defective products, but there were some important differences of detail. For example, the Scottish Law Commission favoured the cessation of liability of component manufacturers on the incorporation of their product into another, and also took the view that limitation periods should be left to national laws and that no cut-off period was desirable. Also, the Pearson Commission and the Law Commissions were against any ceiling being placed upon the amount of compensation payable in respect of personal injury or death. However, the central difference between the other proposals and the Directive is the latter's inclusion of the development risks defence.

UNITED STATES PRODUCT LIABILITY LAW

Application of common law principles of strict liability for defective products has been an important feature of American law for the past 30 or so years. However, the development of this branch of the law can be traced back to the decision in *Thomas* v. *Winchester*[44] in 1852. A poison, belladona, was falsely labelled by the seller as extract of dandelion. It was sold to a pharmacist, who in turn sold to a customer. On the basis that the defendant's negligence had put human life in imminent danger, liability was imposed; a mis-labelled poison created such danger, but a defective carriage, as in *Winterbottom*, above, did not. In *Loop* v. *Litchfield*[45] there was a defect in a small balance wheel used on a circular saw. This defect was pointed out to the buyer by the manufacturer. Five years later, the machine having been leased by its purchaser to another, the wheel broke. Holding that the manufacturer was not liable to the lessee, the

[44] 6 N.Y. 397 (1852).
[45] 42 N.Y. 351 (1870).

court excluded the wheel from the imminently dangerous
category. Three years later the New York court followed *Loop*
to find that a steam boiler which exploded was not in the
Thomas v. *Winchester* imminently dangerous category.[46] Then,
in 1882, in a decision which prefigured that in the English case
of *Heaven* v. *Pender*, above, it was held in *Devlin* v. *Smith*,[47]
that the constructor of a scaffold was liable for the death of a
painter who was killed when the scaffold gave way while he was
painting the dome of a court building. Having built the scaffold
for the use of the workmen, the contractor owed them a duty to
build it with care, irrespective of his contract with their master.
Then, in *Statler* v. *Ray Manufacturing Co.*[48] an exploding coffee
urn was held to be imminently dangerous if not carefully and
properly constructed.

The major landmark of the development of United States
product liability law is, however, the case of *MacPherson* v.
Buick Motor Co.,[49] where an

> "improvident Scot squandered his gold upon a Buick and so
> left his name forever imprinted on the law of products
> liability."[50]

One of the car's wheels was made of defective wood and the
plaintiff was injured when the spokes collapsed and he was
thrown out and injured. Approving the dicta of Brett M.R. in
Heaven v. *Pender*, referred to above, although accepting that it
may need some qualification, Cardozo J. stated:

> "We hold, then, that the principle of *Thomas* v. *Winchester*
> is not limited to poisons, explosives, and things of like
> nature, to things which in their normal operation are
> implements of destruction. If the nature of a thing is such
> that it is reasonably certain to place life and limb in peril
> when negligently made, it is then a thing of danger."[51]

Despite the refusal of some courts to accept the extension of the
law represented by *MacPherson*, the decision "swept the
country"[52] and paved the way for the freedom so eagerly
exploited by later courts in product liability cases.

[46] *Lossee* v. *Clute* 51 N.Y. 494 (1873).
[47] 89 N.Y. 470 (1882).
[48] 88 N.E. 1063 (1909).
[49] 217 N.Y. 382 (1916).
[50] Prosser, *op.cit.*, at 1100.
[51] 217 N.Y. 382, at 389.
[52] Prosser, *op.cit.*, at 1100.

The establishment in *MacPherson* of a broad negligence basis for liability for defective products soon gave way to the imposition of strict liability. At first this was restricted to food, but was quickly extended to other products. Writing in 1960, Dean Prosser noted seven recent cases as authority for the view

> "that the seller of any product who sells it in a condition dangerous for use is strictly liable to its ultimate user for injuries resulting from such use, although the seller has exercised all possible care, and the user has entered into no contractual relationship with him."[53]

Observing that the effect of these decisions was no longer to confine strict liability to articles for internal consumption, or to inherently dangerous products, the Dean went on:

> "Seven such cases, in so short a time, may very well be said to amount to a Trend. It would be rather easy to find fault with several of these decisions, which have displayed much more in the way of enthusiasm for the result to be reached than of accuracy in the citation of precedent. But taken in the aggregate, they give the definite impression that the dam has busted, and those in the path of the avalanche would do well to make for the hills."[54]

One of the key decisions, earlier than the cases referred to by the Dean, in the translation from negligence to strict liability was *Escola* v. *Coca Cola Bottling Co. of Fresno*,[55] although it is memorable less for its particular finding that *res ipsa loquitur* ought to be applied in a fairly liberal fashion in products cases, than for the modernity of the opinion of Traynor J. in his concurring judgment. Noting some decisions which based manufacturers' liability upon negligence, he stated:

> "Even if there is no negligence, however, public policy demands that responsibility be fixed wherever it will most effectively reduce the hazards of life and health inherent in defective products that reach the market. It is evident that the manufacturer can anticipate some hazards and guard against the recurrence of others, as the public cannot. Those who suffer injury from defective products are unprepared to meet its consequences.

---

[53] *Ibid.* at 1112.
[54] *Ibid.* at 1113.
[55] 24 Cal. 2d. 453, 150 P. 2d. 436 (1944).

The cost of injury and the loss of time or health may be an overwhelming misfortune to the person injured, and a needless one, for the risk of injury can be insured by the manufacturer and be distributed among the public as the cost of doing business. It is to the public interest to discourage the marketing of products having defects that are a menace to the public. If such products nevertheless find their way into the market it is to the public interest to place the responsibility for whatever injury they may cause upon the manufacturer, who, even if he is not negligent in the manufacture of the product, is responsible for its reaching the market. However intermittently such injuries may occur and however haphazardly they may strike, the risk of their occurrence is a constant risk and a general one. Against such a risk there should be a general and constant protection and the manufacturer is best situated to afford such protection."[56]

Policy considerations were equally influential to the Supreme Court of New Jersey in a further landmark decision, *Henningsen v. Bloomfield Motors Inc.*[57] Here, a man bought a car as a gift for his wife. Ten days after delivery a defect in the steering mechanism caused the car to veer into a wall. The husband recovered on the basis of implied warranty for his consequential losses, but of greater significance is that the court allowed the wife to recover, also in implied warranty, against the manufacturer and against the retailer:

"Thus, where commodities sold are such that if defectively manufactured they will be dangerous to life or limb, then society's interests can only be protected by eliminating the requirement of privity between the maker and his dealers and the reasonably expected ultimate consumer. In that way the burden of losses consequent upon use of defective articles is borne by those who are in a position to either control the danger or make an equitable distribution of the losses when they occur.... We see no rational doctrinal basis for differentiating between a fly in a bottle of beverage and a defective automobile. The unwholesome beverage may bring illness to one person, the defective car, with its great potentiality for harm to the driver, occupants

---

[56] *Ibid.*
[57] 32 N.J. 358, 161 A. 2d. 69 (1960).

and others, demands even less adherence to the narrow barrier of privity."[58]

Just three years later, in *Greenman* v. *Yuba Power Products Inc.*,[59] the final piece of the jigsaw of development from liability for inherently dangerous products to generalised strict tortious liability was put into place. Mrs. Greenman bought her husband a "Shopsmith," which was a combination power tool capable of being used as a saw, drill and wood lathe. Two years later, in 1957, a piece of wood flew out from the machine, while the plaintiff was working on it, striking him on the forehead. He sued both retailer and manufacturer, in each case asserting breach of warranty and negligence. At first instance, the court found the retailer not liable, but held that the manufacturer was liable. The manufacturer and the plaintiff appealed, the latter seeking reversal of the judgment in favour of the retailer, but only if the manufacturer's appeal was successful. Holding the manufacturer liable, Judge Traynor reinforced his dictum in *Escola*, above:

> "... [T]o impose strict liability on the manufacturer under the circumstances of this case, it was not necessary for plaintiff to establish an express warranty.... A manufacturer is strictly liable in tort when an article he places on the market, knowing that it is to be used without inspection for defects, proves to have a defect that causes injury to a human being. Recognized first in the case of unwholesome food products, such liability has now been extended to a variety of other products that create as great or greater hazards if defective.... Although in these cases strict liability has usually been based on the theory of an express or implied warranty running from the manufacturer to the plaintiff, the abandonment of the requirement of a contract between them, the recognition that the liability is not assumed by agreement but imposed by law..., and the refusal to permit the manufacturer to define the scope of its own responsibility for defective products...make clear that the liability is not one governed by the law of contract warranties but by the law of strict liability in tort...."[60]

Thus, the law has developed from a traditional negligence theory, on through a system based on express and implied

---

[58] *Ibid.* at 383 and 83.
[59] 59 Cal. 2d. 57, 27 Cal.Rptr. 697 (1963).
[60] *Ibid.* at 63 and 701.

warranties in contract, and finally to a regime of strict liability in tort. At present the three theories of liability co-exist, but most of the successful product liability actions are founded on strict tort, for obvious reasons. More recent cases which are of significance will be discussed at appropriate places in later chapters, although it ought to be observed that United States tort law is in a state of continuing development, with more than one quarter of states having enacted tort reform measures in the first half of 1988 alone.

As it currently stands, the negligence base of liability is broadly similar to that in the United Kingdom and needs no further treatment here. The use of express and implied warranties in contract is of course not new either, but in the United States it is marked by a radical departure from the basic contractual rule that only the parties to the contract can sue, and be sued, in the event of a breach. This departure is clearly illustrated in *Henningsen* v. *Bloomfield Motors Inc.*, above, where both the manufacturer and the retailer were held liable on the basis of an implied warranty of merchantability. There were, however, a number of complications associated with the express and implied warranty ground of liability, and the last 30 or so years have seen the development of strict liability in tort, founded on cases like *Greenman* v. *Yuba Power Products Inc.*, referred to above, and now codified in the Second Restatement of Torts of 1965.

The Second Restatement, not binding unless adopted by state courts or legislatures, but commonly adhered to, provides for liability where damage is caused by an "unreasonably dangerous" defective product:

> "s.402A. Special Liability of Seller of Product for Physical Harm to User or Consumer
> (1) One who sells any product in a defective condition unreasonably dangerous to the user or consumer or to his property is subject to liability for physical harm thereby caused to the ultimate user or consumer, or to his property, if
>> (a) the seller is engaged in the business of selling such a product, and
>> (b) it is expected and does reach the user or consumer without substantial change in the condition in which it is sold.
> (2) The rule stated in subsection (1) applies although
>> (a) the seller has exercised all possible care in the preparation and sale of his product, and

  (b) the user or consumer has not bought the product
      from or entered into any contractual relation with
      the seller."

Prior to comments a to q on the section, which contain quite
full discussion of its intended import, there appears the
following caveat:

  "The Institute expresses no opinion as to whether the rules
  stated in this section may not apply
      (1) to harm to persons other than users or consumers;
      (2) to the seller of a product expected to be processed
          or otherwise substantially changed before it
          reaches the user or consumer; or
      (3) to the seller of a component part of a product to
          be assembled."

The interpretation of section 402A by United States courts is
considered more fully at appropriate points in the forthcoming
discussion.

  Some of the cases in which damages have been awarded have
caused great alarm to manufacturers and their insurers but an
even more alarming feature of American product liability law
has been the magnitude of damages awarded. In the famous
"Pinto" case,[61] a passenger in a Ford Pinto car who suffered
burns to over 90 per cent. of his body when the car burst into
flames when rammed from the rear, was originally awarded
compensatory damages of $2,842,000 and punitive damages of
$125,000,000. This latter sum was later reduced, on appeal, to
$3,500,000. In product liability cases, American courts do not
baulk at awarding damages of one million dollars or more.

  Recent years have seen a crisis in American product liability.
Manufacturers have been faced with inflated insurance costs,
causing increased prices, and in some cases have been unable to
obtain liability insurance, thereby jeopardising the availability of
compensation to injured customers. One United States Senator,
Commerce Secretary Malcolm Baldrige, went as far as to say
that:

  "product liability problems are affecting both the nation's
  productivity and its ability to compete with exports."[62]

---

[61] *Grimshaw* v. *Ford Motor Co.* 119 Cal.App. 3d. 757 (1981).
[62] Quoted in *Foresight, International Journal of Insurance and Risk Management,*
September 1981.

Late in 1975 the United States government set up the Interagency Task Force on Product Liability, to investigate the causes of the crisis. Its findings, published in 1977, vindicate some, but not all, of the claims made about the effect of strict product liability.[63] More recently, the United States Tort Policy Working Group has urged legislative reform, recommending in particular, a return to a fault-based system of compensation for product liability. For some years Federal legislation has been proposed in an attempt to remedy the perceived excesses of the strict liability regime. Current drafts of the legislation would use negligence as the standard in design defect and failure to warn cases. However, one Bill, H.R. 1115, the first to pass the House of Representatives, would broadly adopt section 402A while making some concessions to the manufacturing lobby. In the light of the history of attempts at Federal reform, there remain major doubts as to whether this draft legislation will reach the statute book.

The problems encountered in the United States in its experience of strict product liability will be of some relevance to the operation of the new regime in this country. However, it must be pointed out that a number of features of the American legal system exacerbate these difficulties, and indeed, may collectively have been a more significant causal factor of the crisis than the substantive law. A broad indication of these features is all that need be given:

(1) American product liability cases are heard in front of juries, who decide on questions of fact and on the extent of any award of damages. Experience shows that juries tend to sympathise with the victim rather than producer, are unwilling to find the injured person contributorily negligent, and are prepared to make high awards of damages;

(2) American law allows for awards of punitive damages. In 1987, a Washington court awarded $95m damages to an eight-year-old boy who had suffered birth defects caused by an anti-nausea drug taken by his mother

---

[63] Interagency Task Force on Product Liability, US Dept. of Commerce, Final Report of the Legal Study, (1977). In response to the Task Force Report, the Commerce Dept. issued, in 1979, a Model Uniform Product Liability Act (MUPLA). A number of attempts to pass Federal legislation based upon MUPLA have been made. For a brief history of these attempts at Federal legislation, see Twerski, (A Moderate and Restrained Federal Product Liability Bill: Targeting the Crisis Areas for Resolution), 18 Univ. of Mich. J. of Law Ref. 575 (1985).

during pregnancy. $20 million of the award was compensatory, the rest punitive.[64]

(3) Attorneys in product liability claims often enter into contingency fee arrangements with clients, under which normally between 20 per cent. and 50 per cent. of any award of damages goes to the attorney. It has been argued that some attorneys may be prepared to file claims for inflated amounts, in the hope of increasing the seriousness of the case in the eyes of the jury, or potentially increasing their own rewards;

(4) Principles of product liability law have been developed in different ways in the various states. Some attempt to remedy this latter difficulty is presently being undertaken with the proposal for Federal Product Liability legislation, but the United States system has yet to address itself to the other factors.

PRODUCT LIABILITY—AN OVERVIEW OF THE NEW RULES

The general effect of Part I of the Consumer Protection Act 1987 is to establish a system of strict, rather than fault-based, liability in respect of loss caused by defective products. Existing tort and contract remedies remain available, but are now supplemented by a new conceptual structure which is intended to focus primarily on the condition of a product rather than upon the conduct of its producer. However, the spirit of the reasonable man has not been fully exorcised and, as we shall see, some of the language and concepts of negligence underlie and in some instances re-appear in the new rules.

Section 2, containing the central provisions on product liability, imposes liability for damage caused wholly or partly by a defect in a product upon the producer, importer or an "own-brander" (someone who has held himself out to be the producer) of the product.

The term "product" is widely defined in the legislation. Article 15 of the Directive permits a Member State to include primary agricultural products and game within the scope of the implementing legislation but the United Kingdom Government was persuaded against inclusion.

Primarily, liability is likely to be visited upon the producer. This will of course generally be the manufacturer but the

---

[64] See report in the "Financial Times" July 16, 1987. This is believed to be the second largest award for damages in the history of US product liability.

definition of producer also deals with raw materials in which case the person who "won or abstracted" the substance is the producer. Similarly, those who process products which have not been manufactured, won or abstracted (for example, agricultural produce) are producers. Certain "own branders" and importers (into the EEC) also incur liability. Those who simply package goods, without processing, are not producers, but such persons are not wholly outwith the scope of the Act since a supplier can be liable if he fails to identify the person who supplied the product to him.

The existence of a "defect" is the basis of liability under the Act. Under section 3, there is a defect in a product if the safety of the product is not such as persons generally are entitled to expect. "Safety" includes risk of damage to property. The section goes on to provide that all of the circumstances shall be taken into account including: the manner in which and purposes for which the product has been marketed, and the use of warnings or instructions; what might reasonably be expected to be done with or in relation to the product; and the time when the product was supplied by its producer to another. Defectiveness is not to be inferred solely from the fact that a product supplied after the product in question is more safe.

"Damage" is defined to mean death or personal injury or any loss of or damage to any property (including land). But this definition is subject to important qualifications: damage to the defective product itself, including damage caused by a component part, is not recoverable; furthermore, damage to property which is not of a type ordinarily intended for private use, occupation or consumption is outwith the ambit of the Act. Article 9 of the Directive excludes liability to compensate for damage to individual items of property worth less than 500 ECU and this is implemented by the Act, where the relevant figure is £275.

When damage is suffered which is not within the scope of the Act (for example, damage to commercial property and pure economic loss) recovery will continue to be governed by the preexisting rules.

Unlike Germany, Denmark and possibly the Republic of Ireland, our Government has decided against setting a financial limit upon the producer's total liability. Since such a limit would have had, at most, a marginal impact on the cost of insurance cover and could result in some victims either not obtaining compensation, or all victims receiving a sum less than their loss, the Government's decision is to be welcomed. The Law Commissions reached a similar conclusion.

If the producer successfully argues that an adequate warning was given, or that the plaintiff misused the product, or that at the time when the product was supplied it satisfied safety expectations, then, as indicated earlier, the product will not be defective. The producer may also adduce the plaintiff's contributory negligence in mitigation of damages. Moreover, section 4 of the Act lists a number of specific defences including the defence of "development risks," the inclusion of which was a condition of the United Kingdom's acceptance of the Directive.

Section 7 prohibits the limitation or exclusion of liability under the Act by any contract term, notice, or other provision.

By virtue of section 6(5) and Schedule 1, important amendments are made to law on prescription and limitation. In broad terms, there is for the purpose of liability under the Act a three-year limitation period for the commencement of actions running from the date on which the pursuer became aware, or should reasonably have been aware, of (i) the damage; and (ii) that it was caused by the defect; and (iii) the identity of the producer.

Further, the obligation to make reparation for damage caused wholly or partly by a defect in a product is extinguished after 10 years from the time when the product was supplied (as defined in section 4(2) of the 1987 Act). This does not however mean that all products must be expected to last for 10 years—for many products a significantly shorter life expectancy obtains and in such cases this fact will be of importance in determining whether the product is defective. Liability for defects occurring more than 10 years after supply must be addressed under the general law and fall outwith the Act.

CONCLUSION

A statute which creates a new conceptual structure in the law on liability for defective products, introducing strict rather than fault-based liability, is of potentially major importance. Exactly what difference it effects in the law of tort is a moot point, and many would argue that the trend in negligence law, with appropriate invocation of the doctrine of *res ipsa loquitur*, would have led to a similar end. However, much uncertainty shrouds the question of the impact of the new strict liability regime. For example, it is not clear whether efforts by insurance companies and by the Law Societies to raise the awareness of the public about potential legal remedies will actually result in greater claims-consciousness and therefore increased litigation. The result could be that the current figures which show that a large percentage of those suffering injury do not seek legal redress may change dramatically. A further uncertainly is that many product-related accidents involving injury occur at the workplace. Most of these will trigger liability under statutes such as the Factories Acts or the Employers' Liability (Defective Equipment) Act 1969, and it is not expected that injured employees will pursue the producer under the new Act.

However, the creation of a separate scheme of compensation for one type of loss, that caused by defective products, can only be justified if it results in a real improvement upon the protection afforded by the general law. The extent to which the new regime realises this aim will now be assessed.

Chapter 2

THE CONCEPTUAL BASIS OF PRODUCT LIABILITY

At the core of a product liability regime is the definition ascribed to the term "defective," since defectiveness is the basis of any claim. In keeping with its central importance, the problem of defining defectiveness has exercised the minds of legal scholars perhaps more than any other aspect of product liability law.[1]

The aim of this Chapter is to analyse the various theories which have been proposed regarding the proper interpretation of defectiveness, and to suggest a workable approach for the strict liability system in the United Kingdom. There will be some brief discussion of the pre-existing legal position and of the theoretical nature of the contract/tort dichotomy. Recommendations for a strict product liability scheme in this country will then be examined including the relevant provisions of the 1987 Act in the light of the considerable experience of American product liability law. Also, the fact that many theories on the meaning of defectiveness are expressed in terms of cost-benefit analysis will lead to a consideration of the ability of courts properly to make such an analysis, and hence reach rational decisions. The main alternative to a cost-benefit approach will then be considered.

DEFECTIVENESS—THE CONTRACT/TORT DICHOTOMY

It has become an axiom of jurisprudence that contract law

---

[1] See, *e.g.* Birnbaum, "Unmasking the Test for Design Defect,: From Negligence [to Warranty] to Strict Liability to Negligence" 33 Vand. L.Rev. 593 (1980); Clark, "Products Liability: Oklahoma's Defective Test Limitations" 39 Okla. L.Rev. 318 (1986); Keeton, "Manufacturers' Liability: The Meaning of Defect in the Manufacture and Design of Products" 20 Syracuse L.Rev. 559 (1969); Keeton, "Products Liability and the Meaning of Defect" 5 St. Mary's L.J. 30 (1973); Montgomery and Owen, "Reflections on the Theory and Administration of Strict Tort Liability for Defective Products" 27 S.C.L. Rev. 803 (1976); O'Connor, "Adding a Risk/Utility Analysis to the Consumer Expectation Test in Design Defect Cases" 28 Ariz. L.R. 459 (1986); Wade, "Strict Tort Liability of Manufacturers" 19 S.W.L.J. 5 (1965); Wade, "On the Nature of Strict Tort Liability for Products" 44 Miss. L.J. 825 (1973); Wade, "On Product 'Design Defects' and Their Actionability" 33 Vand. L.Rev. 551 (1980).

regulates obligations which have been voluntarily assumed, in contrast with the law of tort which is concerned with obligations imposed by law. A consequence is that contract law is about

> "giving effect to the private autonomy of contracting parties to make their own legal arrangements."[2]

Of fundamental importance are the terms of the agreement between the parties since in the event of any dispute these can be used as evidence of what the parties intended, and expected, from the bargain. If the agreement is breached the remedy of monetary damages will often be sought, and the level of the award will reflect the value of the frustrated expectations of the innocent party. This protection of the economic interests of contracting parties by allowing financial compensation for disappointed expectations or loss of bargain is the primary policy aim to the law of contracts. It has also been said to have a "deterrent or hortatory" function by providing incentives for parties to pay their debts and honour their promises.[3]

In tort disputes there is usually no agreement between the parties and hence no easy way of ascertaining the expectations of the injured party. Instead, tortious liability is imposed in accordance with societal standard of fairness and reasonableness. Traditionally, these standards have been determined by balancing the magnitude of the risk inherent in the conduct at issue against the societal benefits or utility of that conduct.

This balancing process is seldom explicitly recognised by courts, but it is implicit in the conceptual infrastructure of negligence. Some analyses of the theoretical basis of negligence have sought to identify the various factors which require to be balanced in the risk-benefit computation.[4]

A cost-benefit approach to negligence has not always merely been implicit, however, and in a number of cases a more structured approach is discernible. Thus, in *Morris* v. *West Hartlepool Steam Navigation Co.*[5] Lord Reid stated that it was the duty of an employer

> "in considering some precaution should be taken against a foreseeable risk, to weigh, on the one hand, the magnitude

---

[2] See Atiyah, "Contracts, Promises and the Law of Obligations" (1978) 94 L.Q.R. 193.

[3] *Ibid.* at 198.

[4] See, *e.g.* Atiyah, *Accidents, Compensation and the Law* (4th ed., 1987), Chap. 2; and text accompanying nn. 18–22, below.

[5] [1956] A.C. 552.

of the risk, the likelihood of an accident happening and the possible seriousness of the consequences if an accident does happen, and, on the other hand, the difficulty and expense and any other disadvantage of taking the precaution."[6]

Individual factors from Lord Reid's formula, such as the probability or likelihood of harm arising, have been decisive in certain cases, including *Bolton* v. *Stone*[7] where the chance of injury was so remote as to justify a lack of precautions. Conversely, in *Paris* v. *Stepney B.C.*[8] the magnitude of the harm which could occur proved decisive in establishing liability. On the other side of the balancing equation, there have been cases where the benefits of the product justified the risk,[9] and cases where the focus has been upon the practicability of taking precautions. Thus, for example, it is not negligent to fail to take precautions which were not feasible at the relevant time. A key question will often be the expense of taking precautions. There have been cases in which courts have held that certain precautions should have been taken despite their relative expensiveness.[10] On the other hand, a relatively expensive precaution will not be required where the risk of injury is small.[11]

It is tempting to deduce from this utilitarian balancing process that, in deciding tort disputes, courts not only decide upon the dispute before them, but also set standards for future conduct, since such decisions will have an impact on design choices by future manufacturers.

The historical distinctiveness between contract and tort is evidenced by the separate tests for defectiveness which they employ. In the product liability context, contractual remedies usually arise from breach of section 14 of the Sale of Goods Act 1979. The test here is whether or not the product was "of merchantable quality" or "fit for its purpose," both of which are interpreted in terms of consumer expectations, which can be ascertained from the terms of the bargain. In negligence, liability is predicated upon breach of a duty of care. The case is centred upon the conduct of the producer, rather than the

---

[6] At 574.
[7] [1951] A.C. 850. See also *Fardon* v. *Harcourt-Rivington* (1932) 146 L.T. 391.
[8] [1951] A.C. 367. See also *Wright* v. *Dunlop Rubber Co.* (1972) 14 K.I.R. 255.
[9] *Roe* v. *Minister of Health* [1954] 2 Q.B. 66.
[10] Examples include: *Latimer* v. *A.E.C.* [1953] A.C. 643; *Henderson* v. *Carron Co.* (1889) 16 R. 633.
[11] *Wyngrove's Executrix* v. *Scottish Omnibuses* 1966 S.C.(H.L.) 47.

condition of his product; societal interests, rather than consumers' expectations, are paramount.

The paradigm of contract law is therefore that the disappointed party can obtain damages for the difference between the actual value of the product and its value had it complied with reasonable expectations. Any compensation for injury caused by the product is in the form of consequential damages. In tort, on the other hand, foreseeable costs and benefits are weighed, and when benefits are outweighed liability will ensue. It is thus axiomatic that contract is about product merchantability or fitness whereas tort is about product safety.

"Defective" in a strict liability regime

The Consumer Protection Act 1987 implements the Directive's definition of defect in section 3:

> "3—(1) Subject to the following provisions of this section, there is a defect in a product for the purposes of this Part if the safety of the product is not such as persons generally are entitled to expect; and for those purposes "safety," in relation to a product, shall include safety with respect to products comprised in that product and safety in the context of risks of damage to property, as well as in the context of risks of death or personal injury.
>
> (2) In determining for the purposes of subsection (1) above what persons generally are entitled to expect in relation to a product all the circumstances shall be taken into account, including:
>
> (a) the manner in which, and purposes for which, the product has been marketed, its get-up, the use of any mark in relation to the product and any instructions for, or warnings with respect to, doing or refraining from doing anything with or in relation to the product;
>
> (b) what might reasonably be expected to be done with or in relation to the product; and
>
> (c) the time when the product was supplied by its producer to another; and nothing in this section shall require a defect to be inferred from the fact alone that the safety of a product which is supplied after that time is greater than the safety of the product in question."

At first sight, it could be concluded that since the crux of the definition is the "consumer expectation test," the strict tortious liability notion of defectiveness has become imbued with a concept derived from the law of contract. However, the explanatory passages of the proposals make it clear that this was not the intention. The EEC explanatory memorandum which accompanied the first version of the Directive categorically states that the definition of defectiveness is based on the safety of the product, and that it is

> "irrelevant whether a product is defective in the sense that it cannot be used for its intended purpose. Such a concept of defectiveness belongs to the law of sale."[12]

The Law Commissions developed this further:

> "In our consultative document we suggested that there were two possible approaches to the definition of defect. One was to make the definition turn on safety; the other was to make it turn on merchantability. Having regard to our general conclusion in this report that strict liability should be confined to personal injuries, the latter approach is less suitable. Moreover as we pointed out in our consultative document, such an approach has conceptual and practical difficulties. The main problem is that the standard of merchantability required depends on the terms and circumstances of the contract under which the product is supplied including the price."[13]

A similar view was expressed by the Government in its Consultative Note on the implementation of the Directive:

> "The defectiveness of the product will be determined not by its fitness for use...but by the level of safety that is reasonably expected of it. An inferior quality product is not considered "defective" for the purpose of this Directive unless it actually introduces a risk of injury."[14]

The major difficulty with the definition of defect in the 1987 Act is that it fails to provide a readily ascertainable objective standard against which a manufacturer, or indeed a court, can measure the safety of a product. What then are our judges to make of this criterion of the "safety which persons generally are

---

[12] Explanatory Memorandum, Art. 4. References are to the Explanatory Memorandum issued along with the first version of the Directive.

[13] Cmnd. 6831 (1977), para. 46.

[14] Dept. of Trade and Industry, "Implementation of the EC Directive on Product Liability," An Explanatory and Consultative Note, (November 1985), para. 55.

entitled to expect"? An analysis of American product liability law will shed some light on this problem.

THE AMERICAN POSITION

Strict liability in tort did not emerge as a discrete theory but is historically rooted in implied contractual warranty. Tracing the development of "defectiveness" in strict tort, Wade states[15]:

> "The initial approach to the problem was in the language of warranty cases. It was said that there was an implied warranty that the goods were of merchantable quality, or were suitable for the purpose for which they were sold.... The reasonable expectations of the buyer were utilized as guidelines in making the determination."

This contract law approach was married to a traditional tort concept—unreasonable danger—to provide the bifurcated test for defectiveness which appears in section 402A of the Second Restatement of Torts: liability will arise where a product is in a "defective condition unreasonably dangerous" to persons or property and thus causes harm.

Interpretation of the criterion in section 402A for liability has been the cause of considerable problems for American courts. Some have taken the view that the whole of the phrase "defective condition unreasonably dangerous" provides the test for liability while others have relied upon "defective condition" alone or "unreasonably dangerous" alone. In one of the leading cases, the "unreasonable danger" test was rejected on the grounds that it

> "burdened the injured plaintiff with proof of an element which rings of negligence."[16]

This absence of judicial consensus on the proper conceptual basis of defectiveness is reflected by the diversity of views espoused by American commentators and has fostered a healthy literature on the subject.[17]

DEFECTIVENESS—A COST-BENEFIT ANALYSIS

If, in keeping with the theory of strict liability, the reasonable

---

[15] Wade, "On the Nature of Strict Tort Liability for Products" 44 Miss.L.J. 825 at 829 (1973).

[16] *Cronin* v. *J.B.E. Olsen Inc.* 8 Cal. 3d. 121, 501 P. 2d. 1153.

[17] See n. 1, above.

man and his attendant spirits such as foreseeability and existence of duty are to be exorcised from this area of the law, then an alternative conceptual structure to that of negligence is required. The preponderance of opinion amongst American authors on the subject is in favour of a cost-benefit approach. These writers consider strict liability in tort as a development from negligence and have thus sought to extrapolate from section 402A's criterion for liability a list of the various factors which have to be weighed in a cost-benefit analysis. These "decisional models" bear many similarities to those suggested by Judge Learned Hand, and others, for the resolution of negligence disputes.

Judge Learned Hand's test was formulated in a decision[18] on whether it was negligent for the owners of a barge to leave it unattended for some hours in a busy harbour. The barge had broken away from its moorings and then collided with another ship. In the course of his judgment, Judge Learned Hand stated:

> "Since there are occasions when every vessel will break from her moorings, and since, if she does, she becomes a menace to those about her, the owner's duty, as in other similar situations, to provide against resulting injuries is a function of three variables: (1) The probability that she will break away; (2) the gravity of the resulting injury, if she does; (3) the burden of adequate precautions. Possibly it serves to bring this notion into relief to state it in algebraic terms: if the probability be called P; the injury L; and the burden B; liability depends upon whether B is less than L multiplied by P: *i.e.* whether $B < PL$."[19]

Judge Learned Hand's formula is simply another way of expressing a cost-benefit approach to decision-making in negligence cases, where the benefits are those consequent upon accident avoidance and the costs are the costs of avoiding the accident.

The decisional models used by judges in deciding upon defectiveness in product liability cases[20] can be treated simply as more refined revisions of Judge Learned Hand's model. In

---

[18] *United States* v. *Carroll Towing Co.* 159 F. 2d. 169 (2d. Cir. 1947).

[19] At 173.

[20] Montgomery and Owen, *op. cit.*, 815, n. 42. Some would argue that a range of tests is available to courts: see Clark, *op. cit.*, n. 1, above, listing as alternatives cost-benefit; consumer expectations; intended use; the hybrid test; and the two-prong test.

general, it is fair to conclude that cost-benefit analysis was always, if often implicit, a decision-making tool in negligence but that it has become more explicitly recognised in strict liability in tort.

The supposed distinction between a strict liability decisional model and a negligence model is that in the latter, the costs and benefits to be balanced are subject to the foreseeability rule whereas in the former, the manufacturer is deemed to have had absolute prevision or prescience of all the harm caused by the product.[21] Therefore, in negligence, cost-benefit analysis is applied to the conduct of the producer whereas in strict liability it is applied to the performance of the product.

A number of commentators have suggested alternative decisional models, in varying degrees of sophistication. Of these so-called decisional models, that suggested by Wade has proved to be the most influential, many courts having explicitly adopted it.[22] The following factors require to be weighed in the cost-benefit or risk-utility analysis:

(1) The usefulness and desirability of the product—its utility to the user and to the public as a whole.

(2) The safety aspects of the product—the likelihood that it will cause injury, and the probable seriousness of the injury.

(3) The availability of a substitute product which would meet the same need and not be unsafe.

(4) The manufacturer's ability to eliminate the unsafe character of the product without impairing its usefulness or making it too expensive to maintain its utility.

(5) The user's ability to avoid danger by the exercise of care in the use of the product.

(6) The user's anticipated awareness of the dangers inherent in the product and their avoidability, because

---

[21] *Ibid.* at 829.

[22] See, *e.g. Finnegan* v. *Havir Manuf. Corp.* 60 N.J. 413, 290 A.2d. 286 (1972); *Phillips* v. *Kimwood Machine Co.* 269 Ore. 485, 525 P.2d. 1033 (1974); *Driesonstok* v. *Volkswagenwerk A.G.* 489 F.2d. (4th Cir. 1974); *Caterpillar Tractor Co.* v. *Beck* 593 F.2d. 871 (Alas. 1979); *Suter* v. *San Angelo Foundry Machine Co.* 81 N.J. 150, 406 F.2d. 140 (1979); *Bowman* v. *General Motors Corp.* 427 F.Supp. 234 (E.D. Pa. 1977); *Cepeda* v. *Cumberland Engineering Co.* 76 N.J. 152, 386 A.2d. 816 (1978). The Supreme Court of New Jersey has frequently referred to Wade's seven factors listed in the text: see, *e.g. Feldman* v. *Lederle Laboratories*, 97 N.J. 429, 479 A.2d. 374. For a recent example of a court reviewing the question of whether a consumer expectation test or a risk benefit test ought to be used, see *Nesselrode* v. *Executive Beechcraft Inc.* 707 S.W. 2d. 371 (Mo. 1986).

of general public knowledge of the obvious condition of the product, or of the existence of suitable warnings or instructions.

(7) The feasibility, on the part of the manufacturer, of spreading the loss by setting the price of the product or carrying liability insurance.

The key question is whether courts should set product safety standards by using such complex cost-benefit calculations. Many problems arise if such a role is assigned to courts, not least that judges may lack the technical expertise to set product safety standards.

Complexity of the cost-benefit approach

There is a major mathematical difficulty inherent in the cost-benefit approach to decision-making, judicial or otherwise—the balancing process can properly be carried out only if like is balanced against like. Thus, the factors to be balanced should be quantified in the same or equivalent units of measurement. In many areas of decision-making, for example, public policy, quantities must be expressed in financial terms. The factors are "monetarised" and money costs are weighed against money benefits to give a rational economic model for the decision. It is clear from product liability cases that courts do not attempt to take cost-benefit analysis to these lengths. Indeed, they are patently ill-equipped to do so. Take, for example, two of the factors present in the basic risk-utility calculus—the cost of injuries and the utility of the product. Welfare economists would argue that monetary values could be ascribed to these factors—despite the absence of a recognised market for them—although there would probably be considerable disagreement as to the proper method of calculation. However, it is clearly ludicrous to expect courts to make such a computation.

The alternative to this monetarisation of factors is simply to trade off costs and benefits in accordance with the decision-maker's own conception of their relative values. This is even more haphazard than the monetary model, but seems to be the type of cost-benefit analysis carried out by courts.

If we accept that both negligence and, more overtly, strict product liability employ a cost-benefit approach to judicial decision-making, we should realise that the method is at least imperfect, if not crude and irrational.

It has been cogently argued that, in the light of the complex risk-benefit balancing process suggested as a test for defectiveness, product liability design-defect[23] cases are incapable of meaningful adjudication. However, a number of recent design-defect cases in the United States have been decided by the application of a multi-factor decisional model. It is true, however, that there will be some design-defect cases which are highly complex. Quantification and balancing of risk-benefit factors, such as the usefulness and desirability of the product, could be almost impossible. If such cases are to admit of rational adjudication, then a test other than the cost-benefit calculus may be required. The "consumer expectation test" is sometimes posited as a workable alternative.

THE CONSUMER EXPECTATION TEST

It was noticed earlier that the crucial wording of section 402A of the Second Restatement of Torts bases liability on a finding that a product is "in a defective condition unreasonably dangerous to the user or consumer," and that both "defective condition" and "unreasonably dangerous" are defined in terms of the expectations of the consumer. Comment i to section 402A explains the test in the following terms:

> "The article must be dangerous to an extent beyond that which would be contemplated by the ordinary consumer who purchases it, with the ordinary knowledge common to the community as to its characteristics."

Moreover, all proposals for a strict liability regime in this country predicated liability upon the absence of the "safety which a person is entitled to expect," and the 1987 Act uses a similar form of words.

On a superficial analysis this test seems worthwhile, upholding a firm tenet of strict liability—attention is focused on the condition of the product rather than the conduct of the manufacturer. Further, the test explicitly recognises the contract history of section 402A's strict liability. However, it has been much criticised despite having been applied in a number of cases.[24]

---

[23] See Henderson, "Judicial Review of Manufacturers' Conscious Design Choices: The Limits of Adjudication" 73 Colum. L.Rev. 1531 (1973).

[24] Fischer, "Products Liability—The Meaning of Defect" 39 Mo. L.Rev. 339 at 348, (1974), cases cited at n. 76. See also *Kaufman* v. *Meditech Inc.* 353 N.W. 2d. 297, 300 (N.D.1984); *Accord Aller* v. *Rodgers Machinery Manufacturing Co.* 268 N.W. 2d. 830 (Iowa 1978); *Barnes* v. *Vega Indus. Inc.* 234 Kan. 1012, 676 P.2d. 761 (1984); *Hancock* v. *Paccar Inc.* 204 Neb. 468, 283 N.W. 2d. 25 (1979); *Stackiewicz* v. *Nissan Motor Corp.*, 686 P.2d. 925, 928 (Nev. 1984); *Seattle First Nat'l. Bank* v. *Tarbert* 86 Wash. 2d. 145, 542 P.2d. 774 (1975); *Mississippi & Toliver* v. *General Motors Corp.* 482 S.2d. 213 (Miss. 1986). For a discussion of the application of the consumer expectation test in Oklahoma, see *Lamke* v. *Futorian Corp.* 709 P.2d. 684 at 687 (Okla. 1985). See also, Clark, *op. cit.*, n. 1, above.

One difficulty is that a consumer may know of a defect or danger inherent in a product, because it is obvious or has been drawn to the user's attention by a warning. In such circumstances the user cannot expect a greater degree of safety than his knowledge of the defect or danger allows. Accordingly, such products may not be found to be defective. *Vincer* v. *Esther Williams All Aluminium Swimming Pool Company*[25] clearly illustrates this point. The case concerned a swimming pool, situated above ground, access to which was by a retractable ladder. A two-year-old child climbed the ladder, which had been left in the down position, and fell into the pool sustaining severe brain damage. It was claimed that the pool had a design defect in that fencing around it could have been extended to include a safety gate at the top of the ladder. The court rejected this contention:

> "the test in Wisconsin of whether a product contains an unreasonably dangerous defect depends upon the reasonable expectations of the ordinary consumer concerning the characteristics of this type of product. If the average consumer would reasonably anticipate the dangerous condition of the product and fully appreciate the attendant risk of injury, it would not be unreasonably dangerous and defective."[26]

Berry v. *Eckhardt Porche Audi Inc.*[27] provides a further illustration. It was argued that a car was defective because a warning buzzer, which was supposed to indicate that seat belts were unfastened, failed to operate. It was held that the ordinary consumer is aware of the dangers of not wearing a seat belt. Thus it could be said that a product does not have to be particularly safe, as long as it matches consumer expectations.[28]

Another problem with the consumer expectation test is the logical difficulty of applying it to cases where bystanders, rather than users, suffer injury. Bystanders may have no knowledge of the existence of the product and therefore no expectations regarding its safety. Further, many products created in this technological era are too complex for a consumer to form any rational impression of the safety to be expected. This is, of course, particularly true of design or warning defects, but will

[25] 69 Wisconsin 2d. 326, 230 N.W.2d. 794 (1975).
[26] *Ibid. per* Hansen J. at 332.
[27] 578 P.2d. 1195 (Okla. 1978).
[28] Clark, *op. cit.*, n. 1, above, at 322.

also be true of new products. The consumer will have no real idea about the level of safety or danger of the product. There will also be circumstances in which expectations exist, but the user can do nothing to avoid the danger for example where a workman is obliged to use a particular piece of equipment. However, the wording in the 1987 Act, which speaks of "persons generally," should preclude enquiry into the expectations of the particular consumer.

Nonetheless, there remains some question as to whether the consumer expectation test is subjective or objective. For example, in *Lester* v. *Magic Chef Inc.*,[29] Justice Praeger, in his dissenting judgment, stated:

> "The consumer expectation test is not an *objective* test. In my judgment the ends of justice require an objective test, not a subjective one, in the area of product liability. A subjective test in this area of the law is not really a test at all. It is an unbridled license to the jury to 'do good' in the particular case. It has been described as 'haphazard subjectivity.' Since it depends on the particular jury's concept of what may be in the consumer's mind, the test is bound to produce inconsistent jury verdicts in comparable cases. This is unfair both to injured plaintiffs and to defendant manufacturers."[30]

It is clearly preferable that the particular consumer's personal knowledge, experience or lack of the same, ought not to intrude into the question of defect, and that subjectivity of this type should be precluded, as it is in the definition adopted in the 1987 Act. However, subjectivity of another variety has also been persuasive to those seeking to reject the consumer expectation test. Those drafting the Model Uniform Product Liability Act stated:

> "The consumer expectation test takes subjectivity to its most extreme end. Each trier of fact is likely to have a different understanding of abstract consumer expectations. Moreover, most consumers are not familiar with the details of the manufacturing process and cannot abstractly evaluate conscious design alternatives."[31]

In view of these difficulties the draftsmen favoured a risk-benefit

[29] 641 P.2d. 353 (1982).
[30] At 363.
[31] S. Rep. No. 476, 98th Cong. 2d. Sess. (1984).

approach to defectiveness although it ought to be observed that the weighing of risks against benefits has its own degree of subjectivity of this type, since each judge will give particular weight to each aspect of the "decisional model" in a subjective fashion. A number of courts also have eschewed the consumer expectation criterion.[32] It could be argued, however, that at least some of the criticisms of the test result from a misunderstanding of its application. The expectations concerned are not those which the particular consumer actually had but are those which the average consumer was *entitled* to have. Thus, a bystander may have no knowledge of the existence of a product but he has a general expectation of, or entitlement to, being safe in its presence. Complex or technological products give rise to the same generalised expectancy or entitlement. If courts are required to go further, and assess the expectations of a particular consumer, the question of how these expectations are to be measured will arise. Clearly, an agreement between the parties will provide the best basis for ascertaining expectations.

There is, however, a fundamental difficulty with a liability criterion which is based upon the expectations of the consumer, especially where it is the expectations of persons generally which are relevant. The difficulty is that the test is fundamentally inexplicit. It could be argued that the actual language of the consumer expectation test is simply a semantic veneer covering what is in reality a cost-benefit test. On this analysis, the test in the 1987 Act is simply a statutory statement of the objective standard already in use in the law of negligence.[33] One writer has taken the view that:

> "What reformers really mean when they say that a product meets 'expectations of safety' is that on balance its benefits outweigh its costs.... It would have made much greater sense simply to couch the liability criterion in terms of costs and benefits as such and drop the concept of expectations altogether."[34]

Indeed, any liability test short of absolute liability could be perceived as ultimately cost-benefit based. However, the distinction between a cost-benefit approach and a consumer expectations approach may really be one of style rather than

---

[32] Fischer, *op. cit.*, cases cited at n. 103.
[33] See Miller and Lovell, *Product Liability and Safety Encyclopaedia*, Pt. III para. 14.
[34] Stapleton, "Products Liability Reform—Real or Illusory?" [1986] C.L.J. 392, at 405.

substance. The consumer expectation test more readily enables courts to proceed upon intuition or common experience. This is less so with the much more structured, although still not scientific, cost-benefit criterion. It remains to be seen whether, as is arguable, the application of the consumer expectation test will result in the exclusion of considerations such as the costs and benefits of particular designs. If so, there is more room for inconsistent findings in comparable product liability cases.

THE TIME AT WHICH "DEFECTIVENESS" IS ADJUDGED

One of the key issues in deciding whether a product has a defect is the question of the relevant time for the making of the cost-benefit analysis, or for the assessment of consumer expectations (assuming that this latter does involve a difference in approach). Should the safety of the product be measured as at the time when it was put into circulation, or some later stage, for example the date of trial? The proposals for reform[35] and the DTI Explanatory and Consultative Note[36] are clear that the relevant time should be the date when the product was put into circulation.

Section 3 of the 1987 Act states that, in determining the safety which persons generally are entitled to expect, the circumstances to be taken into account include:

"the time when the product was supplied by its producer to another"

and

"and nothing in this section shall require a defect to be inferred from the fact alone that the safety of a product which is supplied after that time is greater than the safety of the product in question."

How is this provision to be applied in practice? Setting aside for the purpose of the discussion the point that the Act applies only to products which are put into circulation after the commencement date of the legislation, suppose that in 1975 a manufacturer of refrigerators designed a fridge with a door which opens from the inside. A child suffocates in a fridge made in 1974 and which lacks the safety device. Will liability be

---

[35] See, *e.g.* para. 42 of the Explanatory Report on the Draft Directive of 1976; and Cmnd. 6831 (1977), para. 49.
[36] Para. 52.

precluded since at the time of production no fridges had the safety precaution and hence "persons generally" could not expect an inside-opening door? Or will a court be prepared to stigmatise the design as defective and hold that the safety device, although not incorporated in other models of the same vintage, was within reasonable expectations? This raises a central issue in product liability: will product safety standards be set by prevailing industry practice or by the courts? For the new Act to have any real bite, judges must be prepared to depart from industry standards. Moreover, if after-acquired knowledge is not to be taken into account, then the new regime offers no incentive for the producer to recall a product which such knowledge shows to be unsafe, and seek to make it more safe.

It seems clear, therefore, that consideration will have to be given, in many product liability cases, to the existing state of the art in relation to the production of the product, at the time when the product was put into circulation. This causes the new strict liability regime to suffer from one of the same major drawbacks as a tort regime—

> "the need to reconstruct the state of the art at a point often considerably in the past out of information which is usually complex and costly to gather, and often more within the knowledge of the defendant than the plaintiff."[37]

This question of the time at which defectiveness is to be judged will be revisited in Chapter Six in the context of development risks and state of the art evidence. At this stage it can be concluded that by using the relevant time as the time when the product was supplied (that is, put into circulation), the Act's regime has not really here departed from the existing fault criterion.

It has been noticed that in the United States there are two main theories on the conceptual basis of strict liability for defective products. One approach involves the extrapolation of a set of factors which have to be balanced in a cost-benefit computation, and the other involves comparison between the performance of the product and the expectations of the consumer. The balancing of risks against benefits has become a standard tool in the analysis of negligence cases. In strict liability the computation is rather different from that used in negligence. In the former the producer, as noticed, is imputed with absolute prevision of all harm the product actually causes,

---

[37] Stapleton, *op. cit.*, at 413.

whereas in the latter the "risks" element in the balancing process is evaluated in terms of reasonable foreseeability. However, for both the thrust is towards product safety.

In many cases this balancing process will be applied without difficulty but in others, complexity will cause serious judgmental problems. The consumer expectation test is sometimes presented as a workable alternative to the risk-benefit calculus, but it too has an inherent limitation in that courts may reach differing verdicts in comparable cases.

A "Two-Prong" Test for Defectiveness

In *Barker* v. *Lull Engineering Co. Inc.*[38] the California Supreme Court addressed the problem of design defectiveness and concluded that a product would be defective (a) if the product failed to perform as safely as an ordinary consumer would expect when used in an intended or reasonably foreseeable manner, or (b) if the benefits of the challenged design are outweighed by the risk of danger inherent in such a design. Clearly, the court contemplated that proof of either would result in a finding of defectiveness. Consumer expectations ought not, reasoned the court, to provide a "ceiling" on manufacturers' responsibility, but should be treated as a "floor."[39]

Judge Wisdom framed the issue in a slightly different form, but made essentially the same point, in *Welch* v. *Outboard Marine Corp.*[40] Commenting upon the basis of liability, he said:

> "A product is defective and unreasonably dangerous when a reasonable seller would not sell the product if he knew of the risks involved or if the risks are greater than a reasonable buyer would expect."

Judges in the United Kingdom can, it is suggested, opt for a consumer expectations, or cost-benefit, or two-pronged approach to defectiveness—the 1987 Act allows all the circumstances to be taken into account in determining defectiveness. It is suggested that the hybrid or two-pronged approach to defectiveness seems to be a worthwhile replacement for an exclusive cost-benefit or consumer expectations test and could provide a workable interpretation of the definition of defect

---

[38] 20 Cal. 3d. 413, 143 Cal.Rptr. 225 (1978).

[39] At 421 (Cal.3d.), 451 (P.2d.).

[40] 481 F.2d. 252 (5th Cir. 1973), see the discussion in Montgomery and Owen, *op. cit.*, at 843–845.

under the 1987 Act. It is not suggested that this compromise would preclude problems of complexity in product liability cases, but it would at least allow courts to take advantage of an alternative ground where such problems arise. At all events, some flesh needs to be put on the bare definition in the Act and a cost-benefit approach seems to be a sensible way to do this.

Strict Liability or Negligence—Does it make any Difference?

(a) *Imputed knowledge of defect and harm*

It was noted earlier that a costs versus benefits approach is implicit in the negligence criteria for defectiveness, and that such an approach has on occasion been made explicit. Given that many courts use a cost-benefit test for defectiveness in strict liability and that such a test may feature in the new regime of the United Kingdom (either as an alternative to the consumer expectation test or indeed as its very substance), the question arises as to what differences, if any, will result from the new test for defectiveness.

It could be argued that our new regime will involve no real change in deciding upon defectiveness. Thus, it has been stated that:

> "it is by no means clear... how the test is to be distinguished from its present use in the law of negligence"[41]

and that:

> "... the underlying rationale for a comparison between the risks and benefits in a product appears to demand adherence to principles most familiar to the law of negligence."[42]

Before evaluating the worth of these assertions it is helpful to identify what purported difference there is between the two schemes of liability.

Dicta in the important case of *Feldman* v. *Lederle Laboratories*[43] illustrate the point:

---

[41] Newdick, "The Future of Negligence in Product Liability," (1987) 103 L.Q.R. 288 at 304.
[42] *Ibid.* at 305. See also Stapleton, *op. cit.*
[43] 479 A.2d. 374 (N.J.1984).

"Generally speaking, the doctrine of strict liability assumes that enterprises should be responsible for damages to consumers resulting from defective products regardless of fault. The doctrine differs from a negligence theory, which centers on the defendant's conduct and seeks to determine whether the defendant acted as a reasonably prudent person. This difference between strict liability and negligence is commonly expressed by stating that in a strict liability analysis, the defendant is assumed to know of the dangerous propensity of the product, whereas in a negligence case, the plaintiff must prove that the defendant knew or should have known of the danger."[44]

For manufacturing defects, as opposed to design defects or defects arising from a failure to warn, the difference is of some importance since it cancels the need on the part of the plaintiff to establish that the defendant knew or should have known of the danger. But in such cases there is already a strong tendency for courts (even under a negligence theory of liability) to impose liability almost as a matter of course.[45]

Does the distinction between strict liability and negligence make any difference in design defect or failure to warn cases? Again, the *Feldman* decision offers some guidance:

"When the strict liability defect consists of an improper design or warning, reasonableness of the defendant's conduct is a factor in determining liability.... The question in strict-liability design-defect and warning cases is whether, assuming that the manufacturer knew of the defect in the product, he acted in a reasonably prudent manner in marketing the product or in providing the warnings given. Thus, once the defendant's knowledge of the defect is imputed, strict liability analysis becomes almost identical to negligence analysis in its focus on the reasonableness of the defendant's conduct."[46]

What then is the significance of imputing to the defendant knowledge of the defect and also, it would seem, of the harm caused by it? Put simply, the need to establish foreseeability of the defect and of the harm is elided under strict liability, although traditional principles of causation will continue to be applied to the link between the defect and the damage.

---

[44] *Ibid.* at 386.
[45] See Newdick, *op. cit.*, at 290–292.
[46] *Feldman*, above, n. 43, at 386.

The imputed knowledge characteristic of strict liability has much less significance, however, where a conscious, deliberate design choice has been made. Thus, if a product was deliberately designed in the full knowledge of the risk and consequences of the design, there is no need to impute any knowledge, and the distinction between negligence and strict liability ceases to be of real importance. Here the manufacturer effectively submits his own cost-benefit appraisal of the product as being correct, and it is that appraisal upon which the court must adjudicate.

(b) *Reasonableness of the manufacturer's conduct*

It was important to the court in *Feldman* to emphasise that the idea of imputing, to the manufacturer, knowledge of the danger and the resultant harm still leaves room for an assessment of the reasonableness of the manufacturer's conduct. This is of interest because it runs counter to the supposed distinction between strict liability's focus on the product and the focus, under the law of negligence, upon the conduct of the manufacturer. Speaking of their test for liability, outlined above the *Feldman* court stated:

> "This test does not conflict with the assumption made in strict liability design-defect and warning cases that the defendant knew of the dangerous propensity of the product, if the knowledge that is assumed is reasonably knowable in the sense of actual or constructive knowledge."[47]

This is a matter of some difficulty and requires some analysis. The court's view can be summarised as follows: a manufacturer is assumed to know of the dangerous propensity of his product but only if that danger is reasonably knowable. There is very little difference between assuming that a manufacturer knew of reasonably knowable dangers and charging him with having had within his contemplation reasonably foreseeable dangers. If the approach of the *Feldman* court is accepted, reasonableness of the manufacturer's conduct is a vital ingredient in strict liability and accordingly it is only the reversal of the burden of proof as to what was knowable which distinguishes the *Feldman* test from that of the law of negligence.

Will this reversal in the burden of proof be a significant aid to the injured party? On the face of it, the answer is in the

---

[47] *Ibid.*

affirmative, but it seems to be rather a two-edged sword: the manufacturer will be better equipped to identify what was reasonably knowable at the date of circulation, and if the plaintiff wishes to contest this he must of course advance evidence that the danger *was* knowable. This necessitates the plaintiff's advisers engaging in research as to available knowledge at the date of circulation. Reversal in the burden of proof is therefore of some significance in such circumstances but will not wholly preclude proof problems for the plaintiff.

Thus, in major categories of product liability cases—design-defects and failure to warn (the latter being really just a subset of the former)—the move to strict liability will, if *Feldman* is representative, have little impact. It would be misleading to assert, however, that the *Feldman* retrenchment does represent the state of strict liability for product defects in all jurisdictions in the United States. For example, many courts[48] have applied a consumer expectation test—which is very similar to the test in the new United Kingdom regime—*without* seeking to extrapolate a cost-benefit analysis. Although more intuitive and less scientific than cost-benefit, it could be argued that the consumer expectation test is a more appropriate vehicle for delivering strict liability since it leaves less scope for assessment of the reasonableness of the manufacturer's conduct.

Other courts, as has been noticed,[49] allow the plaintiff to recover using either a risk-utility balance or a consumer expectation test. Further, there is a substantial body of case law which supports an *ex post* risk utility analysis, where time-of-trial knowledge of product risks is imputed to the defendant.[50] Some jurisdictions, such as New Jersey, have, as was noted in

---

[48] See n. 24, above.
[49] *Barker* v. *Lull Engineering Co. Inc.* 20 Cal. 3d. 413, 143 Cal.Rptr. 225 (1978); *Welch* v. *Outboard Marine Corp.* 481 F.2d. 252 (5th Cir. 1973); see also, *Caterpillar Tractor Co.* v. *Beck* 593 P.2d. 871 (Alaska 1979); *Ontai* v. *Straub Clinic and Hospital Inc.* 66 Hawaii 237, 659 P.2d. 734 (1983); *Cremeans* v. *International Harvester Co.* 6 Ohio St. 3d. 232, 452 N.E. 2d. 1281 (1983).
[50] See Wheeler, "Comment on Landes and Posner," (1985) XIV Jnl. of Leg. Studs., 575. Examples include: *Anderson* v. *Heron Engineering Co.* 198 Colo. 391, 604 P.2d. 674 (1979); *Ulrich* v. *Kasco Abrasives Co.* 532 S.W.2d. 197 (Ky. 1976); *Elmore* v. *Owens-Illinois, Inc.* 673 S.W.2d. 434 (Mo. 1984); *Jackson* v. *Coast Paint and Lacquer Co.* 499 F.2d. 809 (9th Cir. 1974); *Berkebile* v. *Brantly Helicopter Corp.* 462 Pa. 83, 337 A.2d. 893 (1975); *Carter* v. *Johns-Manville Sales Corp.* 557 F.Supp. 1317 (E.D. Tex. 1983); *Boatland Houston Inc.* v. *Bailey* 609 S.W. 2d. 743 (Tex. 1980).

Feldman, withdrawn somewhat from this position.[51] Thus, the overall picture remains unclear.

In the United Kingdom, however, there will be significantly less scope for disparity. Since the time at which the product was put into circulation is to be relevant to the question of defectiveness an *ex post* analysis will not be used here. Accordingly, the new regime may not have advanced much from the position which obtains under the current law of negligence. To have any real chance of moving away from this reasonableness criterion, British courts would have to give the plaintiff the opportunity of recovery on the alternative grounds of risk-utility analysis or consumer expectations. This would allow courts to avoid the difficulties which particular fact patterns pose for either test. For example, where the danger is patent but the product is nonetheless arguably dangerous, consumer expectations should not alone be used to indicate a finding of no liability, and the product should be exposed to a risk-utility analysis. Conversely, where the application of a risk-utility analysis will be highly complex, or where it would be similar in application to its use in the law of negligence, true strict liability can be imposed using a consumer expectation test. The "strictness" of our new regime will depend partly upon how the courts address the problem. Hitherto, there have been few cases in negligence law in which manufacturers' conscious design choices have been reviewed by United Kingdom courts. The move to strict liability may well help to generate the view that such design choices are open to argument before our courts.

---

[51] See also *O'Brien* v. *Muskin Corp.* 94 N.J. 169, 463 A.2d. 298 (1983).

Chapter 3

THE PRODUCT AND THE CHAIN OF LIABILITY

In common parlance, the term "product" indicates an item which has been manufactured and is then sold, perhaps through an intermediary, to the consumer. Since no separate scheme of product liability exists under the general law of negligence, there has been no need for British courts, in negligence cases, to offer a definition of "product." Under the new rules, however, "product" is a central concept—if no "product" is involved then the new regime's strict liability will not be attracted. What should be the boundary between products and other things? Should the term "product" include all goods? Ought there to be any exemptions? What about component parts and raw materials? Such questions will be considered in the present chapter.

Another of its aims is to identify the persons who should be liable for defective products. The chain of distribution will often be more complex than manufacturer-retailer-customer. For example, wholesalers, distributors, importers, employers, persons who brand their own products and retailers may all be involved in the marketing chain. In a product liability regime, the question arises as to who in this chain of manufacture and distribution ought to incur liability in respect of a defective product.

The Pre-Existing Legal Position

The law previously recognised no separate area of product liability. This was not always so. Mr Winterbottom's bad leg[1] was an impediment from which English law did not recover until *Donoghue* v. *Stevenson* in 1932, having spent more than a century with an apparent dichotomy between "dangerous chattels" and other goods.

General negligence principles have been applied to what could be called product liability cases. The general law is fully explained in other works and there is no need to rehearse it here. It will suffice to observe that negligence principles have

[1] *Winterbottom* v. *Wright* (1842) 10 M. & W. 109.

been sufficiently flexible to allow United Kingdom courts to cope with modern, mass produced, products. Thus, liability has been imposed primarily upon manufacturers and component manufacturers. Distributors and retailers will usually have satisfied their obligation to take reasonable care by having purchased from a reputable supplier, unless the defect was discoverable on the exercise of due care. Until 1969, the liability of employers was co-extensive with that just stated, but the Employer's Liability (Defective Equipment) Act 1969 imposes a form of strict liability on employers in respect of defective tools or other equipment. The Act provides[2]:

> "Where (a) an employee suffers personal injury in the course of his employment in consequence of a defect in equipment provided by his employer for the purposes of the employer's business; and (b) the defect is attributable wholly or partly to the fault of a third party (whether identified or not) the injury shall be deemed to be also attributable to negligence on the part of the employer . . ."

The right of the employer to seek a contribution from his supplier is expressly preserved. "Equipment" is defined as including "any plant and machinery, vehicle, aircraft and clothing," thus leaving a number of other products or materials used at work to be covered by the common law. There is recent case law to the effect that a ship is not equipment.[3]

Before progressing to the changes in the law, one final point, affecting all those in the chain of supply who sell goods, should be made. A person who is injured by goods which are in breach of the safety regulations made under the Consumer Protection Act 1961 or the Consumer Safety Act 1978 may bring an action for breach of statutory duty against any seller in the chain of supply. The regime of regulations under these Acts has been consolidated and improved by the Consumer Protection Act 1987, but the right to raise a civil action is unaffected by this change. In the words of the Pearson Commission:

> "In effect, the seller is strictly liable if he sells goods in breach of the regulations."[4]

---

[2] s.1.
[3] See *Coltman* v. *Bibby* [1987] 1 All E.R. 932.
[4] Cmnd. 7054 (1978), para. 1213.

Further, the right of action is not confined to the buyer. Since over 30 sets of regulations have been made under these Acts,[5] it can be appreciated that, in relation to certain products, a measure of strict liability already existed.

The Consumer Protection Act 1987 repeals the Consumer Safety Act 1978 and the Consumer Safety (Amendment) Act 1986, and the regulation-making powers have been extended. The 1987 Act also provides for a general safety requirement[6] whereby a person shall be guilty of an offence if he supplies consumer goods which are not reasonably safe having regard to all the circumstances. However, breach of the general safety requirement will not (unlike breach of regulations) ground a civil action for breach of statutory duty.

PROPOSALS FOR CHANGE

Liability of manufacturers

The major proposals for change of the law on product liability all agreed on the imposition of strict liability on the manufacturer, or to use the preferred term, the producer, of a defective product. The term "producer" is not without ambiguity since the maker of the finished product may simply be an assembler of component parts. Indeed, component parts may themselves have been assembled from sub-components. As well as this, there may be no actual manufacture involved, as is the case with animal and vegetable produce.

The EEC Directive virtually echoed the Strasbourg definitions. Thus, the producer would be:

> "the person who manufactured the end product and put it into circulation in the form in which it was intended to be used."[7]

This would apply to assemblers of component parts, but primary agricultural products (unprocessed animal and vegetable produce) were exempted although individual states could derogate from this exemption.

The Pearson Commission concluded that sureness of remedy had to be balanced against the resultant increase in cost, and

---

[5] These cover, *inter alios*, nightdresses, heaters, electric blankets, cosmetics, toys, fireworks, upholstered furniture, and asbestos products.

[6] Pt. II of the Act, implementing the proposals set out in the White Paper "The Safety of Goods," Cmnd. 9302, (1984).

[7] Explanatory memorandum accompanying the first draft Directive, III.3. See the Bulletin of the European Communities, Supplement 11/76.

recommended that both producers of finished products and component producers should be strictly liable, although distributors should not.

Some of the proposals gave special consideration to producers of particular products. An instance already mentioned is the treatment of producers of primary agricultural products in the EEC Directive, who have been exempted from the new regime of strict liability. Disagreeing, the Pearson Commission recommended that such producers should be included:

"shell fish, for example, are known carriers of disease."[8]

Producers of moveable products which have been incorporated into immoveables and producers of pharmaceuticals also merited special discussion. In the case of the former, the majority view, that strict liability ought to be applied, prevailed. As for pharmaceuticals, it was argued that the development of new drugs would be unduly inhibited. However, the Pearson Commission felt that drugs represented the class of product in respect of which the greatest public pressure for compensation had been felt—*viz.* the Thalidomide tragedy, and that no special treatment could be justified. The Directive includes such products in its scheme of liability.

Liability of component producers

Despite their express or implied adherence to a policy of channelling liability towards the producer of the finished product all proposals, as already indicated, would also have imposed strict liability on component producers, although the Scottish Law Commission would have had that liability cease when the component or constituent material was incorporated into the finished product.

The arguments advanced by the Scottish Law Commission in support for this view include: that to provide otherwise would run contrary to the channelling argument; to provide otherwise would lead to:

"a duplication or multiplication and cumulation"

of insurance in respect of the same risk; for many components there are a large number of potential uses and therefore the extent of the risk is unknown or a matter of speculation at the time of manufacture.[9] However, in recognition of the fact that

[8] Cmnd. 7054 (1978), para. 1246.
[9] Cmnd. 6831 (1977), para. 77–82.

this view was, in terms of all the proposals, in the minority, the Commission went on to say that if strict liability were to continue after incorporation of a component part then the definition of "defect" should be reconsidered so as to be restricted to "normal" uses of the component part.

Only the Directive thought it necessary to expressly exculpate the component producer from liability where the component had been produced in accordance with a design or specification instructed by the final producer. In such circumstances, the others observed, the component part would not be "defective" within the meaning ascribed to that term.

Liability of distributors

The term "distributors" is used in this context to include those in the marketing and distributing chain other than producers, component producers or retailers. The proposals were united in recommending the imposition of liability upon an own-brander (one who holds himself out as a product's producer) and importers.

Liability of retailers

Each of the proposals would exclude retailers from the scheme of strict liability except in respect of own brand products and products where the retailer did not disclose the identity of his supplier within a reasonable time. This latter extension of liability will cause some anxiety to all suppliers, who will now require to maintain full records of their sources in order to escape liability under the Act. However, it will be recalled that sellers are already strictly liable to buyers under the Sale of Goods Act 1979.

Liability of employers

None of the proposals sought to alter the present liability of an employer in respect of defective products used at work, except that an employer would be a supplier and so if he could not name the producer, importer or own brander, or name his own supplier, then the employer would incur liability. Given the existence of the Employer's Liability (Defective Equipment) Act 1969 this slight change will have little impact.

"PRODUCT" AND PERSONS LIABLE UNDER THE 1987 ACT

"Product"

Section 1(2) of the Act defines the term product to mean:

> "any goods or electricity and (subject to subsection (3) below) includes a product which is comprised in another product, whether by virtue of being a component part or raw material or otherwise."

The interpretation section (section 45(1)) defines "goods" as including:

> "substances, growing crops and things comprised in land by virtue of being attached to it and any ship, aircraft or vehicle."

Some of the terms used in the definition of goods are themselves subject to further definition. Thus, "aircraft" includes gliders, balloons and hovercraft; "ship" includes any boat and any other description of vessel used in navigation; and "substance" means any natural or artificial substance, whether in solid, liquid or gaseous form or in the form of a vapour, and includes substances that are comprised in or mixed with other goods. Vehicle is not defined.

The major consequence of the breadth of meaning ascribed to the term product is that, despite the statute's short title of the Consumer Protection Act 1987, Part I's scheme of strict liability will have a wider application than to consumer goods. As noticed earlier, major disasters stemming from for example chemicals or aircraft could well be litigated under the Act. This is of course the American experience where chemical defoliants, (such as Agent Orange) asbestos, and other toxic substances have posed challenging questions for courts in product liability cases.

The extension of the term "goods" to include moveables which have been incorporated into immoveables is of some interest. This clearly covers moveable items such as window frames, pipes, and central heating systems which have been so incorporated. In this way the Act implements Article 2 of the Directive. Further, building materials themselves fall within the definition. It would also appear that the definition covers moveable structures which have been affixed to land. This would cover not only fixtures within the normal meaning of that term but would also, arguably, include attached structures such as the swings and roundabouts of a children's play park, or the structure and equipment of a ski-lift.

One final matter which has caused some anxiety is the position of those who produce printed textbooks, manuscripts and the like. In their Explanatory and Consultative Note the DTI stated:

"Special problems arise with those industries dealing with products concerned with information, such as books, records, tapes and computer software. It has been suggested, for example, that it would be absurd for printers and bookbinders to be held strictly liable for faithfully reproducing errors in the material provided to them, which—by giving bad instructions or defective warnings—indirectly causes injury. It does not appear that the Directive is intended to extend liability in such situations. On the other hand, it is important that liability is extended to the manufacturer of a machine which contains defective software and is thereby unsafe, and to the producer of an article accompanied by inadequate instructions or warnings, the article thereby becoming a hazard to the user. The line between those cases may however not be easy to draw, particularly in the field of new technology where the distinction between software and hardware is becoming increasingly blurred."[10]

The anxiety of the printing industry is that incidents such as that involving a textbook on chemicals, published in 1979, could recur and could trigger liability under the Act. In the textbook a proportion between two chemical elements was stated as 2:30 rather than 2:3 and there was a major explosion in a school as a result.[11] Publishers' anxiety will not be eased by looking to the meaning of the terms "product" and "producer," for both are clearly wide enough to include textual errors in published works. Nor would the industry be particularly comforted by the Minister's statement that:

"it seems to us reasonably clear that the Directive does not apply to mis-statement."[12]

This view rests in the rather difficult distinction between such things as books or magazines and other products, a distinction which United Kingdom courts may or may not be prepared to recognise. However, given the conservative treatment of liability for mis-statements under current negligence law, it is to be expected that a cautious approach will be taken.

The exemption of game and agricultural produce from strict liability

Section 2(4) of the Act exempts from the Act's scheme of liability any game or agricultural produce which has not undergone

---

[10] Para. 47.
[11] This incident was referred by Clement Freud M.P. at the Committee stage of the Bill in the House of Commons: Daily Report, May 13, 1987, col. 364.
[12] *Ibid.* See also col. 366.

an industrial process. "Agricultural produce" means any produce of the soil, of stockfarming or of fisheries.[13] Game is not defined. This provision purports to implement the Directive. But, Article 2 of the Directive states that:

> "Primary agricultural products means the products of the soil of stockfarming and of fisheries, excluding products which have undergone *initial* processing" (my emphasis).

However, the preamble to the Directive speaks of it being appropriate to exclude liability for agricultural products and game, except where they have undergone processing of an industrial nature which could cause a defect in these products.

A wide range of processing goes on in the food industry. For example, milk is pasteurised; grain is milled; meat is slaughtered and butchered; prior to slaughter, animals are injected with a variety of chemicals for a variety of purposes; vegetables and fruit are sprayed with pesticides, fungicides and insecticides; meat and vegetables are frozen; game is plucked. Which of these are industrial processes? That question is not answered in the definition section of the Act, a matter which caused Lord Denning to observe:

> "...but what is an industrial process?...it is so vague and uncertain that it will give rise to all sorts of litigation."[14]

The nearest statutory usage to industrial process is that in the Clean Air Act 1968 section 1(5) which speaks of "industrial or trade process." This is not defined, and case law[15] on the matter is of no assistance in the present context. Judicial interpretation of "process" indicates that a continuous and regular operation carried on in a definite manner is required.[16]

The Government's view was expressed at the Committee Stage in the Lords.[17]

> "The test is twofold. First, there must have been processing, and for processing to take place some essential

---

[13] s.1(2). The definition raises the interesting question of whether those vegetables grown by a method known as hydroponics, which does not involve any actual soil, are within the meaning of "agricultural produce."

[14] Official Report, Fifth Series, Lords, Vol. 482, col. 1039. See also Vol. 483, col. 721.

[15] *Sheffield City Council* v. *A.D.H. Demolition* (1984) 82 L.G.R. 177.

[16] See, *e.g. Kilbride* v. *William Harrison* 26 B.W.C.C. 197; *Vibroplant* v. *Holland* (1982) 126 S.J. 82.

[17] *Per* Lord Lucas of Chilworth, Official Report, Fifth Series, Lords, Vol. 483, col. 737.

> characteristic of the product must have been altered. . . .
> Moreover, the process must be an industrial one—that is, it
> must be carried on in a large and continuing scale and with
> the intervention of machinery."

This view is reasonable, but a court may not be convinced
that some essential characteristic of the product must have been
altered or that the scale of the operation must be large.

What then is the effect of this exemption for game and
agricultural produce? Every other Member State is set to take a
similar line to that in the new Act. Thus, in policy terms, our
farmers will not be at a competitive disadvantage, which, it was
agreed, would have resulted had there been no exemption.
However, the net effect of the exemption is to pass liability for
defective foodstuffs on to those further along the chain of
supply. Those who freeze or can foods, for example, could be
held liable for defects caused by pesticide residues. It is true
that the pesticide producer would still be liable if the pesticide
was itself defective. However, if it has been used in the wrong
concentration or on the wrong product then it will not be
defective. This leaves the injured person to pursue the farmer in
negligence. Here, one of the Government's own arguments in
favour of the exemption of primary agricultural products proves
to be rather a two-edged sword. It was agreed that one reason
for the exemption was that it is difficult to trace the producer of
primary agricultural products, especially when bulk supplies are
mixed. But where does this leave the injured person? Quite
apart from establishing negligence, he will be faced with the
almost impossible task of tracing the producer.

Unhappily, the exemption for primary agricultural products
must be viewed as a victory for the very strong EEC and United
Kingdom farmers' lobbies over the interests of food consumers.
Problems with misuse of fertilisers, pharmaceuticals and
pesticides are becoming increasingly apparent and it is suggested
that time will show this exemption to have been misconceived.

The chain of liability

As noted in Chapter One, persons other than the producer of
a product may incur liability under the new regime. The Act
achieves this in two ways: first by giving in section 1 an
extended definition to the term producer, and secondly, by
establishing, in section 2, the range of persons who may be
liable and the circumstances in which a mere supplier can have
liability visited upon him. Section 1(2) states:

"'producer,' in relation to a product means—
(a) the person who manufactured it;
(b) in the case of a substance which has not been manufactured but has been won or abstracted, the person who won or abstracted it;
(c) in the case of a product which has not been manufactured, won or abstracted but essential characteristics of which are attributable to an industrial or other process having been carried out (for example, in relation to agricultural produce), the person who carried out that process."

Thus, manufacturers, those who win or abstract raw materials or other substances, and those who process other products can be liable. Again the wording leaves room for interpretation by our courts. What does "essential characteristics" mean? What is an "industrial or other process" (and why not just "a process")?
Section 2 goes on:

"(1) Subject to the following provisions of this Part, where any damage is caused wholly or partly by a defect in a product, every person to whom subsection (2) below applies shall be liable for the damage.
(2) This subsection applies to:
(a) the producer of the product;
(b) any person who, by putting his name on the product or using a trade mark or other distinguishing mark in relation to the product, has held himself out to be the producer of the product;
(c) any person who has imported the product into a member State from a place outside the member States in order, in the course of any business of his, to supply it to another."

Section 2(2)(*b*) is designed to catch "own-branders" of goods but could worry others, for example retail pharmacists who may supply a prescription drug with a label bearing the pharmacist's name. It is suggested, however, that such a person does not hold himself out to be the producer. The position of importers into the EEC is clear from section 2(2)(*c*) but this will raise some interesting conflict of laws issues including those generated by the Civil Jurisdiction and Judgments Act 1982. Under this Act it is possible to sue the importer in the state of his domicile or in the state in which the harm occurs. Judgments given in one state are, in general, enforceable in all the others. Where a product is manufactured in an EEC country, then exported outwith the EEC, and then imported back again it would seem that both the producer and the importer incur liability (jointly and severally).

The inclusion of own-branders and importers in the chain of liability creates serious new burdens for such businesses. It is arguable that the increased insurance costs caused by the new regime of strict liability will have the greatest incidence on own-branders and importers.

Section 2(3) is relatively straightforward and achieves its aims in a fairly succinct manner. It states:

> "Subject as aforesaid, where any damage is caused wholly or partly by a defect in a product, any person who supplied the product (whether to the person who suffered the damage, to the producer of any product in which the product in question is comprised or to any other person) shall be liable for the damage if—
>
> (a) the person who suffered the damage requests the supplier to identify one or more of the persons (whether still in existence or not) to whom subsection (2) above applies in relation to the product;
>
> (b) that request is made within a reasonable period after the damage occurs and at a time when it is not reasonably practicable for the person making the request to identify all those persons; and
>
> (c) the supplier fails, within a reasonable period after receiving the request, either to comply with the request or to identify the person who supplied the product to him."

What this provision does is to visit, upon all of those who supply products, the threat of strict liability for product defects. That threat can be obviated by identifying *either* a person within subsection 2—producer, certain own-branders, or importer into the EEC,—or the person who supplied to the supplier. The aim of the provision is clear but the questions of "reasonable period" and "reasonable practicability" are eminently litigable.

A large range of persons are caught by the definition of supply in section 46 of the Act. The definition includes:

> "doing any of the following, whether as principal or agent, that is to say—
>
> (a) selling, hiring out or lending the goods;
>
> (b) entering into a hire-purchase agreement to furnish the goods;

(c) the performance of any contract for work and materials to furnish the goods;

(d) providing the goods in exchange for any consideration (including trading stamps) other than money;

(e) providing the goods in or in connection with the performance of any statutory function; or

(f) giving the goods as a prize or otherwise making a gift of the goods and, in relation to gas or water, those references shall be construed as including references to providing the service by which the gas or water is made available for use."

However, private sellers will often be able to use a defence in order to avoid liability.

The chief impact of section 2 will be to cause all suppliers (as defined) to maintain records of their own sources of supply, and in order to allow the prescriptive period to expire, those records should go back for 10 years. This will present an onerous extra task for many small suppliers, a large majority of whom will either not be insured or will be under-insured and hence unable to meet a product liability claim. Like the general need for record-keeping which this Act creates, there will be difficulties of document retention and storage. The fact that many modern methods of storing information have limited lives will create a temptation to store information on computer, leading to interesting questions as to the admissibility of evidence when the record is produced for use in a case.

Section 1(3) contains an important provision on the liability of suppliers under the Act:

"For the purposes of this Part a person who supplies any product in which products are comprised, whether by virtue of being component parts or raw materials or otherwise, shall not be treated by reason only of his supply of that product as supplying any of the products so comprised."

This somewhat enigmatic provision was inserted in order to alleviate the position of a supplier who would otherwise incur liability under section 2(3) if he could not identify the person who supplied the product to him. Specifically, it deals with the situation in which a supplier can identify his source in respect of the finished product but cannot identify (and it would of course be wholly unreasonable to expect him to do so) the suppliers of component parts or raw materials which are comprised within that finished product. Let us suppose that I buy a computer which has a defective piece of electronic circuitry, thus causing a fire. Assume that for some reason the producer of the computer is not worth pursuing (for example, where he has gone out of business or has much more limited resources than the producer of components). Were it not for section 1(3) the retail supplier would be liable if he could not identify the supplier of the defective component.

On a cursory reading, it might appear that section 1(3) has the effect of enabling a producer to avoid liability for component parts in his product, which would defeat a major aim of the legislation—that of making producers liable both for finished products *and* components therein. However, the key words are "shall not be treated by reason *only of his supply* of that product." The producer of a finished product has not merely supplied a product, he has produced it and hence is liable for defects in it or in its components.

The subsection also has an effect on the identification of the time when the product was supplied. Where a finished product contains a defective component part then there are two defective products and two times of supply: the time of supply of the finished product, and the time of supply of the component part. Which time of supply is to operate for the purposes of for example, prescription, or for the purposes of the defence given in section 4(1)(d): "that the defect did not exist at the relevant time?" It would seem that the effect of section 1(3) is that the time of supply of components is the time of their supply by the component manufacturer rather than their supply by the producer of the finished product. If this is correct then, if one sues the producer of a finished product which is defective because of a defective component, the time of supply will be the time of supplying the component part rather than the supply of the finished product.[18]

One loophole for the unscrupulous producer, own-brander or importer is exploitation of the ease and inexpensiveness with which limited liability can be acquired. How many will form or buy a company as a vehicle for the marketing of defective or doubtfully safe products? It has been argued that some foreign traders who sell in the United Kingdom market will be tempted, as of course will some indigenous rogues. Company law is notoriously inept at dealing with abuse of the separate corporate personality and limited liability principles, and it is by no means

[18] This is certainly the view of the Lord Advocate: Official Report, Fifth Series, Lords, Vol. 483, col. 751.

clear that the law would be prepared to lift the veil of incorporation in such circumstances.

Section 2(5) restates the now general common law approach in joint fault:

> "Where two or more persons are liable by virtue of this part for the same damage, their liability shall be joint and several."

Similarly, existing rights of contribution and recourse are preserved by section 6.

THE UNITED STATES POSITION—SOME COMPARISONS

(A) *Products*

For many years it seemed that strict liability in the United States was applicable to product-caused harms and that, subject to the usual exceptions, negligence applied elsewhere. This position has been subject to some erosion in the sense that strict liability has been extended beyond the accepted meaning of product. Thus, the concept of product has been extended to incorporeal property[19] and even to land.[20] Phillips[21] sums up the position thus:

> "Products law has been applied to leases, bailments, licences, and in the transfer of goods where no transfer of property interest is contemplated. There is an emerging trend to apply strict products liability law to occupiers of business premises. The law is being extended to testers, franchises, licensees, and it may well soon include mere advertisers. Similarly, the providers of professional services—doctors, lawyers, architects and the like—may be brought within the penumbras of product law."

Perhaps the most challenging questions which product liability has posed for the American legal system as a whole are those

---

[19] *Halstead* v. *U.S.* 535 F.Supp. 782 (D.C. Conn. 1982). For discussion of whether information products such as aircraft instrument approach charts are products see: *Brocklesby* v. *United States* 753 F.2d. 794 (9th Cir. 1985); *Fluor Corp.* v. *Jeppeson Inc.* 170 Cal.App. 3d. 468, 216 Cal. Rptr. 268 (1985).

[20] *Avner* v. *Longridge Estates* 272 Cal.App. 2d. 607, 77 Cal. Rptr. 633 (1969). See also *Becker* v. *IRM Corp.* 38 Cal. 3d. 454, 213 Cal. Rptr. 213 (1985) for an application of strict liability to landlords.

[21] Phillips, "The Status of Products Liability Law in the United States of America," Conference paper presented to S.P.T.L. Colloquium, September 1984.

raised by the so-called toxic torts. Litigation arising from, for example, use of the defoliant Agent Orange, from asbestos, toxic wastes and cigarettes, has strained the United States tort system and raised the crucial question about whether after-acquired information should be used to evaluate product safety. It is interesting to notice that only some of these toxic torts would ground strict liability under the United Kingdom regime. Clearly, the definitions of product and producer in the 1987 Act will not permit the kind of expansion of product liability to which Phillips adverts. In particular, strict liability for toxic wastes will not arise under our new regime unless the product has been supplied in the course of business with a view to profit. Thus, persons injured by toxic wastes such as chemicals which are dumped, or those injured in a trial of a product fall outside the Act. These apparent anomalies are the necessary result of any system which imposes a particularised regime of strict liability, and which thus has to draw boundaries by the use of concepts such as product, producer, defect, supply, and which uses, as the vehicle for change, statute rather than common law.

There is, however, one other divergence of approach to the question of "products" between the United States and the United Kingdom regime which ought, albeit briefly, to be considered. As noted, many courts follow section 402A of the Restatement (Second) on Torts. For present purposes the important wording is:

"One who sells any product in a defective condition unreasonably dangerous . . ."

These words make it clear that strict liability is contingent upon there having been a sale of a product rather than the supply of services, the latter situation being usually a negligence rather than strict liability issue.

Of the types of case in which United States courts have made the products/services distinction three are the most striking: the supply of human blood or blood products; the supply of pharmaceutical services, and the supply of information.[22]

Cases on the supply of human blood products are controversial and indeed infamous, in particular the *Cunningham* decision, adverted to elsewhere,[23] which rejected the unknowability of the defect as a defence to a strict liability claim. Some

---

[22] See generally, Walker, "The Expanding Applicability of Strict Liability Principles: How is a Product Defined?" (1986) 22 Tort and Ins. L.Jnl. 1.
[23] See discussion in Chap. 6.

jurisdictions have applied section 402A's strict liability to blood suppliers[24] while others have characterised the supply of human blood as a service,[25] hence attracting negligence rather than strict liability. But the vast majority of states have solved the problem by legislation to the effect that the supply of human blood is a service rather than a sale. This has been done on policy grounds, including the fear that the availability of medical services might be adversely affected by the imposition of strict liability. For example, the California Court of Appeal[26] in deciding whether or not the supply of blood products to a haemophiliac, who had died after contracting AIDS from the product, attracted strict liability, applied the state legislation[27] to the effect that the manufacture or supply of a blood product was the rendition of a service.

Legislation has not solved the products/services question in other spheres, and it has been left to the courts to proceed on an ad hoc basis. So where plaintiffs have sought to have strict liability imposed upon, for example, pharmacists, some courts have felt able to differentiate pharmacists from other retailers, finding the former to have supplied a service.[28] A leading recent illustration from the California Supreme Court is *Murphy* v. *R.R. Squibb and Sons Inc.*[29] in which a plaintiff sought to hold a pharmacist strictly liable for loss caused by the defective drug, DES. The reasoning of the court in finding a distinction between pharmacists and other retailers rested on the character-isation of pharmacists as professionals. This in itself may be true but when dispensing drugs their activity is often more retail rather than advisory.

The difficulties inherent in the legal treatment of information are exacerbated in the context of information technology. Should manufacturers of computer software be viewed as supplying a product and hence be subjected to strict liability standards? This matter has not yet arisen before the appellate courts in the United States[30] but in some "information product"

---

[24] *Ibid.*; *Brady* v. *Overlook Hosp.* 121 N.J.Super. 299, 296 A.2d. 668 (1972).

[25] e.g. *Perlmutter* v. *Beth David Hospital* 308 N.Y. 100, 123 N.E. 2d. 792 (1954); *Shephard* v. *Alexian Bros. Hosp. Inc.* 33 Cal.App. 3d. 606, 109 Cal. Rptr. 132 (1973).

[26] *Hyland Therapeutics* v. *Superior Court* 175 Cal.App. 3d. 509, 220 Cal. Rptr. 590 (1985).

[27] Cal. Health and Safety Code, para. 1606 (West, 1979).

[28] See, e.g. *Batiste* v. *American Home Prods. Corp.* 32 N.C. App. 1, 231 S.E. 2d. 269 (1977); *Bichler* v. *Willung* 58 A.D. 2d. 331, 397 N.Y.S. 2d. 57 (1977).

[29] 40 Cal. 3d. 672, 710 P.2d. 247, 221 Cal. Rptr. 447 (1985).

[30] Walker, *op. cit.*, at 12.

cases, strict liability has been applied. For example, in *Fluor Corp.* v. *Jeppeson Inc.*,[31] where an airport instrument approach chart did not designate a hill, which was the highest point in the area, the chart was held to be a product for the purposes of strict liability. The primary reasons for the court's decision were that the charts were mass-produced, unlike information supplied "under individually-tailored service agreements,"[32] and that the policy reasons underlying strict liability, in particular the need to afford protection from manufacturing defects, should be considered in deciding whether something is a product.[33] Accordingly, the catastrophic nature of the potential harm was significant.

It is to be expected that any Federal legislation on product liability would retain the need for the sale of a product rather than a service, and would exclude human tissue, organs and blood products from the definition of product.[34]

This products/services dichotomy is also important in United Kingdom law, for example in deciding whether or not the Sale of Goods Act 1979 applies to a particular transaction. Oft cited problem cases include the manufacture and supply of false teeth made to order,[35] the supply of food in a restaurant,[36] the manufacture to specification of a ship's propellor,[37] and the supply and fitting of roofing tiles.[38] There have of course been more clear-cut cases, such as *Robinson* v. *Graves*[39] in which the painting of a portrait was not a sale of goods. In contract, the supply of services is generally governed in England by the Supply of Goods and Services Act 1982. In tort, however, no product/services dichotomy exists. It is of course true that Lord Atken's dictum in *Donoghue* uses the term "product" but the general principles of negligence liability have been interpreted

---

[31] 170 Cal.App. 3d. 468, 216 Cal. Rptr. 268 (1985).

[32] *Ibid.* under reference to *Brocklesby*, n. 19 above, and *Saloomey* v. *Jeppeson & Co.*, 707 F.2d. 671 (2d. Cir. 1983).

[33] *Ibid.* under reference to *Lowrie* v. *City of Evanston* 50 Ill. App. 3d. 376.

[34] See, *e.g.* H.R. 1115, 100th, Cong. 1st. Sess., 133 Cong. Rec. E 930. (daily ed., April 28, 1987). In H.R. 5214, 97th. Cong. 1st Sess., 127 Cong. Rec. H 9529 (daily ed., December 14, 1981), s. 8(4) states that the term "product" does not include human tissue, organs, or human blood and its components.

[35] *Samuels* v. *Davis* [1943] K.B. 526.

[36] *Lockett* v. *A.M. Charles Ltd.* [1938] 4 All E.R. 170.

[37] *Cammel Laird & Co. Ltd.* v. *Manganese Bronze and Brass Co. Ltd.* [1934] A.C. 402.

[38] *Young and Marten* v. *McManus Childs* [1969] 1 A.C. 454.

[39] [1935] 1 K.B. 597.

as covering the whole range of production-related negligent acts.[40] What, then, is the position under the Consumer Protection Act 1987? The answer to this question lies principally in an understanding of the terms "producer" and "own-brander," and of the meaning of the term "supply." These terms were explained earlier. In the present context it is clear that, for example, someone who repairs a product will not be included in the definition of producer. Similarly, the product's designer will be excluded, assuming that he is not also the manufacturer or own-brander. Those who recondition products would fall into the category of producers if their activity could be construed as manufacture of the products. Those who install or fit products manufactured by others will not be producers unless the installation or fitting is into some other finished product: such a person will be liable as an own-brander only if he has held himself out as producer. Difficulties may arise in some cases however: if, in the above example of the portrait, the paint was defective as a result of materials mixed by the artist, would he be regarded as the producer of a product? It is difficult to avoid an affirmative answer to this question.

Thus, many persons performing services will be excluded from primary liability under the new rules. However, they will often be caught as suppliers of the product and hence liable unless they can identify the producer, importer or own-brander.[41] The definition of supply was given earlier, but it is worth noticing that those who hire out goods or perform any contract for work and materials to furnish the goods are suppliers. In summary, one who performs services using products manufactured by another will not be liable (except as own-brander or importer) unless, as supplier, on failure to identify the producer, own-brander or importer.

By way of illustrating the application of the new rules let us take the three United States examples quoted earlier. Human blood, blood products and derivatives, organs, etc., are certainly products within the meaning of section 1(2). Leaving aside the metaphysics, who is the producer? According to section 1(2):

> "in the case of a substance which has not been manufactured but has been won or abstracted, the person who won or abstracted it."

---

[40] See, *e.g. Herschtal* v. *Stewart and Arden Ltd.* [1940] 1 K.B. 155; *Malfroot* v. *Noxel Ltd.* (1935) 51 T.L.R. 551; *Howard* v. *Furness Houlder Argentine Lines Ltd.* [1936] 2 All E.R. 781.

[41] See the Consumer Protection Act 1987, s. 2(3).

Thus, the health authority would be liable for loss caused by defective blood although the development risks defence may apply in some cases.

The position of the pharmacist is fairly straightforward—he will not be a producer unless he manufactures products; he will not be an own-brander simply by putting his name on a product; he may of course be an importer; like other retailers he may incur liability as a supplier. There is no room, it is suggested, for the United States products/services dichotomy in relation to pharmacists in the United Kingdom.

Product liability problems posed by "information" products were also mentioned earlier. Clearly, loss caused by reliance upon the written word may trigger liability for mis-statement, but the printed page is a product and the publisher is its producer. It will take some nimble footwork for the United Kingdom courts to find an escape route for the publisher of written works such as computer software. Courts will certainly be tempted to find an exception for "information products," as the separate treatment of mis-statements at common law shows. The approach of some of the United States courts, based upon the mass-produced nature of the information, and the policy reasons behind the common law development of strict liability, is quite convincing. Books and magazines are, however, also mass-produced, and it would not be open to a United Kingdom court to invoke policy reasons for avoiding the application of the statute. It may well be the case that the exclusion of such things from the scheme of strict liability is not by means of the definition of product, but is on the basis that they were not defective or that the pursuer was contributorily negligent in relying upon the information. Arguably, however, Lord Denning's familiar marine hydrographer,[42] who omits a reef from a published chart causing a ship to sink, will not be liable in negligence but the publishers may find themselves liable under the 1987 Act.

(B) *The chain of liability*

Most of the states in the United States now recognise some form of strict liability for defective products, and many have expressly adopted the provisions of section 402A of the Second Restatement of Torts. This provision imposes strict liability on those who engage in the business of selling a defective product.

---

[42] In *Candler* v. *Crane, Christmas & Co.* [1951] 2 K.B. 164 at 183.

Many states which have enacted or introduced product liability Bills based on section 402A. However, proposals for a Federal product liability statute are being discussed and if these are accepted it is expected that there will be a retreat back to negligence in design defect and warning cases.

Comment c to section 402A gives the justification for the imposition of strict liability on those in the marketing enterprise:

"on whatever theory, the justification for strict liability has been said to be that the seller, by marketing his product for use or consumption, has undertaken and assumed a special responsibility towards any member of the consuming public who may be injured by it; that the public has the right to expect and does expect, in the case of products which it needs and for which it is forced to rely upon the seller, that reputable sellers will stand behind their goods; that public policy demands that the burden of accidental injuries caused by products intended for consumption be placed upon those who market them, and be treated as a cost of consumption against which liability insurance can be obtained; and that the consumer of such products is entitled to the maximum protection against injury at the hands of someone and the proper persons to afford it are those who market the products."

Comment f to the section goes on to identify those persons engaged in the business of selling whom the provision perceives to be strictly liable:

"The Rule stated in this section applies to any person engaged in the business of selling products for use or consumption. It therefore applies to any manufacturer of such a product, to any wholesale or retail dealer or distributor, and to the operator of a restaurant..."

This principle that sellers in the distributive chain should be liable in respect of a defective product has long been recognised in American courts. Examples of manufacturer's liability are legion and many have been cited earlier. There can be no doubt that the majority of product liability claims in the United States are raised against the manufacturer of the defective product— research indicates that 87 per cent. of product liability payments stem from claims made against manufacturers,[43] but there is also

---

[43] Insurance Services Offices (1977): "Product Liability Closed Claim Survey: A Technical Analysis of Survey Results." New York I.S.O.

a clear body of case law which supports the imposition of liability on others in the production and marketing chain.

As in this country, liability will not arise, in negligence, if the distributor was not required to test or inspect the product and had no knowledge of its defectiveness.[44] However, these considerations obviously do not apply under a strict tort theory of liability.

Applications of strict liability outside the field of the selling and marketing of moveables can also be found in United States judgments. In a number of cases, car-hire firms have been held liable, in respect of defects in vehicles hired.[45] Builders of immoveable property (real-estate) have also been subjected to strict liability.

Employers, on the other hand, are usually exempt from a strict liability action. This arises from the "exclusive remedy" rule in relation to work-related injuries which has been incorporated in all state workers' compensation statutes. Broadly speaking, the rule is that state compensation is the sole remedy available from the employer. Common law tort claims against employers ceased to exist following the incorporation of the rule. However, in recent years some claims against employers have succeeded. These are the so-called "dual capacity" suits in which the employer is also the manufacturer and where, therefore, the exclusive remedy rule can be circumvented.

The virtual elimination of employers' common law liability, coupled with the inadequacy of workers' compensation, was probably the single most influential factor in the development of strict liability in tort. Employees who were dissatisfied with state compensation pursued the manufacturers of defective products in order to "top-up" the state's award. What began as a "top-up" measure has burgeoned into a massively important area of litigation.

(C) *Successor corporation liability and market share liability*

(a) *Successor corporation liability.* Some 10 years ago, American courts began to recognise a form of liability which has now become quite widely recognised and which is usually described as "successor corporation liability." This term is used to refer to the situation resulting from a takeover, merger or sale of assets

---

[44] See Miller and Lovell, *op. cit.*, at 310–311.
[45] See, *e.g. Francioni* v. *Gibsonia Truck Corp.* 2 Prod. Liab. Rep. 7911 (1977).

in which a successor business becomes liable for loss caused by defective products marketed by its predecessor. It has been said[46] that the key characteristics of a successful successor corporation claim are (a) an exchange of predecessor assets for successor stock; (b) dissolution of the predecessor shortly after the exchange; and (c) the successor continuity of employees and management. The basic justification for imposing liability commonly is continuity.[47] In *Ortiz* v. *South Bend Lathe*,[48] Fleming J. summed up the situation in vivid terms:

"Product liability today has become an integral part of a manufacturing business and the liability attaches to the business like fleas to a dog, where it remains imbedded regardless of changes in the ownership of the business."

In *Ray* v. *Alad Corp.*,[49] the court identified policy reasons for the imposition of successor corporation liability: first, the remedy which the plaintiff would have had against the predecessor business is no longer available, usually because of its dissolution; secondly, the defendant as successor corporation had the resources to assume the risk spreading role of the original manufacturer; and, thirdly, the defendant having benefitted from the predecessor's goodwill in continuing to produce the same goods, should properly bear the burden of loss caused by previous goods. These considerations have continued to guide courts in successor corporation cases[50] and indeed in some cases courts have applied successor corporation liability where some of the basic characteristics, listed above, were absent.[51] Thus, in some cases, the requirement that assets be exchanged for stock has been ignored[52]; in others, the requirement that the predecessor be dissolved[53] has been

---

[46] See Phillips, "Successor Corporation Liability" 58 N.Y.U.L.Rev. 906 (1983); Roe, "Mergers, Acquisitions and Tort: A Comment on the Problem of Successor Corporation Liability" 70 Va. L.Rev. 1559 (1984).

[47] See Whincup.

[48] 120 Cal. Rptr. 556 (1975).

[49] 560 P.2d. 3 (1977).

[50] See, *e.g. Harnandez* v. *Johnson Press Corp.* 388 N.E. 2d. 778 (1979); *Johnson* v. *Marshall and Hushart Machinery* 384 N.E. 2d. 142 (1978); *Lundell* v. *Sidney Machine Tool Co.* (Calif. Court of Appeal, 2nd. Dist. Div. 1, April 9, 1987.

[51] See generally, Phillips, *op. cit.* n. 21, above.

[52] *Ray* v. *Alad Corp.* n. 117, above; *Turner* v. *Bitum. Cas. Co.* 397 Mich. 406, 244 N.W. 2d. 873 (1976).

[53] *e.g. Tift* v. *Forage King Indus.* 108 Wis. 2d. 72, 322 N.W. 2d. 14 (1982).

dispensed with and the need for management and/or employee continuity has been questioned.[54]

There is currently some doubt as to the limits of the doctrine of successor corporation liability, and the cases have proceeded on rather an ad hoc basis. It is clear, however, that in some states it is simply not imposed, even where the predecessor's assets are used by the successor to produce the same product. Also, most courts continue to insist that the basic characteristics, mentioned earlier, are present before allowing a claim and most courts also require that the same product is produced by the successor. Thus, it can be concluded that the law on successor corporation liability in the United States is in an embryonic state and as yet no viable and consistent principles have been established.

The question of successor corporation liability for predecessor torts simply has not arisen before United Kingdom courts. The reason for this is that in the United Kingdom, because of the transaction costs, the most common method for transferring control of a business is the take-over bid, agreed or contested, by which shares in the target company are acquired either for cash or in exchange for shares in the offeror company.[55] Hence, the target company will commonly remain as a separate legal entity and thus be liable *inter alia* for its own past torts including the manufacture of defective products. However, it is possible for the target company to be extinguished as a legal entity or, indeed, for two companies to merge into a new company. Take, for example, what Palmer's company law describes as "a very popular method of amalgamation."[56]

> "Companies E and F want to amalgamate. A new company, E (Holdings) is formed. E (Holdings) issues shares to the shareholders in E and F in exchange for their shares in E and F. The former shareholders in E and F thus become holders of shares (credited as fully paid) in E (Holdings). E and F are then dissolved and E (Holdings) alters its name to E. The amalgamation is complete."

What then is the position of those (who could be described as involuntary creditors) who have tort claims against the original E or against F in respect of a product marketed prior to

---

[54] See Phillips, *op. cit.* n. 46 above.
[55] See generally, Weinberg and Blank, *Takeovers and Mergers* (Sweet and Maxwell 4th ed., 1979), Chap. 1.
[56] (8th ed., 1987), para. 80–05, example 4.

dissolution? On creditors generally, Palmer offers the following view[57]:

"... their position is that they remain creditors of the transferor company, and have all the rights against that company that their debts confer. It will normally be part of the arrangement that the transferee company agrees to meet the liabilities of the transferor company and gives an indemnity to this effect or, alternatively, that the transferor company retains sufficient assets to meet its liabilities."

But what if the "normal" indemnity is not given, or does not cover tort liabilities, or the assets retained by the transferor company are insufficient to meet tort claims? Similarly, if one company sells assets and goodwill, rather than shares, to another and this results in the dissolution of the former, where do tort victims stand?

The key issue is, of course, whether the predecessor company dissolves. As indicated above, this does happen in some take-over or merger situations. If it does happen, then it is clear that tort claimants against the dissolved company have no remedy, in the absence of an indemnity which can be construed as covering tort liabilities.

(b) *Market share liability.* One of the most fascinating departures from traditional tort principles in United States liability law is the so-called "market share" liability for product defects.

This form of liability, which is particularly likely to arise in "mass tort" claims (*i.e.* where many have been injured by a defective product) is derived from a decision of the California Supreme Court in 1980: *Sindell* v. *Abbott Laboratories*,[58] in which liability was imposed, severally (it seems), on producers of a defective drug without proof of causation and on the basis

---

[57] *Ibid.* at 80–06.
[58] 26 Cal. 3d. 588, 607 P.2d. 924, 163 Cal. Rptr. 132, cert. denied, 449 US 912 (1980). The decision has provoked much criticism: see, *e.g.* Note, "Market Share Liability: An Answer to the DES Causation Problem," 94 Harv.L.Rev. 668 (1981); Note, "Market Share Liability for Defective Products: An Ill Advised Remedy for the Problem of Identification," 76 N.W. Univ. L.Rev. 300 (1981); Teff, "Market Share Liability—A Novel Approach to Causation," (1982) 31 I.C.L.Q. 840. Other techniques have been employed by courts to avoid problems of identification in DES cases: see Winslow, "Market Share Liability, etc.," 8 J. of Prod. Liability 167. See also *Abel* v. *Eli Lilly & Co.* 343 N.W. 2d. 164, 469 US 833 (1984); *Bichler* v. *Eli Lilly & Co.* 436 N.E. 2d. 182 (1982).

of percentage of market share. The case was a class action concerning the drug Diethylstilbestrol (DES), a synthetic oestrogen used to prevent miscarriage, which can cause cancerous vaginal and cervical growths, occasionally fatal, in daughters exposed to it while *in utero*. These cancerous growths are of the type adenocarcinoma, which until the 1970s was rare, and which manifests itself at the earliest 10–12 years after birth, and commonly more than 20 years later. It seems that somewhere between 200 and 300 companies actually produced DES although in the present case only five of the major producers were involved as defendants at the final stage. The court considered an earlier case, *Summers* v. *Tice*,[59] in which two defendants, who had each fired shotguns in the direction of the plaintiff, were held jointly and severally liable for the resulting harm even though it was impossible to establish whose gun caused the injury. The court shifted the burden of proof of causation to the defendants, effectively obliging each to establish that his act was not the cause of the harm. In *Sindell*, the court considered that is could not apply the *Summers* ratio, since in *Summers* the harm had certainly been caused by one of the defendants, while in *Sindell* it was not clear that any of the five defendants had actually produced the particular pills which had caused the injury. Thus, in *Summers* the person responsible was being made liable, while in *Sindell* the producer of the offending substance may have escaped all liability. Nevertheless, the court in *Sindell* was prepared to find *all* the defendants prima facie liable.[60]

> "But we approach the issue of causation from a different perspective: we hold it to be reasonable in the present context to measure the likelihood that any of the defendants supplied the product which allegedly injured the plaintiff by the percentage which the DES sold by each of them for the purpose of preventing miscarriage bears to the entire production of the drug sold by all for that purpose. Plaintiff asserts in her briefs that Eli Lilly and Company and five or six other companies produced 90 per cent. of the DES marketed. If at trial this is established to be the fact, then there is a corresponding likelihood that this comparative handful of producers manufacture the DES which caused plaintiff's injuries, and only a 10 per cent.

---

[59] 33 Cal. 2d. 80, 199 P.2d. 1 (1948).
[60] 26 Cal. 3d. 588 at 611–612.

likelihood that the offending producer would escape liability...

The presence in the action of a substantial share of the appropriate market also provides a ready means to apportion damages among the defendants. Each defendant will be held liable for the proportion of the judgment represented by its share of that market unless it demonstrates that it could not have made the product which caused plaintiff's injuries. In the present case, as we have seen, one DES manufacturer was dismissed from the action upon filing a declaration that it had not manufactured DES until after plaintiff was born. Once plaintiff has met her burden of joining the required defendants, they in turn may cross-complaint against other DES manufacturers, not joined in the action, which they can allege might have supplied the injury-causing product."

The court concluded that:

"...under the rule we adopt, each manufacturer's liability for an injury would be approximately equivalent to the damages caused by the DES it manufactured..."[61]

What are we to make of such an approach to causation? There are, as the court conceded, practical problems in defining the market and the market share. As Teff notes,[62]

"some companies were major national suppliers of DES; others operated only in a regional market, and their respective shares may have varied considerably over time and from place to place."

These certainly are difficult obstacles, but it seems that the court would absolve from liability those producers whose product could not have been used by the plaintiff, for example, where it could not have been obtained from the source from which she obtained it, or where the producer only commenced manufacture after the injury was sustained. It must be presumed, however, that such producers will be liable in respect of other plaintiffs, since in such other cases they will be unable to disprove the presumption of causal link. There will also be major difficulties in applying the court's criterion that a "substantial percentage" of the producers should be joined in the action.

---

[61] *Ibid.*
[62] *Op. cit.*, at 843.

It is clear that the inability of a plaintiff to identify the producer of the offending product will increasingly feature in product liability cases of the "mass tort" or "toxic tort" type. Can *Sindell* be justified as the proper judicial response in such circumstances? Hart and Honore say of the decision[63]:

> "Hence in effect the court dispenses with the need to prove fault and causal connection and instead treats the manufacturers of the drug as collectively insuring in proportion to the market share of each, those who suffer harm after using the drug."

However, it is suggested that in the particular circumstances of the case—an unidentifiable producer of a particular defective product which has a proven propensity for harm—market share liability was a novel and just solution, albeit one which ought to be applied very sparingly.

Conclusion

Any particularised scheme of liability brings in its train definitional problems. Although the Act gives a wide meaning to the term product, the production and sale of land or buildings, of incorporeal moveables and of "pure" services will fall outside the scheme of liability; nevertheless, the full range of goods and substances falls within the statutory definition, including moveables incorporated into immoveables and products supplied with services. In general, the definition of product is satisfactory and there should be little scope for litigation in which plaintiffs seek artificially to fit their claim into the new regime; the boundaries are quite clearly drawn.

Difficulties with imposing liability on a range of persons have been addressed earlier. The new rules will have quite a marked impact in this regard, since the general principles of negligence liability would preclude a finding of fault where a reputable manufacturer had been used or where inspection by the distributor was impossible. One immediate effect of the new provisions will be to cause distributors and retailers to maintain full records of their sources, undoubtedly a burden, but a necessary one, on the smaller business.

It could be suggested, however, that the Act does not go far enough, and that all of those in the manufacturing and marketing chain (including distributors and retailers—even

---

[63] *Causation in the Law* (2nd ed., 1985), p. 424.

where they can identify their sources) should be subject to strict liability in respect of defective products which they sell. As noted, this is the American approach. The effect of this would be to create an economically motivated safety consciousness amongst all product sellers. On the positive side, distributors and retailers, having been required to compensate an injured party, would exercise a contractual right to an indemnity, thereby effecting the transfer of the responsibility to the ultimate producer. However, as the proposals point out, a broader scheme of liability involves a concomitant increase in costs.

The principal theme of the economic argument against a broad spectrum of liability is that, since all in the marketing chain would have to insure against liability, and since ultimately the public would have to pay for the strict liability regime, there will be an unconscionable rise in product prices. This, it is claimed, would put British manufacturers at a competitive disadvantage and would fuel inflation. However, spokesmen from the insurance industry have stated that, since the average cost of product liability premiums is so small, an increase in insurance costs would not significantly affect product prices.[64] Commenting on the United States position, the Interagency Task Force states that:

"...the alleged product liability insurance crisis has not resulted in a substantial increase in the cost of products."[65]

The argument that all those in the producing and marketing enterprise should incur strict liability is a strong one. All product sellers are already strictly liable in contract and under consumer safety legislation. Presumably insurance is carried for these risks. Widening this insurance provision to cover injury to non-purchasers would be the effect of a strict liability regime. Arguably, there would be no significant increase in costs. Although superficially inequitable, such a change could be argued to be a major step towards the furtherance of the primary policy aim—accident prevention. In any event, a sense of justice would be preserved by the existence of contractual and tortious rights of indemnity. Further, product sellers and distributors would have an incentive to monitor the safety

---

[64] See Editorial, 76 Law Soc. Gazette, June 1979.
[65] Interagency Task Force on Product Liability, US Dept. of Commerce, Final Report of the Legal Study (1977).

aspects of products which they stock, and would cease to deal with unreliable producers, thus furthering policy aims.

Why then does our new regime impose strict liability on distributors and sellers only where original producers cannot be identified? The answer, it would seem, is that notions of culpa still lurk, albeit at some depth, in the philosophy behind the new rules. There is great force in the argument that the primary creator of the risk should, in tort, bear a greater burden than that borne by the agency of its distribution.

Chapter 4

THE ROLE OF WARNINGS IN PRODUCT LIABILITY

The question of whether or not potential dangers or defects
inherent in the use of a product have been brought to the
attention of the user by an adequate warning or set of
instructions for use, is an important aspect of product liability
law. Many product liability claims have focused upon this issue,
and have involved an allegation that a manufacturer has failed
to warn of a defect or danger. It is clear that this emphasis on
warnings will continue in a strict liability regime. As one
commentator notes:

> "The popular solution to every alleged design defect
> problem seems to be 'Warn against it.' Like mother's
> chicken soup it is the panacea for all ills."[1]

Thus, the role of warnings in product liability law, although
not on the face of it a major element in the new legislation,
should not be under-estimated. In this Chapter that role is
examined in detail. It will be argued:

(a) that in the United States, despite the advent of strict
liability and the much-vaunted "product liability crisis"
(allegedly caused by strict liability), cases based on
failure to warn are not tried under proper strict
liability principles (even where the court purports to
apply strict liability) but under principles of negligence.
The result of this is that after almost 30 years of strict
liability, on the failure to warn issue United States law
is for most jurisdictions really no stricter than our own;
and

(b) that, notwithstanding this lack of progress, there are a
number of difficulties inherent in using the failure to
warn ground of liability which will probably be
exacerbated under a strict liability regime in this
country, and which should cause our judges to tread
warily when dealing with litigation in this area.

[1] See Twerski et al., "The Use And Abuse of Warnings In Product Liability—
Design Defect Litigation Comes of Age" 61 Cornell L.Rev. 495, (1976), at
500.

A COMPARISON BETWEEN UNITED STATES AND UNITED
KINGDOM "FAILURE TO WARN" CASES

The producer's knowledge of the danger

(a) *General principles.* In both the United Kingdom and the
United States liability in negligence for failure to warn exists
only in respect of dangers which the manufacturer knew, or
ought to have known, about. There can be no liability where
the danger is scientifically undiscoverable or unknowable since
the duty is to take only reasonable care. In any event, it would
seem logically absurd to impose liability on a manufacturer for
failing to warn of a danger about which he could not have
known.

One of the leading authorities on failure to warn is *Vacwell
Engineering Ltd.* v. *B.D.H. Chemicals Ltd.*[2] The defendants
supplied the chemical boron tribromide to Vacwell in glass
ampoules labelled "harmful vapour." It was not known to the
suppliers that the chemical reacted violently with water. A
scientist accidently dropped an ampoule into a sink containing
other ampoules and the resulting explosion killed him and
caused great damage to the plaintiff's factory. The manufacturers were held to have been negligent in failing to give an
adequate warning of the dangerous properties of the chemical,
which had been pointed out in scientific journals and therefore
ought to have been known. Liability was imposed both in tort
and in contract (under section 14 Sale of Goods Act 1979). It is
clearly established that this contractual liability is strict and that
B.D.H. would still have been liable had the dangerous
properties of the chemical been unknown and undiscoverable.
Another example is *Fisher* v. *Harrods Ltd.*,[3] in which retailers
were found liable for failing to warn of the dangers occasioned
by a jewellery cleaning fluid coming into contact with the eyes.
In most instances, however, the duty to warn will fall upon the
manufacturer rather than the retailer.

In the American law of negligence the principle is the same as
in United Kingdom cases; liability is imposed in respect of all
foreseeable product risks which have not been adequately

---

[2] [1971] 1 Q.B. 88. See *Wormell* v. *R.H.A Agriculture (East) Ltd.* [1987] 1
W.L.R. 1091. See also *Ellis* v. *International Playtex Inc.* 745 F.2d. 292 (4th Cir.
1984) for a US example of an inadequate warning constituting a breach of
implied warranty of merchantibility.
[3] [1966] 1 Lloyd's Rep. 500; 110 S.J. 133.

warned against. At first sight, it might be thought that strict liability in tort would be applied to the failure-to-warn situation, and that this would differ from the approach taken in negligence. Section 402A of the Restatement (Second) of Torts, in Comment j, states that:

> "in order to prevent the product from being unreasonably dangerous the seller may be required to give directions or warnings on the container as to its use."

However, the comment goes on effectively to return to negligence by introducing the concept of foreseeability: the seller must warn:

> "if he has knowledge, or by the application of reasonable, developed human skill and foresight should have knowledge of the presence of the danger."

Thus, even under the strict liability principles of section 402A attention is focused on the conduct of the manufacturer as in negligence and not on the product, as a strict liability regime logically requires. This was clearly illustrated in *Karajala* v. *Johns-Manville Products Corp.*[4] where the court stated that failure to warn leads to:

> "liability for damages under strict liability in tort... Of course a manufacturer is only required to warn of foreseeable dangers."[5]

Similarly, the Illinois Appellate Court found that there was no duty to warn of the possibility of "severe and persistent welting" caused in some users by an aerosol spray, unless the manufacturer knew or had reason to know that a substantial number of the population was allergic to the product.[6]

Nevertheless, United States courts have from time to time imposed true strict liability in failure to warn cases. In *Berkebile* v. *Brantly Helicopter Corp.,*[7] for example, the plaintiff claimed, *inter alia*, that a failure by helicopter manufacturers properly to warn of safety procedures to be carried out following engine failure had caused her husband's death. The court stated:

---

[4] 525 F.2d. 155 (8th. Cir. 1975).
[5] *Ibid.* at 158–159. It is clear that the duty to warn is a continuing duty so that latent defects which become known to the manufacturer ought to be warned against; see, *e.g. Comstock* v. *General Motors* 358 Mich. 163, 99 N.W. 2d. 627 (1959); *Cover* v. *Cohen* 61 N.Y. 2d. 261, 473 N.Y.S. 2d. 378 (1984).
[6] *Presbrey* v. *Gillette Co.* 105 Ill.App. 3d. 1082, 435 N.E. 2d. 513 (1982).
[7] 462 pa. 83, 337 A.2d. 893 (1975).

"It must be emphasised that the test of the necessity of warnings or instructions is not to be governed by the reasonable man standard.... Rather, the sole question here is whether the seller accompanied his product with sufficient instructions and warnings to make his product safe."[8]

But this case is illustrative of the exception rather than the rule. In the vast majority of cases, while purporting to apply strict liability principles, the courts have held that a manufacturer is liable only for a negligent failure to warn.

In the context of warnings, this question of the distinction between negligence and strict liability has been extensively litigated in New Jersey. That litigation will now be examined.

(b) *The Beshada-Feldman split: "All the King's horses...."* The question arises whether strict liability should apply, on failure to warn grounds, where the manufacturer could not have known of the dangers of his product. In *Beshada* v. *Johns-Manville Prods. Corp.*[9] the Supreme Court of New Jersey answered this question in the affirmative, finding a manufacturer of asbestos liable for loss caused by the product. But, just two years later, in *Feldman* v. *Lederle Laboratories*[10] the same court answered the same question in the negative. Thus, asbestos manufacturers in New Jersey were subjected to strict liability irrespective of whether the dangers could have been known, while drug manufacturers were, in *Feldman*, bound to warn only of known dangers. This line of litigation has very recently visited the United States Court of Appeals[11] where the asbestos manufacturers claimed that the New Jersey Supreme Court's decisions unconstitutionally discriminate among categories of civil litigants because no rational basis for the discrimination can be posited, and that by failing to give adequate reasons for its action the state court violated the Due Process Clause of the Fourteenth Amendment.

In *Beshada* the sole question was whether the defendants in a strict liability case based on failure to warn could avail themselves of a state of the art defence by asserting that the danger of which they failed to warn was undiscovered at the

---

[8] At 903. The court also stated that "To require foreseeability is to require the manufacturer to use due care in preparing his product." *Ibid.* at 899.

[9] 90 N.J. 191 (1982).

[10] 97 N.J. 429 (1984).

[11] *Danfield* v. *Johns-Manville Sales Corp.* 829 F.2d. 1233 (1987).

time the product was marketed and that it was also undiscoverable given the state of scientific knowledge at that time. *Beshada* was six consolidated cases against manufacturers and distributors of asbestos products, where it was alleged that asbestosis, mesothelioma and other asbestos related illnesses had been contracted as a result of exposure to asbestos. There was a substantial factual dispute about what the defendants knew and exactly when they knew it. However, the court in *Beshada* felt that it need not resolve the factual issues raised and predicated its decision on the assumption that the defendants' version of the facts was accurate (*i.e.* that the dangers were unknown and unknowable at the relevant time). Having reviewed the authorities, the court rejected the defendants' arguments that a warning was not possible and similarly rejected the contention that the imputation of knowledge which strict liability implies related only to knowledge of the product's dangerousness that existed at the time of manufacture. Thus the court held that a state of the art defence should not be allowed in failure to warn cases.

The court went on to assert that state of the art is essentially a negligence defence which seeks to explain why defendants are not culpable for failing to provide a warning, but that in strict liability cases culpability is irrelevant:

> "when the defendants argue that it is unreasonable to impose a duty on them to warn of the unknowable they misconstrue both the purpose and effect of strict liability. By imposing strict liability, we are not requiring defendants to have done something that is impossible. In this sense, the phrase 'duty to warn' is misleading. It implies negligence concepts with their attendant focus on the reasonableness of defendant's behaviour. However, a major concern of strict liability—ignored by defendants—is the conclusion that if a product is in fact defective, the distributor of the product should compensate its victims for the misfortune that it inflicted on them."[12]

Policy aims such as risk spreading, accident prevention and avoidance of difficulties in fact finding, led the court to the firm conclusion that liability ought to be imposed.

In this way, *Beshada* represents a staunch adherence to a fundamentalist doctrine of strict liability, untrammeled by negligence ideas. It should be noticed that the decision was not

[12] 90 N.J. 191 (1982) at 204–205.

intended to be limited to asbestos cases—it applied to all product liability suits. Later decisions, it will be observed, have, however, sought to restrict *Beshada* to asbestos. Despite the court's indication that language such as "duty to warn" is inapposite in a strict liability context, the decision attracted severe criticism for its apparently contradictory finding of a need to warn of unknown dangers.

In an attempt to overturn the effect of *Beshada*, a Bill was introduced, soon after the decision, in the New Jersey legislature, but was never enacted.[13] The torrent of criticism generated by the decision helped to cause the New Jersey Supreme Court to depart from *Beshada* at an early opportunity.

The occasion arose in *Feldman* v. *Lederle Laboratories* above. In brief, the facts were that a child suffered grey discolouration of the teeth consequent upon the use of a tetracycline antibiotic. In an action based upon strict liability for failure to warn, the *Feldman* court refused to follow *Beshada*, and stated:

> "We do not overrule Beshada, but restrict Beshada to the circumstances giving rise to its holding."[14]

The exact meaning of this rather enigmatic statement has perplexed later judges, but its major impact has been to restrict the *Beshada* decision to asbestos cases. The court in *Feldman* decided that in "warning" cases available knowledge is a relevant factor in measuring the reasonableness of the manufacturer's conduct.

The key question is:

> "Did the defendant know, or should he have known, of the danger, given the scientific, technological and other information available when the product was distributed; or, in other words, did he have actual or constructive knowledge of the danger?"[15]

As was noted in the earlier discussion of *Feldman*, one characteristic which distinguishes a strict liability action from one of negligence is the burden of proof. Accordingly, the court held that it was for the defendant to establish that:

---

[13] s.1465 201st. N.J. Leg., 1st. Sess. (1984). However, in 1987 New Jersey enacted a statute adopting a conservative approach to product liability: N.J.S.A. 2A; 58C–1 (L.1987 c.197).

[14] 97 N.J. (1984) 429, 479 A.2d. 374 at 388.

[15] *Ibid.* at 386. (A.2d report).

"the information was not reasonably available or obtainable and that it therefore lacked actual or constructive knowledge of the defect."[16]

Thus, the apparently key element in strict liability, imputation to the defendant of knowledge of the product's dangerousness, was to be restricted to available knowledge:

"A warning that a product may have an undiscoverable danger warns one of nothing."[17]

Before briefly noting the appellate court's discussion of the *Beshada-Feldman* dichotomy, one last case should be mentioned. In *Fischer* v. *Johns-Manville Corp.*[18] the court determined that at least one manufacturer did know of the hazards of asbestos at or before the time of distribution of the product. The court decided that personal injury plaintiffs could obtain punitive damages where a manufacturer failed to warn of a reasonably knowable danger. Clearly, one avowed aim of *Beshada*—to simplify product liability actions by not spending sufficient trial time in the investigation of what was known at a particular time—is seriously damaged by *Fischer* since plaintiffs are now being encouraged to investigate the knowledge issue in the hope of triggering a punitive award.

This troubled area of case law was bound to produce further litigation. In September 1987, the United States Court of Appeals for the Third Circuit in *Danfield* v. *Johns-Manville Sales Corp.*[19] was asked to decide whether the *Beshada-Feldman* dichotomy violated the constitution by discriminating against asbestos manufacturers and by being inadequately justified by the state court.

Over 30,000 asbestos-related personal injury claims were listed in the United States in 1986, and a court has estimated that by the year 2010 that figure will have risen to 210,000.[20] Just one month after the apparent retrenchment of *Feldman*, an asbestos manufacturer sought to rely upon that decision in order to avail himself of the state of the art defence. A motion to introduce the relevant evidence was denied by the trial court which relied upon *Beshada* to assert that asbestos manufacturers could not use the defence. The state court affirmed this

---

[16] *Ibid.* at 388.
[17] *Ibid.* at 387.
[18] 103 N.J. 643, 512 A.2d. 466 (1986).
[19] See n. 11, above.
[20] *Re School Asbestos Litigation* 789 F.2d. 996 at 1000. (3d. Cir. 1986).

decision.[21] In later cases, asbestos manufacturers again sought to introduce state of the art evidence, alleging that they were being discriminated against. The district court decided this matter, en banc, in *Re Asbestos Litigation (1986)*[22] for the purpose of issuing a ruling applicable to all pending asbestos cases. By a majority of eight to six the court held that the treatment of asbestos manufacturers by the New Jersey courts did not violate the constitution. The matter was then appealed to the United States Court of Appeals, which again by majority (2:1) upheld the decision of the state court.

Judge Weis decided that:

> "the policies of risk-spreading, compensation for victims, and simplification of trials in the highly unusual circumstances of asbestos claims furnish an adequate, albeit minimal, basis for eliminating the state of the art defense in these cases and preclude a successful equal protection challenge to the New Jersey Supreme Court decision abolishing that defence."[23]

In a powerful dissent, however, Hunter J. argued that there was no rational basis for the denial of a state of the art defence to asbestos manufacturers. He found the New Jersey court to be in breach of the constitution:

> "Today this court has noted that the manufacturers of one product may not use the state of the art defence. That product is asbestos. The court has said to asbestos manufacturers: there are too many asbestos cases, these cases have clogged up the court calendar, schedules and statistics; the proof of state of the art is too time-consuming and concerned with too many variables; and, in any event, we do not think you could prove the defence even if we gave you the chance. This one number class of defendants is deprived of a potentially exculpatory defense in the interest of expediency and calendar control. The manufacturers of all other products—including Agent Orange, the Dalkon Shield and DES—may use the defense, even if they are also clogging up the court calendar and causing statistical chaos. Only the asbestos industry is treated differently. This is just plain wrong and I dissent."[24]

---

[21] *In the Matter of Asbestos Litigation Venued in Middlesex County* 99 N.J. 204, 491 A.2d. 700 (1984).

[22] 628 F.Supp. 774 (D.N.J. 1986).

[23] *Danfield*, n. 11 above, at 1244.

[24] *Ibid.* at 1252.

The final result cannot be rationally justified. Whatever rationale is to be given to the law in this area, it can hardly be one based upon the kind of product involved. To have different shades of strict liability for different types of product is a wholly irrational and indefensible policy.

The user's knowledge of the danger

Both United Kingdom and United States law also recognise that a manufacturer is not required to warn of a danger or defect which is obvious or is a matter of common knowledge.[25] Thus, for example, in *Farr* v. *Butter Bros.*[26] where an experienced steel erector continued to work on a crane which he knew to be defective and was killed by a falling jib, the court held that there was no duty on the defendant to warn the plaintiff in respect of known dangers. Courts in the United States have normally followed the same principle. Thus, there are many cases in which users of ready-mixed concrete have sustained burns from lime in the product and been denied recovery on the ground of "obvious or known danger."[27]

The advent of strict liability has not affected this principle: the Restatement (Second) of Torts states that there is no duty to warn where:

> "the danger, or the potentiality of danger is generally known and recognised."[28]

In any event, a product which carries an obvious risk of harm is probably outwith the definition of defective (the so-called "consumer expectation test") under which, in the United Kingdom, a product must provide the safety which persons generally are entitled to expect, while in the United States, a product has a defect when it is:

> "dangerous beyond that contemplated by the ordinary consumer who purchases it, with the ordinary knowledge common to the community as to its characteristics."[29]

---

[25] Miller and Lovell, *Product Liability*, (Butterworths, 1977), p. 239; Noel, "Products Defective Because of Inadequate Directions or Warnings." 23 S.W.L.J. (1969), at 272 *et seq.*

[26] [1932] 2 K.B. 606.

[27] Noel, *op. cit.*, cases cited at 272, n. 102.

[28] s. 402A, Comment j.

[29] *Ibid.* Comment i.

Thus, for example, in *Genaust* v. *Illinois Power Co.*[30] the court found that strict liability did not impose a duty to warn where:

> "the possibility of injury results from a common propensity of the product which is open and obvious."[31]

However, the danger itself may be known to the user but he may not know the means of avoiding the risk, in which case a warning or instructions may be required. Also, in both systems it is clear that use of a product known to be dangerous may result in a finding of contributory negligence rather than the total preclusion of liability. In *Devilez* v. *Boots Pure Drug Co.*,[32] for example, the plaintiff accidently spilled corn solvent on his genitals and recovered damages from the manufacturer on the grounds of failure to warn, although he was held to have been 25 per cent. contributorily negligent.

However, there has, at least in the United States, been some recognition of the undesirable consequences of the general application of the rule that there can be no recovery where the danger was known. The problem was articulated as early as 1966 by Harper and James:

> "The bottom does not legally drop out of a negligence case against the maker when it is shown that the purchaser knew of the defective condition. Thus, if the product is a carrot-topping machine with exposed moving parts, or an electric clothes wringer dangerous to the limbs of the operator, and if it would be feasible for the maker of the product to install a guard or safety release, it should be a question for the jury whether reasonable care demanded such a precaution, though its absence is obvious. Surely reasonable men might find here a great danger, even to one who knew the condition; and since it was so readily avoidable they might find the maker negligent."[33]

This view was vindicated in *Micallef* v. *Miehle Co.*[34] where the plaintiff noticed a foreign body (known in the printing trade as a "hickie") on a printing press. He informed his foreman that he intended to "chase the hickie," *i.e.* attempt to remove it.

---

[30] 62 Ill. 2d. 456, 343 N.E. 2d. 456 (1976).
[31] *Ibid.* at 463.
[32] (1962) 106 S.J. 552.
[33] 2 Harper and James, *Torts*, Chap. 28.5.
[34] 39 N.Y.2d. 376, 348 N.E. 2d. 571, 384 N.Y.S.2d. 115.

While engaged in this activity the plaintiff suffered injury. It was held that the obviousness of the danger of such an activity would not preclude recovery. Other factors, including the feasibility and reasonableness of a design modification (for example, by the incorporation of a safety guard) were relevant.

In summary, it could be argued that the manufacturer is required to warn any user whom he knows or ought reasonably to expect to be less informed than himself as to the dangers associated with the product.[35]

(a) *Who should be warned?* Again for both systems, the general rule is that the ultimate user of the product should receive any warning. However, this rule is tempered by the doctrine that only foreseeable users need be warned and is of no application in a situation where a responsible intermediary has been warned.

Thus, for example, in *Beadless* v. *Severel*,[36] the Illinois Appellate Court held that the manufacturers of a refrigerator were liable to a second-hand purchaser for failing to warn of the possibility that poisonous carbon monoxide might be emitted from the burner if it was not regularly cleaned. A warning given to the first purchaser was insufficient.

Other cases indicate that in many circumstances the manufacturer will be exculpated where he has warned persons other than the ultimate user. For example, a warning given to an employer may suffice. In *Foster* v. *Ford Motor Co.*[37] a warning of the danger of a tractor overturning when operated in a particular way was given to the purchaser. The court found that the manufacturer had no duty to warn an employee who was injured when the tractor fell on him. In *Jackson* v. *Coast Paint and Lacquer Co.*[38] the court stated that:

> "a warning to an employer would be sufficient if (1) the actual user was controlled or supervised by the employer, and (2) it would be difficult or unduly expensive to warn the actual user."[39]

In circumstances in which a product is normally used by skilled persons, it has been held in the United States that there

---

[35] See generally, Madden, "The Duty to Warn in Products Liability: Contours and Criticism" 89 West Va. L.Rev. 221 (1987) at 234.

[36] 344 Ill.App. 133, 100 N.E.2d. 405 (1951).

[37] 139 Wash. 341 (1926).

[38] 499 F.2d. 809 (1974).

[39] *Ibid.* at 812–813.

is no need to warn an unexpected, unskilled purchaser. Thus, in *Canifax* v. *Hercules Powder Co.*[40] a manufacturer of a fuse for dynamite caps was not liable for failure to warn of the short burning time of the fuse.

It might be thought that the "foreseeability of user" doctrine, with its connotations of negligence, would be irrelevant in a strict liability regime, where the issue should simply be the condition of the product rather than the conduct of the manufacturer. It seems, however, that this question has received little discussion in a strict liability context, with the exception of *Jackson* (above) where the manufacturer of paint was held liable for damage caused by fumes given off from the product. The court, focusing on the condition of the product, held that a warning should have been put on the container. This accords with the requirements of section 402A of the Restatement (Second) of Torts, Comment j of which states:

> "In order to prevent the product from being unreasonably dangerous, the seller may be required to give directions or warning, on the container, as to its use."

Decisions such as *Jackson* apart, the advent of strict liability has made no real difference to the "who should be warned" issue.

The principle that a manufacturer will not incur liability where he has warned a responsible or learned intermediary is also recognised both in the United Kingdom and the United States. Courts have recognised, among others, doctors, teachers and hairdressers as such intermediaries.[41] Thus, for example, in *Holmes* v. *Ashford*[42] the manufacturers of hair dye were not liable for injury caused to the plaintiff's scalp since the container in which it was supplied to hairdressers, and the accompanying literature, warned of the danger. The hairdresser was a responsible intermediary and in the circumstances a warning to him was sufficient.

There are a number of American illustrations of this point, including a case in which the user of an intra-uterine contraceptive device failed in an action based on failure to warn of possible dangers inherent in using the product. Since the product was obtainable on prescription only, the manufacturer's

---

[40] 237 Cal. App. 2d. 44, 46 Cal. Rptr. 552 (1965).
[41] See Miller and Lovell, *op. cit.*, pp. 245–246.
[42] [1950] W.N. 269.

duty was held to have been discharged when the doctor was warned.[43]

(b) *Adequacy of warning.* Both systems attach significance to the question of whether or not a particular warning is adequate in the circumstances. In *Vacwell Engineering Ltd.* v. *B.D.H. Chemicals Ltd.* (above) the words "harmful vapours" did not give adequate notice of the explosive properties of the product on its contact with water. This area has been developed further in the United States. Thus, a warning must be sufficiently prominent: in *Maize* v. *Atlantic Refining Co.*[44] a warning of the dangers of inhalation of carbon tetrachloride, again in very small letters, was held to be inadequate. Its inadequacy was exacerbated by a positive representation of safety in the product's name—Safety-Kleen.

As in *Vacwell*, the warning must be commensurate with the degree of danger involved. In *Tampa Drug Co.* v. *Wait*,[45] another case involving carbon tetrachloride, the warning that vapours from the liquid were harmful was insufficiently intense. Warning of the life-threatening nature of the danger should have been given. Similarly, "effervescence" did not give adequate warning of a blinding explosion.[46] Industry custom, standards and regulations as regards information given with products are recognised in both systems as indicative, though inconclusive, of whether the requisite care has been taken.[47]

Again, strict liability has had little impact on this particular aspect of the warning issue. It may be that the standards of reasonable care and "defective condition unreasonably dangerous" exact the same requirements.

Misuse

Under the law of negligence, it is clear that if a dangerous use is reasonably foreseeable and has not been warned against, liability can arise. For example, in *Hill* v. *James Crowe (Cases) Ltd.*,[48] it was foreseeable that a lorry driver engaged in loading wooden cases on to a lorry would stand upon the cases.

---

[43] *McKee* v. *Moore* 648 P.2d. 21 (Okla. 1982.). 45. 41 A.2d. 850 (Pa. 1945)

[44] 41 A.2d. 850 (Pa. 1945). Where appropriate, safe methods of use should be stated: see, *e.g. Murray* v. *Wilson Oak Flooring Co.*, 475 F.2d 129 (7th Cir. 1973).

[45] 103 So.2d. 603 (Fla. 1958).

[46] *Bean* v. *Ross Manufacturing Co.* 344 S.W. 2d. 18 (Mo. 1961).

[47] See Noel, *op. cit.* pp. 285 *et seq.*, and Miller and Lovell *op. cit.* pp. 264 *et seq.*

[48] [1978] 1 All E.R. 812.

Accordingly, the manufacturers of the cases were held liable for injury caused when a case gave way. Despite its apparent breadth of meaning, in this context the concept of foreseeability is, at least in the United Kingdom, used with caution and a clearly abnormal misuse will not ground liability.

In the United States, Comment j to section 395 of the Restatement (Second) of Torts 1965 deals with misuse in the law of negligence:

> "In the absence of a special reason to expect otherwise, the maker is entitled to assume that his product will be put to a normal use, for which the product is intended or appropriate; and he is not subject to liability when it is safe for all such uses, and harm results only because it is mishandled in a way which he has no reason to expect, or is used in some unusual or unforeseeable manner."

Since foreseeability is inherently so important to the question of misuse, the strict liability standard laid down in section 402A of the Second Restatement is, on this matter, very similar to that in negligence. Comment h to section 402A states:

> "A product is not in a defective condition when it is safe for normal use and consumption. If the injury results from abnormal handling, as where a bottled beverage is knocked against a radiator to remove the cap, or from abnormal preparation, as where too much salt is added to food, or from abnormal consumption, as where a child eats too much candy and is made ill, the seller is not liable. Where, however, he has reason to anticipate that danger may result from a particular use, as where a drug is sold which is safe only in limited doses, he may be required to give adequate warning of the danger ... and a product sold without such a warning is in a defective condition."

Given the similarity in these criteria, the trend in United States product liability cases has been to predicate liability for abnormal use on the foreseeability or otherwise of such use. Where a particular use is unforeseeable, the product will commonly be found not to have been defective, although some courts prefer to speak of such misuse as a defence to a product liability action. Where a particular use is foreseeable, the manufacturer should have warned against dangers inherent in such a use or so designed his product as to preclude the danger. This principle is well documented in decisions dating back some 50 years, although its application has been at the mercy of particular interpretations of foreseeability, resulting in some quite surprising decisions.[49]

The approach taken in *Sawyer* v. *Pine Oil Sales Co.*,[50] where a housewife who splashed cleaning fluid in her eye was unable to recover damages for a permanent injury because:

> "the cleaning preparation was not intended for use in the eye"[51]

was rapidly abandoned. Thus, in *Haberly* v. *Reardon Co.*,[52] an assistant painter who was injured by strong chemicals contained in paint when a dripping brush came into contact with his eye, was able to recover on the basis of failure to warn:

> "... while all would agree that neither paint nor cleaning fluid is intended for use in the eye, it may well be foreseeable that such materials may be splashed into someone's eye in one way or another."[53]

Full recognition of the potential breadth of the concept of foreseeability brought about a similar reversal in a pair of cases involving ingestion of domestic cleaning products by children. In *Boyd* v. *Frenchee Chem. Corp.*[54] a young child died as a result of consuming a shoe cleaner which contained poisonous ingredients. Despite the absence of a warning the manufacturers were exculpated. In a similar case some 20 years later,[55] a child died from chemical pneumonia following consumption of furniture polish. This time the producer was found liable. The court stated that the manufacturer must:

> "be expected to anticipate the environment which is normal for the use of his product and where, as here, that environment is the home, he must anticipate the reasonably foreseeable risks of the use of his product in such an environment... and to warn of them, though such risks may be incidental to the actual use for which the product was intended."[56]

---

[49] See Madden, *op. cit.*
[50] 155 F.2d. 855 (5th Cir. 1946).
[51] *Ibid.* at 856.
[52] 319 S.W. 2d. 859 (Mo. 1958).
[53] See Noel, "Recent Trends in Manufacturers' Negligence as to Design, Instructions and Warnings" (1965) 19 S.W.L.J. 43 at 54 *et. seq.*
[54] 37 F.Supp. 306 (E.D.N.Y. 1941).
[55] *Spruill* v. *Boyd-Midway Inc.* 308 F.2d. 79 (4th Cir. 1962).
[56] *Ibid.* at 83–84.

In *LeBouef* v. *Goodyear Tyre and Rubber Co.*,[57] two people who had been drinking since 9 p.m. left at 5 a.m. the next morning for a dance in a local town. The car was driven at 100–105 miles per hour, and the tyre tread on one tyre separated from the tyre carcass resulting in a crash in which the driver died and the other person suffered serious injury. Holding that the manufacturer ought to warn against reasonably foreseeable uses of his product, the court found for the plaintiffs. Contributory negligence by the driver, either in the form of intoxication or of exceeding the speed limit, was no defence. The car was designed and marketed as a high speed vehicle and so unsafe operating speeds for its tyres ought to have been warned against.

While the above examples may create the impression that foreseeability is too wide a concept it should be noted that other courts have taken a more restrictive view of its meaning. Thus, for example, in *Mazzola* v. *Chrysler France S.A.*[58] the owner of a Simca car replaced an inlet hot water hose, which passed from the front of the car through the passenger compartment to the rear engine, with a different type from the original. The new hose was not suitable, water escaped, and the user was scalded. He brought an action for damages against the car manufacturer, alleging that the water heating system in the car was defective. The court found for the manufacturer, stating:

> "The manufacturer was not required to foresee that there would be . . . substituted an entirely different type of hose for the Simca hose."[59]

In a similarly restrictive treatment of foreseeability, it was decided in *Landrine* v. *Mego Corp.*[60] that, where a child ingested a balloon taken from a toy consisting of a doll which simulated the blowing up of the balloon, there had been unforeseeable misuse:

> "No duty to warn exists where the intended or foreseeable use of the product is not hazardous. . . . Digestion of a balloon is not an intended use, and to the extent it is a foreseeable one, it is a misuse of the product for which the guardian of children must be wary."[61]

---

[57] 623 F.2d. 985 (5th Cir. 1980).
[58] 407 F.Supp. 24 (1978), *affirmed* 607 F.2d. 997 (1979).
[59] *Ibid.* at 28.
[60] 95 A.D. 2d. 759, 464 N.Y.S. 2d. 516 (1983).
[61] *Ibid.* at 759–760.

These examples show the interaction of the concept of defect with the duty to warn and with action which may be construed as contributory negligence. However, it is difficult to draw any firm conclusion from the case law, given the variety of interpretations of foreseeability. The Consumer Protection Act speaks of "what might reasonably be expected to be done with or in relation to the product" as a factor in determining defectiveness. Presumably, it is the manufacturer's expectations which are relevant, although this is not clear. It is also unclear whether the test in the legislation is intended to be less extensive or as extensive as the concept of foreseeability. If anything, the wording suggests a criterion at least as extensive as foreseeability, although it is to be expected that courts in the United Kingdom will avoid the more exotic interpretations of that term illustrated by some of the United States examples quoted above.

Defences

In the failure to warn context there is a much-reduced scope for the application of recognised defences like contributory negligence and *volenti non fit injuria*. The reason for this is that if the allegation is that no warning of a defect or danger is given then, in most circumstances, the user could have no knowledge of the existence of any danger. Having no knowledge of any danger, he is not in a position voluntarily to assume the risk. Similarly, it is difficult to establish that a user failed to take adequate care for his own safety in a situation where he had no knowledge of the potential danger. Admittedly, there is some room for these defences in a failure to warn case. For example, a warning which is inadequate may have been given, the effect of which would be to cause the user to suspect that there was some danger inherent in the use of the product—although having been inadequately warned he will not be aware of the full extent of the danger. Instances of this will however be relatively rare.

Notwithstanding the apparent lack of opportunity to use such defences, courts in both the United Kingdom and the United States have been willing to apply them in the failure to warn context.[62]

---

[62] See, *e.g. Devilez* v. *Boots Pure Drug Co.*, (1962) 106 S.J. 552; *Carmen* v. *Eli Lilly & Co.* 109 Ind. App. 76, 32 N.E. 2d. 729 (1941).

A problem with such an approach is the need for any defence at all since, if the warning was adequate, then the product is not defective.

In concluding upon this matter, it is clear that a substantial number of product liability cases are based on the failure to warn ground. The above discussion of these cases indicates two things: (a) the theory of liability under which United States courts purport to adjudicate a failure to warn claim makes little difference to the decision; and (b) despite the advent of strict liability in the United States, both systems adhere to the same legal principles; accordingly, the argument that a strict liability regime in the United Kingdom will result in many of the problems which have beset United States product liability law cannot, at least in failure to warn cases, be valid.

However, as the discussion of the *Beshada-Feldman* dichotomy shows, United States courts are still struggling with the conceptual treatment of warnings in strict liability. Given the hostility which greeted the *Beshada* decision and the paucity of decisions which have been reached on a similar ratio, it is to be expected that the *Feldman* approach will, in the longer term, prevail. As will be noticed, the statutory regime introduced in the United Kingdom achieves a result very similar to the *Feldman* decision. However, strict liability for product defects in the United States has thrown up problems which have not yet been contemplated under negligence law in the United Kingdom; witness the sheer volume of asbestosis and other so-called "toxic tort" litigation.

One example of particular interest in the context of warnings is where manufacturers of tobacco products have been pursued by "victims" of cigarette smoking. The leading litigation in this area is *Cippolone* v. *Liggett Group Inc.*[63] which had already visited both state and appellate courts on preliminary matters such as discovery of documents and alleged judicial partiality before the recent trial of the underlying product liability issues. *Cippolone* is the first action to be heard from a number of actions filed in the state and federal courts of New Jersey. At least 100 similar cases are awaiting trial in other jurisdictions. In all of these cases, cigarette smokers or their personal representatives claim that smoking-related diseases such as lung cancer resulted from cigarette smoking. These pending actions are commonly grounded in negligence, strict liability and

[63] 822 F.2d. 335, 7 Fed. R. Serv. 3d. 1438 (3d. Cir. 1987).

intentional wrong-doing. One major allegation is that cigarette producers failed adequately to inform smokers of the dangers associated with use of the product, even when warnings were used on the packets. The plaintiffs argue that such warnings were insufficient and were rendered nugatory by the advertising practices of the manufacturers.[64] In *Cippolone*,[65] the jury held that one of the defendants, *Liggett Group Inc.*, was liable for failing to warn smokers, prior to January 1966 when Federal law made warnings mandatory, of the health risks of smoking and for falsely guaranteeing that its products were safe. The other defendants were exculpated on the basis that the deceased had started smoking their brands of cigarette only after 1966. Her decision to smoke and to continue smoking even after the warnings appeared made her 80 per cent. contributorily negligent, reflected in a final award of $400,000 in damages. An appeal is pending.

These cases raise issues of some complexity. In particular, courts will be faced with massive evidential problems regarding causation. Recent decisions in California and Tennessee have rejected damages claims because of failure to discharge this evidential burden, and because the plaintiff was held to have assumed the risk. It is also likely that at least some plaintiffs will argue that the addictive nature of tobacco nullifies the ability of consumers to take heed of warnings. Problems of contributory negligence, assumption of risk and adequacy of warning will be similarly formidable. In addition, the manufacturers will assert that the warnings given comply with and are dictated by legislation, in particular, by the Federal Cigarette Labelling and Advertising Act 1965. Further problems can be expected where "passive smokers" (those who inhale smoke from other people's cigarettes) bring actions.

The sheer complexity of the issues raised by cigarette litigation seems to have escaped the notice of the Pearson Commission, which, speaking of the definition of defect, rather glibly commented that:

> "That definition would allow the producer to show that the victim should have taken heed of warning notices such as those on cigarette packets."[66]

---

[64] *Ibid.*

[65] *Cippolone* v. *Liggett Group Inc.*, 693 F.Supp. 208 (1988). It is thought that the costs of raising the action far exceeded the award.

[66] Pearson Commission, Cmnd. 7054 (1978) para. 1237. See also Stapleton, "Products Liability Reform—Real or Illusory?" Ox. Jnl. of Leg. Studs. 392 at 407.

If successful in the United States, cigarette litigation is bound to arise in this country and the experience of the American courts on "warnings" cases will be of value in determining liability under the 1987 Act. But such litigation in the United Kingdom may well be pre-empted by fuller information on cigarette packets about the health hazards of smoking cigarettes.

Increased emphasis on the warning issue in a strict liability system

It is suggested that, despite similarities in the treatment of warnings in negligence and in strict liability, the move to strict liability for defective products will herald an increase in the emphasis placed on warnings by both courts and producers. The reasons for this are:

1. Producers may use warnings more frequently if potential liability is strict, rather than negligence based.
2. There are a number of advantages inherent in basing a defective products claim on failure to warn.
3. The definition of "defective" emphasises the role of warnings.
4. The "consumer expectation" test for defectiveness may cause manufacturers to rely on warnings.
5. Courts may be tempted to decide cases on failure-to-warn grounds.

(a) *More frequent use by producers.* Arguably, manufacturers who are aware that the exercise of due care will not of itself exculpate them may be tempted to warn users of a product of potential hazards which would not normally be warned against.

For example, a producer of perfume may feel that in a strict liability regime a warning as to flammability is now necessary, or a shoe polish manufacturer may now feel constrained to warn against the harmful effect of ingestion of the product.[67] There has even been a suggestion that producers of beer and other forms of alcohol ought to consider warning against dangers of over-consumption, but even in the United States this product is unlikely to be found to be defective through the absence of a warning.[68]

---

[67] See *Spruill* v. *Boyd Midway Inc.*, n. 55 above.
[68] In addition to the probably insurmountable hurdle of the requirement to prove that such products are defective, the obvious nature of the dangers would prompt defences of misuse, contributory negligence or assumption of risk. See *Maguire* v. *Pabst* 387 N.W. 2d. 565 (1986).

The temptation to warn in such circumstances will obviously be qualified by the desire to maintain product marketability, and also affected by legal constraints on liability such as foreseeability of use, but the possibility of the move to strict liability resulting in greater emphasis on warnings by manufacturers remains a real one.

(b) *Advantages of basing case on failure-to-warn.*[69] The principal advantage inherent in basing a claim on failure to warn is that if the claim is successful, the requirement of establishing defectiveness is automatically satisfied without having to go further.

There is therefore no need to embark upon the difficulty and expense of engaging expert witnesses in an attempt to show the feasibility, or lack of feasibility, of a design alternative. Further, difficulties regarding access to production processes and details of quality control techniques are removed. In any event, the product may have been so badly damaged as to render evidence of defectiveness difficult to secure.

Thus, in *De Vito* v. *United Airlines Inc.*,[70] for example, when pilots were asphyxiated by carbon dioxide in the cockpit, causing a crash, it was simpler to show a duty to warn of the need to provide oxygen masks than to show defectiveness of design. Further, establishing a failure to warn of dangers inherent in the use to which the product was put negates the defence that the use was not foreseeable and virtually eliminates considerations of contributory negligence.

Moreover, it is sometimes difficult to establish that the product was defective at the time at which it was put into circulation, or to rebut claims that the defect was due to a modification of the product or some other misuse. Establishing that there has been a failure to warn obviates these problems.

Finally, a court may be more favourably disposed towards a finding of defectiveness based on failure to warn as opposed to defective design, for the reason that an inexpensive labelling change will enable the producer to correct the defect. The court is thus not forcing actual re-design of the product or a material change in the production process. Thus, even where a whole product line is held to be defective, correction is easy.

(c) *Emphasis on warnings in the definition of "defective."* It is clear that the new strict liability system closely mirrors the

[69] See Noel, *op. cit.* n. 24 above.
[70] 98 F.Supp.88 (E.D.N.Y. 1951).

proposals of the Pearson Commission and is of course based upon the EEC directive of July 1985. At the very nub of the new system of strict liability lies the definition of "defective."

The absence or inadequacy of warnings is elevated to feature in the nucleus of strict liability—the definition of "defect." Section 3(2) of the Consumer Protection Act 1987 implements the Directive's definition stating that the circumstances to be taken into account include:

"(a) the manner in which, and purpose for which, the product has been marketed, its get-up, the use of any mark in relation to the product and any instructions for, or warnings with respect to, doing or refraining from doing anything with or in relation to the product. . . . "

Clearly the shift from the generality of "presentation", used in the Directive, to the detail of the wording on the Act has some advantages. The "manner in which" and "purpose for which" a product has been "marketed" seem to allow greater freedom of movement than simply the "presentation" of the product. Similarly, the provisions as to instructions and warnings are expressed in wide terms.

As originally drafted, the Act would have sought to draw a distinction between liability for loss caused by negligent misstatement and loss caused by instructions, warnings or other information which render the product concerned to be defective. The difficulties of drawing this distinction in the legislation caused the attempt to be abandoned and it will now be a matter for the courts to distinguish between warnings cases and liability for misstatements. This will often be a straightforward enough task, but, as noted in the discussion on the meaning of the term "product," there will be some difficult cases.

Clearly, manufacturers who notice that product defectiveness is contingent at least partly on the presence of a warning will err on the side of safety, and hence will be more willing to use warnings.

(d) *The "consumer expectation" test.* The definition is clear on one fundamental point—that a product will be defective when it does not provide the safety which persons generally are entitled to expect. The main benefit of such a test is that, in keeping with a system of strict liability, considerations of negligence on the part of the producer are supposedly eliminated. The degree of care taken by the manufacturer should cease to be of relevance, what matters is consumers' expectations of safety.

Thus, it could be said that the appropriate principle is that a warning should be given:

"Whenever a reasonable man would wish to be informed of the risk in order to decide whether to expose himself to it."[71]

There is however a major difficulty with such a test. The definition implies that if the defect or danger is obvious or the user knows or should know of it, then the product is not defective within the meaning of the definition since it would be unreasonable for persons generally to expect a greater degree of safety than that which is apparent or known to them. Therefore, when consumers know of a defect or danger, perhaps because attention has been directed to it by a warning, they cannot expect a greater degree of safety than that known. Consequently, the manufacturer will argue that the product is not defective. The effect of this could be to divert the attention of the court to the presence or absence of a warning when the real issue is whether the product's design causes it to be defective or dangerous. Further, if manufacturers can obviate a finding of defective or dangerous design by giving a warning, at much less expense than re-design, they will do so.

Against this, however, it could be said that the consumer expectation test adopted under the 1987 Act does not leave the same room for subjectivity as the American version; the words "persons generally are entitled to expect" should be interpreted so as to allow a court to find that re-design rather than a simple warning is what people are entitled to expect.

(e) *Tempting for courts to decide on failure-to-warn grounds.* Given the relative simplicity of "warnings" litigation, a court may be tempted to deal with a product liability case on the basis of presence or absence of an adequate warning rather than dangerousness or defectiveness of design. One reason for this, noted earlier, is that a finding of defectiveness based on failure to warn is much less serious from the manufacturer's point of view since he thereby incurs the relatively minor expense of labelling or re-labelling the product, rather than the cost involved in a physical re-design of the product.

Another reason is that by focusing on the warning issue the court may not have to deal with detailed and often complex technical evidence regarding the production processes of the

---

[71] *Moran* v. *Johns-Manville Sales Corp.* 691 F.2d. 811 at 814 (6th Cir. 1982).

manufacturer. Litigation would thus be shorter and simpler, with the attendant saving for both the public and the litigants.

Problems associated with focusing on warnings

If, as has been argued, the shift to strict liability involves a concomitant increase in the use of warnings, and hence the attention focused upon them, then there are a number of associated problems which have to be recognised. The underlying difficulty is that by focusing on the warning issue the defectiveness or otherwise of the product's design may be overlooked.

(a) *Efficacy of warnings.* An increased emphasis on warnings, by both courts and manufacturers, would have an adverse effect on the efficacy of warnings generally. Arguably, warnings should be used only when there is no feasible design alternative. If manufacturers use warnings instead of physical re-design then the increased use would devalue the effectiveness of warnings in general and the user would acquire some immunity to the warning message.

The foreseeability of the use to which a product is put also has an important bearing on the warning issue. One of the differences between the definitions of defective given by the Pearson Commission and an earlier draft of the EEC Directive is that the draft directive's version contained the words "being used for the purpose for which it was apparently intended," an attempt to preclude potential difficulties regarding foreseeability of use. Such a provision does not feature in the definition of defective which has been adopted, although "reasonably expected use" has to be taken into account.

Many cases, including some discussed above, illustrate how foreseeability of use affects the warning issue. For example, in *Moran* v. *Faberge Inc.*,[72] two teenage girls were discussing whether or not a candle was scented. Having agreed that it was not, one girl decided to make it scented. She grabbed a bottle of "Tigress" Cologne and began to pour its contents over the wax part of the candle. Flames erupted from the bottle and the other girl was burned. By a majority, the court decided that such misuse of the product was foreseeable, and that a warning as to flammability should have been given.

In other cases, it has been held foreseeable that a chair may be used for standing on as well as sitting, that a girl may spray

[72] 273 M.D. 538, 332 A.2d. 11 (1975).

her hair and dress with inflammable perfume, and that a boy of five wearing an inflammable jacket may play with and around an open fire.[73]

Such decisions may lead manufacturers to warn of all potential hazards associated with use, or misuse of a product. The effect of this would be to again increase the number and scope of warnings given and thereby devalue warnings in general. Users, bombarded by warnings, may not take cognisance of a warning when they most need to do so.

(b) *The "consumer expectation" test and warnings.* As noticed earlier, a product will be defective when it does not provide the safety which persons generally are entitled to expect, it is therefore arguable that if the user knows of a defect or danger in a product, he cannot expect a greater degree of safety than that known to him.

Liability is predicated on the latent or unknown nature of the defect or danger. Consequently, if the attention of the user has been directed to a defect or danger by a warning, or because it is obvious, the court may find for the defendant. This can be so even where a low cost design modification would remove the danger. Thus, in a case where a young girl slipped in the path of a power lawnmower, sustaining leg injuries which resulted in amputation, the giving of a warning coupled with the patent nature of the danger persuaded the court to find for the manufacturer.[74] The presence or absence of safety devices on other power movers, and the ease of such a modification, were held to be irrelevant.

(c) *Cases where an adequate warning would render the product unsaleable.* In some circumstances the imposition of liability on the ground of failure to give an adequate warning will be tantamount to calling for physical re-design, since giving an adequate warning would render the product unmarketable. In such cases judicial emphasis on warnings is regrettable. The court should address itself to the question of the product's design rather than the warning issue, and should be prepared to hold that the design is defective, if such is the case, rather than call for a warning.

(d) *Cases where warnings do not have any effect on the dangerousness of the product.* The rationale behind giving

---

[73] Noel, *op. cit.*, n. 25 above, p. 275.
[74] *Murphy* v. *Cory Pump and Supply Co.* 197 N.E. 2d. 849 (1964).

warnings about products is that the user will thereby be alerted to the dangers associated with using the product. If the ability of the user to take cognisance of a warning is restricted or non-existent, the warning will be of no value. If it is foreseeable that the user may be unable to take heed of a warning then the giving of a warning will not exculpate the manufacturer. Children are one class of foreseeable users whose ability to take cognisance of warnings may be restricted or non-existent. Design modification, for example providing a safety-cap on containers of dangerous products, is again the answer.

Another class of foreseeable users unable to take heed of warnings are those who for reasons of language differences or lack of education cannot understand a warning. In *Hubbard Hall Chemical Co.* v. *Silverman*[75] two Puerto Rican workers died after having come into contact with chemicals used for spraying and dusting crops. The manufacturer's label had warned that protective clothing and a mask should be worn. Liability was imposed on the manufacturer on the ground that the warning was inadequate since it was foreseeable that the product might be used by persons whose reading ability was limited. It has also been suggested that a cause of a major air disaster in 1976 was the inability of Algerian members of the ground crew to follow instructions printed in English upon a Turkish DC–10 aeroplane. A cargo door which had not been properly closed was ripped off and over 300 people were killed.[76]

In some circumstances, such as those in the above cases, using pictorial symbols or warning a responsible intermediary may suffice, but in others re-design is necessary. For example, it may be foreseeable that a sudden or accidental act may occur, rendering it impossible for a warning to be heeded. This could happen where a machine such as, for example, a lawnmower, is inadequately guarded. It is foreseeable that a user, or indeed a non-user, may trip, slip or otherwise accidentally come into contact with dangerous parts of the machine and thus sustain injury. Any warning attached to a machine in such circumstances could not be heeded. The court's attention should again be focused on the safety of the product's design rather than the warnings issue.

CONCLUSION

There are a number of features of the move to strict product

---

[75] 340 F.2d. 402 (1st. Cir. 1965).
[76] See the discussion in "Better Safe than Sorry," "Engineering," February 1988, 65 at 69.

liability which could cause manufacturers and courts artificially to emphasise the presence or absence of an adequate warning. Such extra attention is undesirable.

The definitions of defective put forward by the Pearson Commission and in the EEC Directive, now echoed in the 1987 Act, are capable of being construed in a way which is prejudicial to the consumer where a warning has been given. This construction should be avoided. In interpreting "the safety which persons generally are entitled to expect" the court should focus attention on the product itself rather than any warning given.

Emphasis on warnings in product liability cases does nothing to further the principal policy aim in this field—accident prevention. Manufacturers can best be deterred from marketing dangerous or defective products by a real threat of liability. Allowing producers to obviate potential liability by attaching warnings to such products causes the onus of accident prevention to fall on the user. Removal of the chance of injury, by imposing the burden of accident prevention on the manufacturer, is manifestly more efficient than leaving accident prevention in the hands of the consumer. This can best be achieved if the court concentrates on the product and not on the presence or absence of a warning. Warnings can thus be reserved for circumstances in which the elimination of product risks is not feasible.

Warnings are an effective method of alerting a user to a defect or danger inherent in a product, but if it is feasible for the danger or defect to have been designed out of a product, and reasonable for the consumer to expect it to have been designed out, then the giving of a warning should not exculpate the manufacturer.

As has been noticed, there is a strong argument that such matters as feasibility of design alternatives, reasonableness of the manufacturer's conduct and the importance of knowledge are of necessity negligence issues and hence that cases based on failure to warn ought to be addressed under a negligence theory of liability. Thus, in Smith v. E.R. Squibb & Son Inc.,[77] it was stated that:

> "The test for determining whether a legal duty has been breached is whether the defendant exercised reasonable care under the circumstances. Determination of whether a

[77] 273 N.W. 2d. 476 (Mich. 1979).

product defect exists because of an inadequate warning requires the use of an identical standard. Consequently when liability turns on the inadequacy of a warning, the issue is one of reasonable care, regardless of whether the theory pled is negligence, implied warranty or strict liability is tort."[78]

As the foregoing discussion has shown, the characterisation of "warnings" cases as involving reasonable care has been the approach of most courts. However, a sufficient number of decisions have departed from this view and, as a result, jurisdictions such as New Jersey have found themselves in a state of much confusion. The *Beshada* and *Feldman* decisions highlight this confusion but other decisions have added to the difficulty. For example, in *O'Brien* v. *Muskin Corp.*,[79] it was held that even where an adequate warning was given, and no alternative, safer design was posited by the plaintiff, a manufacturer could still be liable in that the product's risks may outweigh utility. In Texas, the District Court concluded, in *Carter* v. *Johns-Manville Sales Corp.*,[80] that knowledge acquired by a manufacturer, after the product has been made and distributed, could not be imputed to the manufacturer in a case based upon failure to warn. The court reasoned that such a case ought to be decided on negligence principles. However, the court took the view that strict liability should be applied to a design defect case:

"To permit the defendant to defend a strict liability claim by proving that it could not have foreseen the danger, in effect by proving that it was not negligent, would fly in the face of the entire history of the evolution of strict liability in tort."[81]

On the other hand, the court held that under strict liability, a manufacturer in a design defect case has such "after acquired knowledge" imputed to him.

This distinction between failure to warn and design defect cases is probably untenable.[82] A warning is simply an aspect of

---

[78] *Ibid.* at 461.
[79] 94 N.J. 169, 463 A.2d. 298 (1983).
[80] 557 F.Supp. 1317 (E.D. Tex. 1983).
[81] *Ibid.* at 1319.
[82] See the discussion in Twerski, "A Moderate and Restrained Federal Product Liability Bill: Targeting the Crisis Areas for resolution" (1985) 18 Univ. of Mich. Jnl. of Law Reform 575 at 598.

a product's overall design, and so failure to warn claims ought to be decided under identical principles to design defect cases.

The real question is whether such principles ought to come from negligence or from strict liability. It is suggested that warnings issues do not automatically require negligence concepts for their resolution. As cases such as *Feldman* show, "warnings" cases are amenable to adjudication under ostensibly "strict" liability; indeed, *Beshada* illustrates warnings being dealt with under true strict liability principles. However, the actual mechanism of deciding on "warnings" cases in either form of strict liability seems to involve either an overly elaborate approach (warning as one element in a risk-benefit calculus) or an overly simplistic, but general, treatment (consumer expectations).

If the after-acquired knowledge issue is to be resolved in the manner of *Feldman*, then this will result only in shifting the burden of proof. It is only if a *Beshada* approach is used that strict liability achieves its apparent policy aims. If *Feldman* is accepted then the short step forward from negligence which that decision represents seems hardly worth the effort, especially if that step is achieved as in the United Kingdom by means of a wholly new set of legal concepts, many of which will themselves require litigation in order to be clarified. Perhaps a deeper argument has been exposed: the very nature of the concept of a warning is not amenable to the doctrine of strict liability. Warnings are, necessarily, about the manufacturer's knowledge and conduct and no verbal gymnastics can allow "warning" cases to be regulated by pure strict liability principles. Rather, negligence principles—subjected to slight tampering such as a shift in the burden of proof—must be employed. The alternative argument and, it is suggested, the better view, is to accept that "warning" cases are not suitable for adjudication under strict liability unless the logical difficulty about finding liability for failure to warn of the unknowable is ignored. As *Beshada* demonstrates, it is only in this way that true strict liability can be imposed. However, true strict liability of the *Beshada* type would not be applied were the proposals for a Federal uniform product liability Act to be adopted; as currently drafted, this legislation would return to a negligence standard for failure to warn actions.[83]

The question of whether ordinary negligence principles, or *Feldman* strict liability, or *Beshada* strict liability, should govern

---

[83] *Ibid.*

"warnings" cases in product liability is of interest in the wider frame. On a narrower point, it is clear that the Consumer Protection Act 1987 has in effect introduced a *Feldman* standard for strict liability failure to warn cases into the United Kingdom. When deciding upon defectiveness, our courts may apply the consumer expectation test (in section 2's definition of defective) intuitively or they may seek to extrapolate a cost-benefit approach. Either way, if a pursuer argues that the product was defective because of failure to warn and the manufacturer proves that he could not have been expected to have discovered the danger, the claim will fail. This is a result of the development risks defence, adverted to earlier, made available under section 4(1)(*e*) of the Act. That section makes it clear that the burden of proving the defence rests upon the manufacturer. Hence, it can be concluded that the new regime applies the *Feldman* approach in United Kingdom failure to warn cases. There is no doubt that this represents an improvement, from the consumer's point of view, on the law of negligence. But this advance is small and simply does not justify the new conceptual structure, heavy with inherent uncertainties and pregnant with litigation potential, which is the vehicle for its achievement.

Until cases come before the appellate courts, it will not be known whether a cost-benefit or an intuitive approach will be taken to the question of defectiveness. However, in "warnings" cases either approach is likely to result in decisions no different from those obtained by applying negligence principles. Indeed, it is probable that existing negligence cases on warnings will guide our courts in the application of the new, so-called "strict" liability under the Act.

Chapter 5

RECOVERABLE LOSS

One of the fascinations of product liability law is its treatment
of the various types of damage which can be caused by a
defective product. It is generally accepted that a broad
distinction can be drawn between pure economic loss and other
types of damage caused by products (personal injury, property
damage, and economic loss consequential upon personal injury
or property damage) with the general rule that losses of the
former category cannot be recovered. This division, which as we
will discover is rather difficult to draw, is mirrored in the broad
scheme of the Consumer Protection Act 1987, which excludes
recovery of pure economic loss. Also, as the short title suggests,
the Act excludes damage to commercial property.

RECOVERABLE LOSS—THE PRE-EXISTING LAW

The initial difficulty is to draw a distinction between pure
economic loss and other losses. Following *Junior Books* v. *The
Veitchi Co.*,[1] in which the pursuers recovered for economic loss
caused by defects in flooring, it might be thought that pure
economic loss could simply be defined as financial loss caused
solely by the fact that a product, which poses no threat of harm
to person or property, is defective. However, at least some
judges have been reluctant to describe even the loss in *Junior
Books* as purely economic. In *Tate & Lyle Industries* v.
G.L.C.,[2] Lord Templeman (with whose speech both Lord Keith
and Lord Roskill agreed) spoke of the damage in *Junior Books*
as being damage to property, thereby characterising the loss in
that case as other than purely financial. Such a view does seem
to stretch the categories of loss in this area too far and the view
that the loss in *Junior Books* was purely economic is, it is
submitted, the more tenable.[3]

If we accept the definition of pure economic loss just given,
we are still far from a clear picture of the full range of possible

[1] [1983] 1 A.C. 520.
[2] [1983] 2 A.C. 509 at 530.
[3] See discussion in Cane, *United Kingdom Law: Property Damage and Financial
Loss, Colston Symposium* (1984).

losses. There are at least five categories of loss which could be caused by a defective product[4]:

(a) damage to person or property caused by a defective product, and financial losses consequent upon such damage;

(b) the cost of repair or replacement of products so as to remove the danger-threatening aspect of the defect, and financial loss such as loss of profits consequent on the product being unusable;

(c) damage to the product itself caused by the defect in it;

(d) the cost of repair or replacement of products so as to remove a defect which does not pose a threat to person or property;

(e) loss of profits or other financial loss caused solely by the fact that the product is defective; that is, where it poses no threat of damage to person or property or to itself.

The first three types of loss are examples of actual or threatened physical loss and consequential financial loss, as distinct from items (d) and (e) which are types of pure economic loss other than that resulting from physical damage. The last two heads could be viewed as loss resulting from the simple failure of the product to match expectations, and will here be dealt with together following consideration of the other forms of loss.

A. Personal injury, property damage and consequential financial loss

Little need be said about the recovery of damages for personal injury or damage to property since the normal rules of damages in tort apply to such losses when caused by product defects, and since the recoverability of such losses is long established. Full discussion of this matter is covered in the standard texts.[5] Of more interest for our purposes is the recovery of economic loss consequential upon damage to property. As well as the standard requirement of foreseeability of the economic loss, it must be causally proximate to the physical harm.[6] But there is an additional condition of liability.

---

[4] See Cane, "Physical Loss, Economic Loss and Products Liability" 95 L.Q.R. 117 for a full discussion of the position as at January 1979.

[5] See also Miller and Lovell, *op. cit.*, Chap. 16.

[6] See Cane, *op. cit.*, n. 4 above, at 120.

In a series of recent decisions,[7] the appellate courts in Scotland and in England have reasserted the established rule (which had nonetheless contained some room for argument)[8] that only a person with a possessory or proprietary right to the property damaged can sue to recover economic loss consequential upon that damage. Thus, in *The Aliakmon*,[9] Lord Brandon stated:

> "My Lords, there is a long line of authority for a principle of law that, in order to enable a person to claim in negligence for loss caused to him by reason of loss of or damage to property, he must have had either the legal ownership of or a possessory title to the property concerned at the time when the loss or damage occurred, and it is not enough for him to have only had contractual rights in relation to such property which have been adversely affected by the loss of or damage to it."[10]

This principle has recently been applied in three Scottish cases,[11] including *North Scottish Helicopters* v. *United Technologies Corp.*[12] in which the lessors of a helicopter sought to recover for damage to the helicopter and for consequential economic losses, resulting from alleged defects in the rotor brake unit which had, it was argued, caused a fire. On a preliminary proof, the lessors were held to be entitled to sue. The principle has also recently been applied in the Court of Appeal, in *Transcontainer Express Ltd.* v. *Custodian Security Ltd.*.[13] To this general rule there may[14] be some very limited

---

[7] In particular: *Candlewood Navigation Corp. Ltd.* v. *Mitsui O.S.K. Lines Ltd. (The Mineral Transporter)* [1986] A.C. 1; *Leigh and Sillivan Ltd.* v. *Aliakmon Shipping Co. Ltd. (The Aliakmon)* [1986] A.C. 785; *Transcontainer Express* v. *Custodian Security Ltd.* [1988] 1 Lloyd's Rep. 128; *The Kapetan Georgis* [1988] 1 Lloyd's Rep. 352; *Nacap Ltd.* v. *Moffat Plant Ltd.* 1987 S.L.T. 221; *North Scottish Helicopters* v. *United Technologies Corp.* 1988 S.L.T. 77; *Esso Petroleum Co. Ltd.* v. *Hall Russel Co. Ltd.* 1988 S.L.T. 33.

[8] *Per* Slade L.J. in *Transcontainer Express* v. *Custodian Security Ltd.*, [1988] 1 Lloyd's Rep. 128.

[9] [1986] 1 A.C. 785.

[10] *Ibid.* at 809.

[11] *Nacap Ltd.* v. *Moffat Plant Ltd.* 1987 S.L.T. 221; *North Scottish Helicopters* v. *United Technologies Corp.* 1988 S.L.T. 77; *Esso Petroleum Co. Ltd.* v. *Hall Russel Co. Ltd.* 1988 S.L.T. 33.

[12] 1988 S.L.T. 77. The claim failed on the basis that there had been no negligence.

[13] [1988] 1 Lloyd's Rep. 128.

[14] *Per* Lord Fraser in *Candlewood Navigation Corp.* v. *Mitsui O.S.K. Lines Ltd. (The Mineral Transporter)* [1986] A.C. 1 at 25.

exceptions,[15] but these possible exceptions are of no application in the ordinary product liability case.

In one of the few relatively modern product liability cases in which the issue of recovery of consequential financial loss has been discussed, the court was prepared to leave the question open. In *Lambert* v. *Lewis*[16] the House of Lords considered an appeal from a decision that the retailers of a defective towing hitch, who had incurred liability for the deaths caused by the defect, could not pass that liability on to the manufacturers. The House of Lords did not require to decide that particular point, having allowed the retailers' appeal on other grounds. However, Lord Diplock stated that he did not wish the decision to be regarded as approval for the proposition that:

> "where the economic loss suffered by a distributor in the chain between the manufacturer and the ultimate consumer consists of a liability to pay damages to the ultimate consumer for physical injuries sustained by him, or consists of a liability to indemnify a distributor lower in the chain of distribution for his liability to the ultimate consumer for damages for physical injuries, such economic loss is not recoverable under the *Donoghue* v. *Stevenson* principle from the manufacturer".[17]

There is a strong argument that the decisions in *The Aliakmon*[18] and in *Candlewood*[19] solved this issue by denying recovery in the circumstances outlined by Lord Diplock. However, in *The Kapetan Georgis*,[20] a chain claim of the type referred to in *Lambert*[21] was held to be arguable in tort. Thus, it is possible that in a chain claim which originates from a claim based upon physical damage the general rule reaffirmed in the recent cases may admit of exception.

It could be argued, in the wider frame, that the requirement that the loss be consequential upon physical damage is a rather arbitrary and crude test in an area fraught with definitional difficulty and which merits a rather more subtle approach. What

---

[15] Such as *Caltex Oil (Australia) Pty. Ltd.* v. *Dredge Willemstad* (1976) C.L.R. 529.
[16] [1982] A.C. 225.
[17] At 278.
[18] [1986] A.C. 785.
[19] [1986] A.C. 1.
[20] [1988] 1 Lloyd's Rep. 352.
[21] [1982] A.C. 225.

is economic loss in the first place?[22] Any damage to property causes economic loss in the sense that the property is worth less than before the damage; financial compensation is the preferred method of compensating for such harm, and it may seem rather artificial to classify the loss as other than economic. The standard counter argument is of course that a line has to be drawn somewhere, lest the floodgates be opened. Pragmatic considerations, including the need for legal practitioners to be able accurately to advise clients, mean that the physical loss criterion is preferred to a more sophisticated or complex approach. There is, it is suggested, a forceful counter-argument that a generally expressed floodgates fear is a rather inexplicit policy reason for denying or limiting liability; a more sophisticated and rational approach which admits consideration of such factors as the availability of insurance cover and differences between commercial and non-commercial plaintiffs might produce a better formula for drawing the line.

Recent decisions do not however evidence any willingness on the part of the courts in the United Kingdom to develop a more appropriate tool than the physical loss test. For example, in *Muirhead* v. *Industrial Tank Specialities*,[23] the Court of Appeal strongly reaffirmed the predication of economic loss recovery upon the presence of physical damage. The facts of the case are relatively simple and provide an excellent illustration of the dichotomy between types of loss. A wholesale fish merchant lost his entire stock of live lobsters when the process by which the tanks were to be oxygenated failed to perform its task. This failure was traced to defects in the electric motors of water pumps which had cut out when they should have been in operation. Claims against the supplier of the fish storage tank and the supplier of the pumps having proved unsuccessful, the plaintiff was left with an action in tort against the manufacturer of the electric motors. It was established that these motors had suffered frequent failures in operation due to their inability to cope with the voltage range of the United Kingdom electricity supply. Thus there was no real difficulty in asserting a case based upon the defectiveness of the product. The plaintiff

---

[22] See remarks of Lord Roskill in *Junior Books* v. *The Veitchi Co.* [1983] 1 A.C. 520 at 545, where he spoke of the "somewhat artificial distinction between physical and economic or financial loss when the two sometimes go together and sometimes do not—it is sometimes overlooked that virtually all damage including physical damage is in one sense financial or economic for it is compensated by an award of damages. . . . "

[23] [1986] Q.B. 507, [1985] 3 All E.R. 705.

argued that the various losses which he had suffered, including the market value of the lobsters and the cost of cleaning out the lobster tanks, ought to be recoverable in a tort action on the basis, *inter alia*, of *Junior Books*. At first instance, the physical damage to the lobsters was held to be beyond recovery as unforeseeable, but the economic losses were held recoverable on the basis of *Junior Books*. Although in the leading opinion in the Court of Appeal Robert Goff L.J. did not mention the case of *Spartan Steel & Alloys Ltd.* v. *Martin & Co. (Contractors) Ltd.*[24] his two colleagues felt constrained to follow this decision and the court unanimously disallowed recovery in tort for the pure economic loss. In Robert Goff L.J.'s words:

> "I therefore conclude that the manufacturers should be held liable to the plaintiff, not in respect of the whole economic loss suffered by him, but only in respect of the physical damage caused to his stock of lobsters, and of course any financial loss suffered by the plaintiff in consequence of that physical damage."[25]

As O'Connor L.J. made plain, the decision in *Spartan Steel* had to be preferred to that in *Junior Books*:

> "The heads of damage in the statement of claim show that this case is so close to *Spartan Steel and Alloys Ltd.* v. *Martin & Co. (Contractors) Ltd.* [1972] 3 All E.R. 557, [1972] Q.B. 27 that in my judgment it should not be distinguished from that case; until it is overruled we are bound by it. The defendants negligently cut the electricity to the plaintiffs' factory, a batch of metal in the furnace was damaged and they were unable to process four further batches. By a majority this court held that they were entitled to recover the value of the damaged batch, and the consequential loss of profit thereon, but could not recover the loss of profit on the lost batches."[26]

It is regrettable that the court did not attempt a more clear and sophisticated analysis of the issues presented in this case. For example, the plaintiff claimed damages for the cost of the pumps; was this irrecoverable as pure economic loss or recoverable as physical damage to property? What was the

---

[24] [1973] Q.B. 27.
[25] [1985] 3 All E.R. 705 at 719.
[26] *Ibid.* at 720.

product, the pump or the component motor? Was there damage to the defective product itself?

The lack of treatment of these matters in the decision is disappointing, but of more pressing importance for the present discussion is the impact of the case on the recoverability by a consumer of loss caused by a defective product. Any hint that the decision in *Junior Books* created a major inroad into the *Spartan Steel* principle has been rejected, and the position remains that the consumer cannot recover from the manufacturer for loss other than that which is, or which is consequent upon, personal injury or physical damage, unless there was a very close proximity or relationship between the parties and the ultimate purchaser had placed real reliance on the manufacturer rather than the vendor.

In the light of *Muirhead*, it must be concluded that *Junior Books* has had a relatively minor impact upon *Spartan Steel*. In the former case Lord Roskill countenanced the possibility of preferring the dissent in *Spartan Steel* to the majority view,[27] but later decisions have effectively restricted *Junior Books* to its own facts.[28] This has significantly diminished the prospect of any such re-evaluation of the principles laid down in *Spartan Steel*.

B. *Cost of repair or replacement of products which pose a threat of harm to person or property, and consequential loss*

(a) *The wider proposition.* The traditional approach to the question as to whether repair or replacement costs and any consequential financial loss are recoverable in tort has been to assume that the protection afforded by *Donoghue* v. *Stevenson*[29] principles related only to safety deficiencies in products. In the result, such costs were perceived as irrecoverable unless the defective product posed a threat to persons or property. Authority for this proposition can be found in *Spartan Steel* and in particular in *Anns* v. *Merton L.B.C.*,[30] in which the cost of removing a danger caused by an unsafe house was held to be recoverable in tort. The measure of damages in such an instance was the cost of remedying the defectiveness of the product.[31] It

---

[27] [1983] 1 A.C. 520 at 547.
[28] In his speech, Lord Fraser stated that the case was decided "strictly on its own facts": *ibid.* at 533.
[29] 1932 S.C.(H.L.) 31.
[30] [1978] A.C. 728. See also *Dutton* v. *Bognor Regis United Building Co. Ltd.* [1972] 1 Q.B. 373.
[31] See discussion in Cane, *op. cit.*, 95 L.Q.R. 117 at 126.

may be, however, that the danger-threatening defect is irremedi-
able by repair, causing the product to be a total loss. Here,
according to *Batty* v. *Metropolitan Realisations Ltd.*,[32] another
defective premises case, the cost of remedying the defect in the
product is the value of the product itself since removal of the
danger necessitates replacement of the product. In *Batty*, the
plaintiff was permitted to recover in tort (and in contract) damages equal[33] to the value of the property. So, the plaintiff
effectively had a tortious warranty of fitness, allowing him to "get
his money back," as long as the defect in the product created a
risk to safety.

In *Junior Books* both Lord Keith[34] and Lord Roskill[35] were of
the view that recovery from the manufacturer in tort was possible
where the plaintiff had repaired or replaced defective products so
as to remove a threat of danger to person or property. The
matter has also been discussed in an important Canadian decision. In *Rivtow Marine Ltd.* v. *Washington Iron Works*,[36] the
charterers of a barge which was fitted with cranes suffered loss
when it was discovered that the cranes were dangerously defective. The plaintiff charterers were unsuccessful in their claim to
recover in tort for the cost of repair, the court taking the view
that such damage sounded in contract and not in tort. However,
damages for loss of profits during the time when the crane was
undergoing repair was considered to be recoverable in tort. It
was held that the manufacturer and the distributor were liable for
this loss on the basis that they knew about the defective nature of
the crane and ought to have warned the plaintiff of the dangers.
The crane had to be repaired during the busy season rather than
during the slacker times of the year, and in a rather curious
finding, the court held the measure of damages to be the difference between the loss of profits during the time when the crane
was inoperative and the loss of profits had the crane been out of
use during the off-season. But in a powerful dissent,[37] Laskin J.
stated that in his view the manufacturer should incur liability in
tort both for the cost of repair and the loss of profits[38] already
given.

[32] [1978] Q.B. 554.
[33] See Cane, *op. cit.*, 95 L.Q.R. 117 at 127.
[34] [1983] 1 A.C. 520 at 534–536.
[35] *Ibid.* at 542–544.
[36] (1974) 40 D.L.R. (3d.) 530.
[37] *Per* Lord Roskill in *Junior Books* v. *The Veitchi Co.* [1983] 1 A.C. 520 at 544.
[38] It is difficult to understand why Laskin J. did not find liability for all loss of
profits: see Cane 95 L.Q.R. 117 at 138.

"The case is not one where a manufactured product proves to be merely defective (in short, where it has not met promised expectations), but rather one where by reason of the defect there is a foreseeable risk of physical harm from its use and where the alert avoidance of such harm gives rise to economic loss. Prevention of threatened harm resulting directly in economic loss should not be treated differently from post-injury cure."[39]

Moreover, Lord Denning had remarked, albeit *obiter*, in *Dutton* v. *Bognor Regis United Building Co. Ltd.*[40] that the manufacturer ought to be liable for the cost of repair of a defect discovered in time to prevent injury. Thus, there was a steady stream of dicta supporting the wider proposition that recovery was possible both in respect of economic loss comprising the expenditure necessary to make a product safe in the sense of removing its threat to person or property, and expenditure upon repair or replacement.[41] However, in *D. & F. Estates Ltd.* v. *Church Comrs. for England*[42] the House of Lords has cast serious doubt upon this wider proposition.

(b) *The narrow proposition.* In *D. & F. Estates*, plaster inside a flat became loose and some of it fell down. The plaintiffs brought an action for damages in negligence, for the cost, *inter alia*, of remedial work. It was held, unanimously, that the loss sustained in renewing the plaster-work was pure economic loss which was not recoverable under the principle in *Donoghue* v. *Stevenson*. Having reviewed the leading authorities, including those quoted above, Lord Bridge, in the leading speech, summed up the principles thus:

"If the hidden defect in the chattel is the cause of personal injury or of damage to property other than the chattel itself, the manufacturer is liable. But if the hidden defect is discovered before any such damage is caused, there is no longer any room for the application of the *Donoghue* v. *Stevenson* [1932] A.C. 562 principle. The chattel is now

---

[39] (1974) 40 D.L.R. (3d.) 530 at 551–552.
[40] [1972] 1 Q.B. 373 at 396.
[41] Nevertheless, it is important to notice that the majority in *Rivtow* held that a manufacturer would not in general be liable in tort to an ultimate user or consumer for the cost of repairing a dangerously defective article or for the economic loss sustained as a result of the need to effect repairs: *per* Lord Fraser in *Candlewood Navigation Corp. Ltd.* v. *Mitsui O.S.K. Lines Ltd. (The Mineral Transporter)* [1986] 1 A.C. 1 at 23.
[42] [1988] 3 W.L.R. 368.

defective in quality, but it is no longer dangerous. It may be valueless or it may be capable of economic repair. In either case the economic loss is recoverable in contract by a buyer or hirer of the chattel entitled to the benefit of a relevant warranty of quality, but is not recoverable in tort by a remote buyer or hirer of the chattel. If the same principle applies in the field of real property to the liability of the builder of a permanent structure which is dangerously defective, that liability can only arise if the defect remains hidden until the defective structure causes personal injury or damage to property other than the structure itself. If the defect is discovered before any damage is done, the loss sustained by the owner of the structure, who has to repair or demolish it to avoid a potential source of danger to third parties, would seem to be purely economic."[43]

In reaching this view, his Lordship described the decision in *Batty*, above, to which he was a party, as "unsound," and he did not find it necessary to express any concluded view as to how far, if at all, *Anns* involves a departure from this principle.[44] Lord Oliver, in the only other speech, analysed the decision in *Anns* and said:

"A cause of action in negligence at common law which arises only when the sole damage is the mere existence of the defect giving rise to the possibility of damage in the future, which crystallizes only when that damage is imminent, and the damages for which are measured, not by the full amount of the loss attributable to the defect but by the cost of remedying it only to the extent necessary to avert a risk of physical injury, is a novel concept.... For my part, therefore, I think the correct analysis, in principle, to be simply that...the builder of a house or other structure is liable at common law for negligence only where actual damage, either to person or to property, results [from] carelessness on his part in the course of construction."[45]

His Lordship also cast doubt upon the correctness of the decision in *Batty*, and found the boundaries of the doctrine emerging from *Anns* not to be entirely clear.[46] He was generally

[43] *Ibid. per* Lord Bridge at 385.
[44] *Ibid.* at 386.
[45] *Ibid.* at 392.
[46] *Ibid.* at 395.

unwilling to accept the *Anns* approach, but, if *Anns* were to permit recovery

> "liability is limited directly to cases where the defect is one which threatens the health or safety of occupants or of third parties and (possibly) other property. In such a case, however, the damages recoverable are limited to expenses necessarily incurred in averting that danger."[47]

Accordingly, even if the defective plaster posed a threat of danger to person or property, recovery would be limited to the cost of averting the danger—by, for example, removing the plaster—and would not extend to the cost of repair. Thus, it is clear from this decision that financial loss, such as repair costs or loss of profits, consequent upon removal of a danger-threatening defect is beyond recovery in tort.

It will be some time before the precise scope of the principles derived from *Anns* is fully delineated. However, the decision in *D. & F. Estates* shows a marked reluctance to permit recovery in respect of the removal of danger-threatening defects which have not yet caused physical loss. In this way, the House of Lords has declined to provide an incentive, in tort, for the removal of such defects, since repair or replacement costs are beyond recovery.

C. Damage to the defective product itself

Unfortunately, there is a marked lack of Scottish or English authority on this matter, although as will shortly be noticed a number of United States decisions have involved consideration of the issue. It could be argued that any damage to the defective product itself is physical damage and hence is recoverable under traditional rules. Support for this line can be drawn from the treatment of the loss in *Junior Books* as physical damage by the court in *Tate & Lyle*, above, which is consistent with the view of the Lord Ordinary (Grieve), who dealt with the matter at first instance, and who regarded the property damaged by the defenders' alleged negligence as the property supplied by them to the pursuers, that is the upper layer of the floor laid in the factory.[48]

The traditional line of authority supports the proposition that actual damage to person or *other* property (or, as the discussion

---

[47] *Ibid.*
[48] *Muirhead* v. *Industrial Tank Specialities* [1985] 3 All E.R. 705, *per* Robert Goff L.J. at 714.

above shows, possibly a threat of damage) is required before
recovery of damages in respect of loss caused by defective
products. In his dissenting speech in *Junior Books*, Lord
Brandon perceived as central the distinction between a
dangerous product and an unmerchantable one. Speaking of
considerations which ought to limit the duty of care, he said:

> "The first consideration is that, in *Donoghue* v. *Stevenson*
> itself and in all the numerous cases in which the principle of
> that decision has been applied to different but analogous
> factual situations, it has always been expressly stated, or
> taken for granted, that an essential ingredient in the cause
> of action relied on was the existence of danger, or the
> threat of danger, of physical damage to persons or their
> property, excluding for this purpose the very piece of
> property from the defective condition of which such danger,
> or threat of danger, arises."[49]

Here, his Lordship was clearly confining recovery to those
instances in which *other* property was damaged or threatened.
Where the property damaged or threatened by the defect is the
product itself, the question of whether the danger created is a
danger to other property does not admit of an obvious answer,
especially where the danger to the product is caused or
threatened by a defective component part. This matter exercised
the Court of Appeal in *Aswan Engineering Establishment Co.* v.
Lupdine Ltd. (Thurgar Bolle Ltd., third party).[50] Lloyd L.J. put
the difficulties thus:

> "If I buy a defective tyre for my car and it bursts, I can sue
> the manufacturer of the tyre for damage to the car as well
> as injury to my person. But what if the tyre was part of the
> original equipment? Presumably the tyre is *other* property
> of the plaintiff, even though the tyre was a component part
> of the car, and property in the tyre and property in the car
> passed simultaneously. Another example, perhaps even
> closer to the present case, would be if I buy a bottle of
> wine and find that the wine is undrinkable owing to a defect
> in the cork. Is the wine other property, so as to enable me
> to bring an action against the manufacturer of the cork in
> tort? Suppose the electric motors in Muirhead's case had
> overheated and damaged the pumps. Would the plaintiff

[49] [1983] 1 A.C. 520 at 551.
[50] [1987] 1 All E.R. 135.

have recovered for physical damage to the pumps as well as the lobsters?"[51]

Commenting that he did not find these questions easy, Lloyd L.J. drew attention to the curious lack of English authority on this point, in contrast to America with its more highly developed product liability laws. Having noted the presence of United States authority, none of which was cited before the court, Lloyd L.J. concluded, without any real reasons for his view:

> "My provisional view is that in all these cases there is damage to other property of the plaintiff, so that the threshold of liability is crossed."[52]

In *D. & F. Estates*, above, the House of Lords had an opportunity to consider the matter of damage to the building itself. Lord Bridge stated that:

> "...it may well be arguable that in the case of complex structures, as indeed possibly in the case of complex chattels, one element of the structure should be regarded for the purpose of the application of the principles under discussion as distinct from another element, so that damage to one part of the structure caused by a hidden defect in another part may qualify to be treated as damage to 'other property,' and whether the argument should prevail may depend on the circumstances of the case."[53]

Thus, it is quite clear that damage within a defective product may fit into the category of physical damage to other property. But damage to the defective product itself which cannot be treated as damage to other property remains beyond recovery in tort. This is borne out by Lloyd L.J.'s view in *Aswan*[54] that he was

> "assuming in Aswan's favour that the damage was damage to other property, and not a defect in the property itself."

D. & E. Pure economic loss

The decision in *Junior Books*, with its stamp of seminality, at first appeared to have opened the doors to a variety of types of

[51] *Ibid.* at 152.
[52] *Ibid.*
[53] n. 42 above at 386.
[54] [1987] 1 All E.R. 135 at 154.

pure economic losses being recoverable. But the extension of the duty of care apparently achieved by the decision has so far been relatively unexplored. When faced with the inevitable series of claims seeking to take advantage of the apparent relaxation in the rules for recovery wrought by *Junior Books*, the appellate courts have adopted an extremely cautious approach. Their decisions have evidenced not only a reluctance to take advantage of the bridgehead laid down in the case, but, rather, there has been a clear retrenchment to the traditional conservative principle of non-recovery for pure economic loss.

Developments after Junior Books

(a) *The general retrenchment from Anns.* Lord Wilberforce's bipartite formula for the existence of a duty of care had breathed new life into *Donoghue* v. *Stevenson*[55] principles but the Wilberforce test has of late attracted some criticism. It seems to have created too many opportunities for exploitation, and the present Law Lords do not seem to be in the mood for further expansions in negligence liability.

In particular, the view of Lord Keith of Kinkel in *Governors of the Peabody Donation Fund* v. *Sir Lindsay Parkinson & Co. Ltd.*[56] that there is a need to resist the temptation to treat the Wilberforce formula as being of a definitive character, has been approved in later decisions.[57] Further, in *The Aliakmon*, Lord Brandon said of the Wilberforce test:

"... That passage does not provide, and cannot in my view have been intended by Lord Wilberforce to provide, a universally applicable test of the existence and scope of a duty of care in the law of negligence".[58]

His Lordship said that the *Anns* test was the correct approach

"in a novel type of factual situation which was not analogous to any factual situation in which the existence of such a duty had already been held to exist. He [Lord Wilberforce] was not, as I understand the passage, suggesting that the same approach should be adopted to the

---

[55] 1932 S.C.(H.L.) 31.
[56] [1985] A.C. 210 at 240.
[57] See *Candlewood Navigation Corp.* v. *Mitsui O.S.K. Lines Ltd.* [1986] 1 A.C. 1 at 21.
[58] *Leigh and Sillivan Ltd.* v. *Aliakmon Shipping Co. Ltd. (The Aliakmon)* [1986] A.C. 785 at 815.

existence of a duty of care in a factual situation in which the existence of such a duty had repeatedly been held not to exist"[59]

More recently the House of Lords has stated that:

"for the future it should be recognised that the two-stage test in *Anns* is not to be regarded as in all circumstances a suitable guide to the existence of a duty of care."[60]

Nonetheless, the Wilberforce test resulted in recovery for nervous shock to fall to the foreseeability camp[61] and until *Junior Books*, purely economic loss remained as one of the final bastions. That particular citadel has suffered only a very minor breach in its walls.

(b) *The particular retrenchment from Junior Books*. As has already been indicated, the few years which have elapsed since the decision in *Junior Books* has been a time of retrenchment in which the courts have endorsed the more traditional view of the scope of recovery for purely economic loss and have isolated *Junior Books* to its own special facts, just as in negligence generally a period of conservatism has followed one of liberal expansion. In a recent Court of Appeal decision[62] Dillon L.J. felt able to say that:

"My own view of *Junior Books* is that the speeches of their Lordships have been the subject of so much analysis and discussion, with differing explanations of the basis of the case, that the case cannot now be regarded as a useful pointer to any development of the law, whatever Lord Roskill may have had in mind when he delivered his speech. Indeed, I find it difficult to see that future citation from *Junior Books* could serve any useful purpose."[63]

---

[59] *Ibid.*
[60] In the immediate future, it seems likely that the test for existence of duty will be based upon three elements—foreseeability of harm, proximity of relationship between the parties, and whether it is just and reasonable to impose a duty: *Governors of the Peabody Donation Fund* v. *Sir Lindsay Parkinson & Co. Ltd.* [1985] A.C. 210, *Yuen Kun Yeu* v. *Att.-Gen. of Hong Kong* [1987] 3 W.L.R. 776; *Rowling* v. *Takaro Properties Ltd.* [1988] 2 W.L.R. 418.
[61] *McLoughlin* v. *O'Brian* [1983] A.C. 410.
[62] *Simaan General Contracting Co.* v. *Pilkington Glass Ltd.* [1988] 1 All E.R. 791.
[63] *Ibid.* at 805.

In an earlier case, *Muirhead* v. *Industrial Tank Specialities*, discussed above, Robert Goff L.J. considered that the court should treat *Junior Books* as a case in which, on its own particular facts, there was a very close relationship between the parties leading to liability.[64] Indeed, as we have seen, in the case itself Lord Roskill had discerned that the relationship between the parties was

> "as close . . . as it is possible to envisage short of privity of contract".[65]

Moreover, it has been said of two major recent decisions— *Candlewood Navigation Corp.* v. *Mitsui O.S.K. Lines Ltd. (The Mineral Transporter)*[66] and *Leigh and Sillivan Ltd.* v. *Aliakmon Shipping Co. Ltd. (The Aliakmon)*[67]—that they

> "categorically ostracised from the sphere of tort actions for pure economic loss"[68]

This ostracism is, however, incomplete. In the former case *Junior Books* was distinguished as "not in point"[69] while in the latter it was regarded as of "no direct help."[70] Nevertheless, these and other decisions dealing principally with what is described as title to sue[71] have helped to reduce the status of *Junior Books* to a decision turning on its own special facts.

In the product liability context, the Court of Appeal dealt with the problem of recovery for pure economic loss in *Simaan General Contracting Company* v. *Pilkington Glass Ltd.*[72] A contract for the construction of a new building in Abu Dhabi was made between its owner and Simaan as the main contractor. A sub-contractor was engaged for the purpose of installing curtain walling consisting of double glazing units manufactured by Pilkington. These units were found not to be of a uniform shade of green and the owner of the building rejected them. The main contractor sued the manufacturer in tort for the economic loss caused by the goods failing to conform to specification. It was held that the manufacturer

---

[64] [1986] 3 All E.R. 705 at 715.
[65] [1983] 1 A.C. 520 at 546.
[66] [1986] A.C. 1.
[67] [1986] A.C. 785.
[68] Markesinis, *op. cit.*, at 11.
[69] [1986] A.C. 1 24–25.
[70] [1986] A.C. 785 817.
[71] See discussion in Stewart, "Economic Loss From Damage to Others' Property" 1987 S.L.T. 345.
[72] Above, n. 62.

owed no duty of care in tort to the main contractor and hence recovery was barred. *Junior Books* was distinguished as having been interpreted as involving physical damage, and there was no physical damage in the present claim. The goods were as usable as ever and would not deteriorate. There was no threat of damage to person or property. The variation in colour did not make the goods defective; rather, there had merely been a failure to comply with conditions imposed by the Sale of Goods Act 1979.

According to the court, Simaan's real complaint was that the failure of Pilkington's to supply glass of the correct colour had rendered Simaan's contract with the owner of the building less profitable. The law of tort had consistently set its face against this type of claim in this case. The wall was serviceable and merely visually unacceptable. Tort law, it was stated, filled gaps left by other causes of action where the interests of justice so required. Here there was no gap since contractual claims would afford relief further down the chain. The general tenor of the judgments is reminiscent of the approach taken by the United States Supreme Court[73] to the effect that a separation between tort and contract remains desirable, and that an award of damages in a case such as *Simaan* would unreasonably interfere with the terms of the bargain.

Similar considerations also moved the Court of Appeal in another pure economic loss claim, in *Greater Nottingham Co-op.* v. *Cementation Ltd.*,[74] to find that there could be no recovery. In this case, the relationship between the parties was closer than that in *Junior Books* since here there *was* actual privity of contract. However, the court took the view that the terms of that contract ought to delineate the scope of the duties of the parties.[75] Thus, it is clear that the general approach to recovery of pure economic loss is largely affected by pragmatic considerations such as that

> "it is better that lawyers should be able to tell their clients what the law is, even if they cannot assert any rational justification for its consequences."[76]

---

[73] *East River Steamship Corp.* v. *Transamerica Delaval* 106 S.Ct. 2295 (1986).

[74] [1988] 3 W.L.R. 396.

[75] *Ibid.* See, *e.g.* judgment of Woolf L.J. at 418.

[76] See Jones, *op. cit.*, p. 18. In *Muirhead*, above n. 64, Robert Goff L.J. said that dicta of Lord Fraser and Lord Roskill in *Junior Books* "assist us in approaching the present case on a pragmatic basis" (at 715). Dillon L.J. in *Simaan*, above n. 62, at 805–806, also favoured a pragmatic solution. Similarly, in *Candlewood Navigation Corp. Ltd.* v. *Mitsui O.S.K. Lines Ltd. (The Mineral Transporter)*, [1986] 1 A.C. 1 at 11., Lord Fraser justified the general rule, limiting recovery of pure economic loss to persons with a proprietary or possessory title in the property concerned, on the basis that "It should enable legal practitioners to advise their clients as to their rights with reasonable certainty . . . "

This view was echoed by Lord Brandon in *The Aliakmon*[77]:

> "certainty of the law is of the utmost importance, especially but by no means only, in commercial matters. I therefore think that the general rule, reaffirmed as it has been so recently by the Privy Council in *The Mineral Transporter* [1986] A.C. 1, ought to apply to a case like the present one ... "

Applying the general rule referred to in these cases, that only a person with a proprietary or possessory right to property at the time of its damage could sue in respect of that damage, Bingham L.J. in the Court of Appeal in *Simaan* stated[78]:

> "If, contrary to my view, these units can be regarded as damaged at all, the damage (or the defects) would have occurred at the time of manufacture, when they were Pilkington's property. I therefore think that Simaan fail to show any interest in the goods at the time when the damage occurred."

Thus, it would be very misleading to assert at this time that the way is open for a successful claim by a consumer against a manufacturer for damages for pure economic loss caused by a defective product. This was made absolutely plain by the decision of the Court of Appeal in *Muirhead* v. *Industrial Tank Specialities*[79] in which it was held that a manufacturer of goods could be liable in negligence for economic loss suffered by the ultimate purchaser provided there was a very close proximity or relationship between the parties and the ultimate purchaser had placed real reliance upon the manufacturer rather than on the vendor. In *Muirhead*, as indicated above, there was no such proximity or reliance. There was nothing to distinguish the situation of the plaintiff in *Muirhead* from that of an ordinary purchaser of goods who, having suffered financial loss as a result of a defect in the goods, ought to look to the vendor rather than the ultimate manufacturer to recover damages for purely economic loss. Therefore, a latter-day Mrs. Donoghue who receives water instead of ginger beer will still be denied recovery from the manufacturer.

Simaan, however, is illustrative of the general rule as regards recovery for pure economic loss: that in the absence of such

[77] [1986] A.C. 785 at 817.
[78] [1988] 1 All E.R. 791 at 803.
[79] [1985] 3 All E.R. 705.

close proximity and reliance, there can be no recovery for purely qualitative defects or loss caused thereby. The case also shows another[80] attempt to interpret *Junior Books* as involving property damage, but this must stretch the meaning of property damage unacceptably far—in *Junior Books* itself, Lord Keith made it clear that no damage to property was involved:

> "The appellants did not, in any sense consistent with the ordinary use of language or contemplated by the majority in *Donoghue* v. *Stevenson*, damage the respondents' property"[81]

It is commonly asserted that *Junior Books* is dead, and that recent decisions are an attempt to give a decent but secure burial. However, the decision has not been overruled and, as recent cases such as *Muirhead* demonstrate, pure economic loss claims continue to be arguable in tort.

Other recent judgments have attempted to isolate the *Anns* test for existence of a duty of care, but it is suggested that a formula which leaves some scope for imagination and expansion ought to replace it. If not, the argument that recovery has not been allowed in the past and therefore will not be allowed in the future, will prevail. This argument was disparaged, rightly, in *Junior Books*, and some flexibility ought to remain. Policy reasons such as the floodgates fear, the need for reliance, and the wish to maintain a clear distinction between contract and tort have served to restrict liability. While these arguments may be tenable in a commercial context, it could be argued that where a person suffers pure economic loss caused by qualitative defects in a consumer product, none of the policy reasons which has been advanced in order to restrict liability is sufficiently persuasive to disallow recovery.

Proposals for Change

Not all of the proposals for change offered comment on the question of recovery of property damage. For example, the Pearson Report was silent on this issue as its terms of reference

---

[80] In *Tate & Lyle Industries Ltd.* v. *G.L.C.* [1983] 2 A.C. 509, Lord Templeman, with whose speech both Lord Keith and Lord Roskill agreed, described the loss in *Junior Books* as property damage. Also, in *Simaan*, n. 62 above, at 803, Bingham L.J. said: "*Junior Books* has been interpreted as a case arising from physical damage. I doubt if that interpretation accords with Lord Roskill's intention, but it is binding on us."

[81] [1983] 1 A.C. 520 at 536. See also the speech of Lord Roskill at 545.

restricted it to compensation for death or personal injury. The Strasbourg Convention was similarly limited in its application.

The Law Commissions felt that if the scheme of strict liability was to extend to property damage and other types of loss then a number of basic concepts, such as the meaning of defect, the question of contracting out of liability, the imposition of financial limits, the burden of proof and the setting of time limits, would require to be reconsidered, since different considerations were thought to apply depending upon whether property damage and other losses were included. The majority of respondents to the Law Commissions' consultative document who favoured the inclusion of property damage took the view that it should not go beyond personal belongings. The Commissions laid great stress on the question of insurance, taking the view that first-party insurance by the public would cover damage to personal property.

From the original version of the EEC Directive, a scheme of strict liability which included compensation for damage to personal property was recommended, since an adequate system of consumer protection demanded the inclusion of damage to personal property.

Article 9 contains the Directive's definition of "damage," and limits this to death or personal injury, and damage to private property, other than the product itself, excluding damage of less than 550 ECU.

The purported implementation of these provisions of the Directive in the 1987 Act has raised a number of questions about the application of the rules.

THE 1987 ACT

The provisions of the Act on recoverable damage are contained in section 5, and in particular in subsections (1)–(4). The substantive provisions in the remainder of the section, subsections (5)–(7), deal with establishing the date at which damage occurred. These latter provisions do not extend to Scotland but in England are important as regards title to sue, (in that only a person interested in property at the date when it suffers damage has an action), and for establishing the commencement of the running of the limitation period, as well as marking the point at which the question of whether the property was intended for private use or consumption is determined.

Section 5(1) which resembles but does not mirror the provisions in the Directive states:

"Subject to the following provisions of this section, in this Part "damage" means death or personal injury or any loss of or damage to any property (including land)."

Thus it is clear that pure economic loss is entirely outwith the new scheme of liability, as recommended by the various proposals for change in the law. Damages for pain and suffering seem to be included. The Act makes specific provision for the preservation of the rights of relatives to raise an action, and for the rights of a child to sue in respect of disability suffered by the child as a result of the parent being exposed to the product.[82] This latter remedy will of course be of particular importance where a child while in the womb suffers injury caused by defective drugs supplied to a parent.

The general principle of liability expressed in section 5(1) is then subjected to a number of qualifications, which in particular have the effect of excluding from recovery damage to the defective product itself, including damage to a product caused by a defective component part, and damage to commercial property. Damage to private property is recoverable only if it exceeds £275. The inclusion of damage to land would cover, for example, damage to soil by a defective weedkiller.[83] These provisions of the Act, although relatively clear as to their general import, create a number of uncertainties, including the important question as to whether the Act properly implements the Directive. In order to explore these points, the provisions of the Act must be stated in full.

Section 5(2) states:

"A person shall not be liable under section 2 above in respect of any defect in a product for the loss of or any damage to the product itself or for the loss of or any damage to the whole or any part of any product which has been supplied with the product in question comprised in it."

The effect of the provision is clear: damage to the product itself, including damage caused to a product by a component is outwith the Act.[84] Thus, for example, if a defective motor car blows itself up because of a defective battery, which was supplied comprised within the car, any resultant product liability

---

[82] See s.6.
[83] See Blaikie, "Product Liability: The Consumer Protection Act 1987 (Part 1)" 32 J.L.S.S. 325.
[84] Preamble to Directive (85/374/EEC).

litigation will not be under the 1987 Act. The precise dividing
line between when the Act applies and when it does not is of
some interest. What is the position, for example, where the
battery is a replacement which damages the car? Here the car
has not been "supplied with the product in question comprised
in it" and hence the damage to the car will be recoverable,
assuming that we have here damage to property other than the
defective product itself, and that the other aspects of section 5
are satisfied. The damage to the battery by its own self-
destruction will remain outside the scope of the Act.

It was noticed earlier that the Directive differed from the Law
Commissions' recommendations in that the latter would not
have allowed recovery of loss caused by damage to property,
whether or not the property was private. Under section 5(3) of
the 1987 Act, to permit recovery in respect of damage, the
property must be of a description ordinarily intended for private
use, occupation or consumption; and must be intended by the
person suffering the loss mainly for his own private use,
occupation or consumption. Again, the broad import of the
provision is relatively clear: damage to the paintwork of a
private car caused, for example, by a defective washing agent is
recoverable under the Act, while the same damage to a
company vehicle is not; the personal computer which explodes
causing damage to office furniture will require application of the
general law, while if furniture at home is damaged, the Act will
apply.

Interestingly, damage to private property includes land, and
the land must satisfy the tests of being ordinarily intended for
private use, occupation or consumption, and being intended by
the person suffering mainly for such use, occupation or
consumption. The use of a word such as "mainly" in a statute is
troublesome; it seems that this term would allow recovery
where, for example, a television set is used at work having been
taken there from home and is then damaged by a defective
cable which has been attached to it. Similarly, loss caused to a
car which has a small amount of business use and which is
damaged by a defective product is recoverable. Notice also that
the product need not yet actually have been used; the intention
to use it privately is enough. It was argued in the House of
Lords that the use of "intention" in this context meant that the
provision covered only products intended to be used but not yet
actually used. It is doubted whether a court would give the
provision this very limited construction, although the Act does
go further than the Directive here which requires use before

there can be liability.[85] This would of course have been an undesirable restriction on the injured person's remedies; if he had bought a product but had not yet used it when it caused the harm the Directive would not afford protection.

Section 5(4) goes on to implement the Directive's provision that the minimum loss resulting from damage to property which can be recovered is £275. However the drawing of such a line is apt to create almost fortuitous results; damage to a portable television worth £270 by a defective fish tank which leaks on to the set is not recoverable, while damage to a set costing just a few pounds more would be recoverable. A provision of this type is of very dubious merit in a statute which purports to protect consumers and their personal property.

Sections 5(5)–(7) reproduce the wording of section 3 of the Latent Damage Act 1986, and are designed to fix the date when damage is taken to have occurred in a case where the damage could not initially be discovered. As noted earlier, these provisions do not apply to Scotland, where the matter of limitation, including the case of latent damage is dealt with in the Prescription and Limitation (Scotland) Act 1973, as amended.[86]

Particular problems arise as regards cases in which no harm is yet manifest, but, for example, the exposure of the plaintiff to a substance (such as asbestos, DES or the AIDS virus) creates a statistical chance of harm, and the fear of the chance becoming reality results in an action for damages. Arguably, costs incurred in medical monitoring will be recoverable under the general law, as in some American cases.[87] It is clear that the fear itself will not constitute damage recoverable under the 1987 Act, probably not even allowable as an aspect of pain and suffering since it is unaccompanied by personal injury. The intriguing difficulties raised by such cases are not peculiar to product liability and are really a problem for the general law. It is tentatively suggested that where fear is based upon a real statistical chance of harm, damages for the anxiety thereby incurred ought to be recoverable.

---

[85] Art. 9.

[86] By Sched. 1, Pt. II, para. 8 of the Consumer Protection Act 1987.

[87] See Phillips, "The Status of Product Liability Law in the United States of America" Conference Paper presented to S.P.T.L. Colloquium, September 1984, at 7–8. Claims based upon the mere possibility of harm have failed, but if there is reasonable medical certainty then recovery is permitted: see, *e.g. Jackson* v. *Johns-Manville Sales Corp.* 781 F.2d. 384 (5th Cir. 1986); *Hagerty* v. *L. & L. Marine Services, Inc.* 788 F.2d. 315 (5th Cir. 1986).

As a result of the new regime of liability for product defects, there is then a spectrum of recoverability: at one extreme, where the harm is death or personal injury, liability under the Act will co-exist with current, mainly negligence-based, remedies; at the other end of the scale, pure economic loss remains recoverable, if at all, only outwith the new rules. In between, damage of £275 or more caused to personal property attracts potential liability under the Act, while damage to commercial property will be actionable only outwith the regime of the 1987 Act. Damage to the defective product itself is recoverable only under the common law rules, and even then, only if the defect damages, or poses a threat of damage to, person or property, other than the defective item itself.

Since the Act limits recovery to damage to personal property and personal injury, recovery of consequential economic loss, such as loss of profits, is left to the existing rules. Under the general law, compensation for pain, suffering and loss of amenity, is of course recoverable. However, the Explanatory Memorandum issued with the draft directive states that:

> "The term 'personal injuries' comprises the cost of treatment and of all expenditure incurred in restoring the injured person to health and any impairment of earning capacity as a result of the personal injury.
>
> The Directive does not include payment of compensation for pain and suffering or for damage not regarded as damage to property (non-material damage). It is therefore possible to award such damages to the extent that national laws recognize such claims, based on other legal grounds."[88]

It would seem ludicrous to suggest that a separate ground of action must be maintained in order to recover such compensation, and it is suggested that the above comment should not be so construed. However, the last five words of the quote are apt to create ambiguity, as this extract from the Law Commissions' report makes clear:

> " ... in the Explanatory Memorandum that accompanies the EEC Directive it is clearly provided that the term 'personal injuries' ' ... does not include payment of compensation for pain and suffering ... ' If the policy of the Directive is to exclude heads of damage recoverable in the general law of

[88] Explanatory Memorandum, para. 17. This memorandum is set out in full in the Law Commission's Report, Cmnd. 6831 (1977).

tort or delict we think the policy is undesirable and unjustifiable . . . "[89]

It is to be expected that courts in the United Kingdom will take the view that the 1987 Act permits recovery of such compensation, and it is suggested that it was not the intention of the reformers to exclude these damages, despite the apparent contradiction in the Explanatory Memorandum.

As for causation, section 2(1) makes it clear that the damage must have been caused wholly or partly by a defect in a product. This of course preserves the need to establish a causal connection between defect and loss, but the wording of the provision, which differs again from that in the Directive, would seem to have the effect of imposing liability upon the supplier unless he can point to a *novus actus interveniens*, which is the sole cause of the loss and which therefore breaks the chain of causation.[90]

Foreseeability of damage within the Act is not required, since all that needs be established is that the defect caused the damage. Foreseeability remains important of course as regards consequential loss, and as regards damage outwith the Act.

THE AMERICAN EXPERIENCE

A review of the American case law on the issue of recoverable forms of damage reveals, as would be expected, that their courts have had to come to terms with the same kind of problems of categorisation of loss as the courts in the United Kingdom. The Supreme Court has recently had an opportunity to review the area. In *East River Steamship Corp.* v. *Transamerica Delaval Inc.*,[91] an Admiralty case which will be discussed later, three different approaches taken by United States courts to the problem of recovery of loss caused by damage to the product itself were identified: the majority approach; the minority approach; and the intermediate approach. The brief review of the United States cases which follows commences with an overview of these three approaches followed by a more detailed discussion of the issues.

---

[89] Cmnd. 6831 (1977), para. 133. Many states in the U.S.A. have recently legislated to impose a cap on such non-economic damages.

[90] Merkin, "A Guide to the Consumer Protection Act 1987" (Financial Training Publications, 1987). The Directive's provisions are contained in Art. 1 and Art. 8.1.

[91] 106 S.Ct. 2295 (1986).

The majority approach

Seely v. *White Motor Company*,[92] a case from 1965, was taken by the Supreme Court to be illustrative of the majority view that liability in tort ought not to be imposed in respect of pure economic loss. In that case, damages were sought in respect of property damage and economic loss, including the cost of repair, caused by the defective condition of a vehicle manufactured by the defendants. Justice Traynor, a pioneer of the strict tort theory of recovery, refused to allow recovery of the repair costs. Recovery of damages in respect of the physical loss would have been permitted, but the plaintiff failed to establish that a defect in the vehicle caused the physical damage.[93] In the course of his judgment in *Seely*, Justice Traynor explained that physical damage to property was so similar to physical damage to person that the law ought not to distinguish between them.[94]

Later courts have in the main adopted what has been taken to be the *Seely* approach—no recovery in strict tort for purely economic loss. Thus, on this basic dichotomy between pure economic loss and damage to property or personal injury, the trend in the United States has been towards the same result that has occurred here. Accordingly, strict tort allows recovery of the first head of loss in our list—damage to person or property and economic loss consequential thereon.

The minority approach

In reaching his decision in *Seely*, Justice Traynor declined to follow the line taken by the New Jersey Supreme Court which had earlier in the year permitted recovery of pure economic loss. In *Santor* v. *A. & M. Kargheusian Inc.*[95] a carpet manufacturer was held to be strictly liable in tort for defects in a carpet, even though the only damage was damage to the product itself. The plaintiff recovered damages amounting to the difference between what he had paid for the carpet and what it was worth. *Santor* thus became the progenitor of the minority approach, authorising the proposition that:

> "a manufacturer's duty to make non-defective products encompassed injury to the product itself, whether or not the defect created an unreasonable risk of harm"[96]

[92] 45 Cal.Rptr. 17 (1965).
[93] *Ibid.* at 24.
[94] *Ibid.*
[95] 207 A.2d. 305 (N.J. 1965).
[96] *East River*, n. 91 above, at 2301.

Differences of view such as those between *Seely* and *Santor* also rendered uncertain the recoverability of the cost of repairing or replacing products so as to remove the danger-threatening aspect of the defect, and financial loss consequent upon the unusability of the product. Many courts have taken the line that tort does not permit recovery for pure economic loss, such as the cost of repair or replacement, in the absence of any physical damage to person or property.[97] For example, in *National Crane Corp.* v. *Ohio Steel Tube Co.*,[98] recovery in tort was not permitted for replacement costs incurred in order to obviate a threat of potential future physical harm posed by a defective product.[99]

The intermediate approach

Other courts have been willing to adopt a middle course, the intermediate approach, between the apparent *Seely* no-recovery rule, and *Santor's* general recoverability stance. These courts view a product which poses a threat of harm to person or property, and which therefore requires removal of the danger, as being unreasonably dangerous for the purposes of tort recovery,[1] and permit recovery for repair or replacement costs in addition to the much smaller cost of averting the danger. In one of the leading modern decisions in this area, *Pennsylvania Glass Sand Corp.* v. *Caterpillar Tractor Co.*,[2] it was held that recovery in tort was permissible where a defect exposes persons or property to a risk of physical harm, even though no such harm has actually occurred. A similar approach has been taken in several cases[3] in which recovery of pure economic losses, where no actual damage has been suffered, was permitted on the basis that the product (in some cases asbestos) posed a real

---

[97] See Bellehumeur, "Recovery for Economic loss Under a Products Liability Theory: From the Beginning Through the Current Trend" 70 Marq.L.R. 320, in particular, cases cited at n. 8.

[98] 213 Neb. 782, 332 N.W. 2d. 39 (1983).

[99] For a discussion of cases supporting recovery in such circumstances, see Bellehumeur, *op. cit.*

[1] *e.g. Cinnaminson Township Bd. of Educ.* v. *United States Gypsum Co.* 552 F.Supp. 855 (D.N.J. 1982); *School Dist. of Lancaster* v. *ASARCO*, No. 1414, slip op. (Philadelphia C.P., December 6, 1983); *Area Vocational Technical Bd.* v. *National Gypsum Co.*, No. 119, slip op. (Lancaster C.P., September 7, 1983); *Philadelphia National Bank* v. *Dow Chemical Co.* 605 F.Supp. 60 (E.D.Pa. 1985).

[2] 652 F.2d. 1165 (3d. Cir. 1981).

[3] Cases at n. 1, above.

risk of physical harm. Given the policy aims of strict liability in tort, which include the protection of the plaintiff from exposure to an unreasonable risk of injury, this so-called intermediate approach is attractive.

As has been explained earlier, most states have adopted section 402A of the Restatement (Second) of Torts. The seminal decisions in *Seely* and *Santor* were made prior to the adoption of section 402A, but the section's provisions are of no real value in cases involving dangers posed, but not yet manifested as damage, since the section speaks of liability for *physical harm* caused by products which are in a defective condition unreasonably dangerous to the user or consumer or his property.

Section 402A leaves open the further and more troublesome issue of damage to the defective product itself, including damage to a product caused by a defective component part. In *Seely*, defects in a truck caused it to overturn. However, the refusal of the court to allow recovery of the repair costs was not on the basis that the product itself had been damaged. Rather, the court emphasised the nature of the responsibility which a manufacturer undertakes in distributing his products, and distinguished between risk of physical injury and simple expectation losses.[4] This view is simply a reaffirmation of the safety/shoddy distinction which many decisions have taken to underpin the tort/contract dichotomy.

The question of damage to the product itself sits on the border between pure economic loss and damage to property. As is relatively common in such a borderline issue, different state courts have taken differing stances on this matter. In some states, courts have been prepared to characterise damage to the defective product itself as property damage and hence to allow recovery.[5] Other courts have taken the view that damage to the product itself is in the realm of pure economic loss. Accordingly, it is only personal injury or damage to other property which is compensable in such jurisdictions.[6] Thus, where a helicopter was damaged following a crash, there being no damage to person or other property, the plaintiff could not

---

[4] *Seely*, n. 92 above, at 23.
[5] See, *e.g. Bagel* v. *American Honda Motor Co.* 132 Ill.App. 3d. 82, 477 N.E. 2d. 54 (1985); *Vulcan Materials* v. *Driltech Inc.* 251 Ga. 383, 306 S.E. 2d. 253 (1983); *Corporate Air Fleet Inc.* v. *Gates Learjet Inc.* 576 F.Supp. 1076 (M.D.Tenn. 1984); *Pennsylvania Glass Sand Corp.* v. *Caterpillar Tractor Co.* 652 F.2d. 1165 (3d. Cir. 1981).
[6] See the discussion in Bellehumeur, *op. cit.*

obtain compensation under a strict tort theory of liability.[7] In Texas, where that case was decided, the court categorised such a loss as a loss of bargain, compensable under a warranty rather than strict tort theory. Similarly, the law in Minnesota refuses to recognise damage to a product by a defective component part as a compensable loss under strict tort.[8]

Thus, United States decisions show a broad characterisation of damage to the defective product either as pure economic loss, in which case recovery is excluded or as property damage, and so recoverable. However, the simple characterisation of a particular loss caused by damage to the product itself as property damage is not the only requirement for liability. A distinction is drawn between

"the disappointed users... and the endangered ones"[9]

Only the latter are afforded a tort action. The approach of the Alaska Supreme Court is illustrative of this dichotomy.[10] In *Morrow* v. *New Moon Homes Inc.*[11] it was argued that a mobile home which had been purchased by the plaintiffs was defective in a number of respects, including that the home had a leaky roof and cracks in the windows. The losses resulting from these defects, which posed no threat of damage to person or property, were held not to be compensable in tort. In stark contrast, the same court, in another case involving a defective mobile home, allowed recovery: in *Cloud* v. *Kit Manufacturing Co.*[12] the mobile home was completely destroyed when polyurethane foam carpet padding caught fire. Given the well-known dangerous properties of the fumes from burning polyurethane, the court was prepared to accept that there was a risk to persons posed by the defect, and on that basis to depart from the decision in *Morrow* and hence to permit recovery. Echoing the distinction expressed above, but in rather more colloquial terms, the court viewed the distinction between a "lemon" and a dangerous or unsafe product as crucial. There is a difference, according to the court, between damage which is

---

[7] *James* v. *Bell Helicopter Co.* 715 F.2d. 166 (5th Cir. 1983).
[8] See, *e.g. American Home Assurance Co.* v. *Major Tool & Machine Inc.* 767 F.2d. 446 (8th Cir. 1985).
[9] *Russel* v. *Ford Motor Co.* 281 Ore. 587, at 595 (1978).
[10] See discussion of these cases in Bellehumeur, *op. cit.*, at 332 *et seq.*, and in *East River Steamship Corp. et al.* v. *Transamerica Delaval Inc.* 106 S.Ct. 2295 (1986).
[11] 548 P.2d. 279 (Alaska 1976).
[12] 563 P.2d. 248 (Alaska 1977).

qualitative, involving gradual deterioration, depreciation or internal breakage,[13] and damage resulting from some calamitous event. The view taken in Alaska can thus be summed up as follows: if a product creates a potentially dangerous situation, posing a threat of harm to person or property, and loss arises as a proximate result of that danger and under dangerous circumstances, then recovery in tort is allowed.[14] The Alaskan court is not alone in making this division, courts in Georgia and Missouri, among others, having reached the same conclusion.[15]

A rather more sophisticated treatment of this question, which has come to be termed the intermediate approach, was developed in the leading case of *Pennsylvania Glass Sand Corp. v. Caterpillar Tractor Co.*[16] Here, rather than focus on the relatively simple point as to whether sudden accidental loss, as opposed to qualitative deterioration, had occurred, a tripartite approach was taken, which in effect sought to synthesise the criteria developed by other courts. The three factors adduced by the court as requiring examination were: the nature of the defect; the type of risk; and the manner in which the injury arose.[17] The court was anxious to draw the line between contract and tort and stated that the items for which damages are sought, such as repair costs, are not determinative of recovery:

"Rather, the line between tort and contract must be drawn by analyzing interrelated factors such as the nature of the defect, the type of risk, and the manner in which the injury arose. These factors bear directly on whether the safety-insurance policy of tort law or the expectation-bargain protection policy of warranty law is most applicable to a particular claim."[18]

On an analysis of these factors, the court effectively was able to distinguish the unsafe product from the merely shoddy. As regards the nature of the defect, the court indicated that *quantitative* defects ought to be distinguished from *qualitative*

---

[13] See the discussion in *East River*, above, n. 91.

[14] See *Northern Power and Engineering Corp.* v. *Caterpillar Tractor Co.* 623 P. 2d. 324 at 329 (1981).

[15] See *Vulcan Materials Co.* v. *Driltech Inc.* 251 Ga. 383, 306 S.E. 2d. 353 (1983); *City of Clayton* v. *Gruman Emergency Products Inc.* 576 F.Supp. 1122 (E.D.Mo. 1983).

[16] 652 F.2d. 1165 (3d. Cir. 1981).

[17] *East River*, above, n. 91, at 2302.

[18] *Pennsylvania Glass*, above, n. 115 at 1173.

defects. The former create an unreasonable risk of damage to person or property, while the latter entail purely economic losses and create no threat of physical damage to other property or to persons. Thus, recovery is permitted in the case of the former, but not the latter. The second element, the type of risk, also relates to the distinction between risk to safety (of person or property) and risk to the pocket only. Again, risk of the former type created by a defective product is compensable, while the latter is beyond recovery in tort. Finally, the court recognised the calamity or accident criterion, which has been of importance for many other courts. The suddenness, immediacy, violence or calamitous nature of the damage indicates recovery in tort, as distinct from damage which develops and manifests itself only over a period of time.

This decision is of major interest because it shows a departure from the occurrence of sudden, calamitous or accidental harm as being the sole decisive issue, although such a test remains as part of the threefold inquiry. Decisions illustrative of the way in which these factors militate for or against liability include *Bagel v. American Honda Motor Co.*,[19] where the engine of a motorcycle failed to operate after the engine had been running and while still in the garage of the plaintiff. Applying the tripartite approach, this was deemed by the court to be pure economic loss, the manner in which the damage occurred being not such as to pose a threat to the safety of person or property.[20]

There is, however, a major difficulty inherent in a test for liability, especially one which is posited as a means of distinguishing between contract and tort, when that test involves an analysis of interrelated factors. It may even be argued that the separation into three distinct, if related elements is itself artificial as the factors are so inextricably connected as not to be amenable to such a division. At all events it is by no means clear what weight is to be given to any particular facet, or indeed whether the absence of one, such as the "sudden calamity" strand, works to preclude recovery. At best it is suggested that the *Pennsylvania Glass* criteria can only be taken as the starting point for inquiry, leaving later courts to decide on the relative weight to be given to each factor and the need for the presence of all factors. Indeed, the decision has been

[19] 132 Ill.App. 3d. 82, 477 N.E. 2d. 54 (1985).
[20] See also *City of Clayton* v. *Gruman Emergency Products Inc.* 576 F.Supp. 1122 (E.D.Mo. 1983).

said to have "already proved unwieldy in certain fact situations."[21] In some cases[22] the need for a sudden, violent calamity or accident has not been a precondition of recovery and hence it can be seen that *Pennsylvania Glass* ought not to be taken as establishing that all three factors must be present before there can be recovery.

The view of the Supreme Court

Against this rather uncertain background, the United States Supreme Court has recently, in an Admiralty case, reviewed the law on recovery of pure economic loss including the matter of damage to the defective product itself. The decision is of such authority and interest that it is worth exploring the case in some detail. In *East River Steamship Corp. et al.* v. *Transamerica Delaval Inc.*,[23] four oil-transporting supertankers were constructed by a shipbuilding company, which contracted with Delaval to design, manufacture and supervise the installation of the turbines. These turbines, which cost $1.4 million each, were to be the main propulsion units for the vessels. East River chartered one of the tankers, the T.T. Brooklyn, and other operators chartered the three other vessels. In three of the ships an escape of steam from the high-pressure turbine was found to have caused damage to other parts of the turbine. The fault was traced to the virtual disintegration of the first-stage steam reversing ring. The other vessel was put into service some years after the others and did not suffer from the same defect, which had by then been designed out. However, a further defect, this time in the installation of the astern guardian valve, was identified. So, the charterers of the first three ships sued for the cost of repairing the ships and for income lost while the ships were out of service, arguing that Delaval were strictly liable in tort. The charterer of the other vessel could not argue that the product itself was defective and instead alleged negligence in the installation of the valve. Claims based upon contractual warranty were untenable as the limitation period had elapsed. At first instance and then in the Court of Appeals, the claims were held not cognisable in tort. The claims were held to concern product quality. However, one judge in the Court of Appeals, Becker J., felt that:

---

[21] See also, Bellehumeur, *op. cit.*, at 357.
[22] See cases cited at n. 1, above.
[23] 106 S.Ct. 2295 (1986).

"the exposure of the ship to a severe storm when the ship was unable to operate at full power due to the defective part created an unreasonable risk of harm"[24]

But, in the Supreme Court's view, if the development of product liability

"were allowed to progress too far, contract law would drown in a sea of tort. See G. Gilmore, The Death of Contract, 87–94 (1974). We must determine whether a commercial product injuring itself is the kind of harm against which public policy requires manufacturers to protect, independent of any contractual obligation."[25]

The court noted that the traditional property damage claim involved damage to "other property," and that in the present case there was no such damage: the chief allegations were that "each supertanker's defectively designed turbine components damaged only the turbine itself."[26] Since each turbine was supplied as an integrated package, each was a single unit. In this context the court cited with approval dicta in *Northern Power & Engineering Corp.* v. *Caterpillar Tractor Co.*,[27]

"Since all but the very simplest of machines have component parts, [a contrary] holding would require a finding of property damage in virtually every case in which a product damages itself. Such a holding would eliminate the distinction between warranty and strict products liability".

Consequently, damage to the product itself ought to sound in contract but not in tort:

"Obviously, damage to a product itself has certain attributes of a products-liability claim. But the injury suffered—the failure of the product to function properly—is the essence of a warranty action, through which a contracting party can seek to recoup the benefit of its bargain."[28]

The court went on to create the distinction, discussed above, between the majority land-based approach, and the intermediate and minority views.

[24] *East River*, n. 91 above, at 2297.
[25] *Ibid.* at 2300.
[26] *Ibid.* at 2300.
[27] 623 P. 2d. 324 at 330 (Alaska 1981).
[28] *East River*, n. 91 above, at 2300.

The Supreme Court then rejected both the intermediate and the minority land-based approaches as unsatisfactory:

> "The intermediate positions, which essentially turn on the degree of risk, are too indeterminate to allow manufacturers easily to structure their business behaviour. Nor do we find persuasive a distinction that rests on the manner in which the product is injured."[29]

Going on to recognise that damage may be qualitative in the sense that it results from internal breakdown or gradual deterioration, as opposed to sudden, accidental or calamitous damage the court referred to the decisions in *Morrow*, above and *Cloud*, above. This dichotomy was not found to be helpful:

> "But either way since by definition no person or other property is damaged, the resulting loss is purely economic. Even when the harm to the product itself occurs through an abrupt, accident-like event, the resulting loss due to repair costs, decreased value and lost profits is essentially the failure of the purchaser to receive the benefit of its bargain—traditionally the core concern of contract law."[30]

Thus, the court held that a manufacturer in a commercial relationship has no duty under either a negligence or a strict products-liability theory to prevent a product from injuring itself.

Much of the court's reasoning in *East River*, as has already been noticed, is based on safeguarding the present nature of the contract/tort dichotomy. Accordingly, it was felt that in a case such as this the reasons for imposing a tort duty were weak in contrast to the strong reasons for leaving the injured parties to their contractual remedies. The court felt that the increased cost which the public would have to bear for the price of products if the producer were liable in tort for injury to the product itself were not justified. In addition,

> "damage to a product itself is most naturally understood as a warranty claim. Such damage means simply that the product has not met the customer's expectations, or, in other words, that the customer has received 'insufficient product value'."[31]

---

[29] *Ibid.* at 2302.
[30] *Ibid.*
[31] *Ibid.* at 2303.

In places, the judgment hints that the commercial nature of the transaction in the present case was important as regards the question of recoverability:

> " ... the main currents of tort law run in different directions from those of contract and warranty, and the latter seem to us far more appropriate for commercial disputes of the kind involved here ... The expectation damages available in warranty for purely economic loss give a plaintiff the full benefit of its bargain by compensating for lost business opportunities. (See Fuller and Perdue, The Reliance Interest in Contract Damages: 1, 46 Yale L.J. 52, 60–63 (1936)."[32]

This point was developed by the court and is undoubtedly a major reason for disallowing recovery in cases such as the present. The function of tort damages is to compensate the victim, in order to put him in the position he was in prior to the injury. This contrasts with the function of contract damages which is to put the disappointed party in the position he would have been in had the other side not broken the contract. Moreover, the rules regarding remoteness of damage are rather more stringent in a contract claim than in a tort action. The twin notions of privity of contract and recoverability only of loss which is foreseeable in the sense of being a serious possibility, limit the potential figure in a warranty claim.[33] These notions offer a limitation for the manufacturer which tort products liability law, where potential liability to the public generally is involved, does not possess. Foreseeability, in such a situation, "is an inadequate brake."[34]

Again, then floodgates fears were persuasive in restricting recovery of purely economic loss:

> "Permitting recovery for all foreseeable claims for purely economic loss could make a manufacturer liable for vast sums."[35]

In the result, the court could find no good reason to extricate the parties from the bargain which they had made, concluding:

[32] *Ibid.* at 2304.
[33] See *Hadley* v. *Baxendale* (1854) 9 Ex. 341.
[34] *East River*, n. 91 above, at 2304.
[35] *Ibid.*

"Thus, whether stated in negligence or strict liability, no products-liability claim lies in Admiralty when the only injury claimed is economic loss."[36]

It is difficult to assess the precise impact of this recent decision. On the one hand, it is a decision of the Supreme Court, and the tenor of at least certain aspects of the judgment is that uniform rules should apply to commercial and non-commercial plaintiffs, in Admiralty or in general product liability. Thus, the intermediate land-based approach in *Pennsylvania Glass* is disparaged as unsatisfactory, as is the minority view. The policy reasons which the court offers in support of its decision, principally the need to maintain a separation between tort and contract, apply equally well to non-commercial plaintiffs. But it is not clear whether the court sought to overrule *Pennsylvania Glass* and the cases, cited earlier, in which recovery of economic loss, for example where the product poses a threat to person or property, had been allowed. On the other hand, it could be argued that the decision in its key passages speaks only as regards commercial plaintiffs, or only as regards the Admiralty jurisdiction. It may be that in the same way that *Junior Books* was perceived as being dangerously innovative and hence was restricted by later courts, *East River* may be viewed as overly conservative and subjected to similar restrictions.

East River has, however, already been applied to defeat claims for damage caused solely to the product. For example, in *Shipco 2295 Inc. et al* v. *Avondale Shipyards Inc. and Allgemeine Elektricitats Gesellschaft Telefunken*,[37] the United States Court of Appeals for the Fifth Circuit refused claims by charterers for damages in tort for repair costs and loss of profits caused by alleged defects in tankers and in their steering systems. The court took the view that the product in the instant case, as in *East River*, was each vessel itself:

> "In attempting to identify the product, our analysis leads us to ask what is the object of the contract or bargain that governs the rights of the parties? The completed vessels were obviously the objects of the contract. Shipco ... did not bargain separately for individual components of each vessel. We are persuaded that those same vessels that were the object of the contract must be considered 'the product'

---

[36] *Ibid.* at 2305.
[37] 825 F.2d. 925 (1987).

rather than the individual components that make up the vessels."[38]

Thus, no "other property" was damaged. The damages sought by the plaintiffs-appellees were of the same type as that characterised in *East River* as economic loss:

"*East River* teaches that such economic loss to the product bargained for, the vessels in this case, cannot be recovered in tort."[39]

In summary, many courts in the United States have adopted the *Seely* approach, which would exclude recovery of pure economic loss but would permit recovery for damage to the product itself. But a further line is drawn by most courts: harm to property by simple deterioration, or internal breakdown, cannot be recovered; but loss caused by damage to the product which is caused or threatened by a dangerous defect, is recoverable. Other courts, in the minority, allow recovery of pure economic loss. Conversely, *East River* is representative of the rather unsubtle view, espoused by another minority, that damage to the product itself even when caused by a defective component part is beyond the reach of tort compensation.

As a common law system, America ostensibly uses a more empirical form of judicial reasoning than civilian systems. However, as is most patently clear from the whole development of product liability at common law, no rigid principle of *stare decisis* exists in the United States.[40] Thus, it is possible that an Admiralty decision, which involved a commercial product, will be of limited persuasive value in other state or federal courts trying cases of manufacturers' liability.

But, at least in Admiralty cases involving commercial products, clarity has replaced the relative uncertainty of approaches such as that in *Pennsylvania Glass*. Do the policy reasons promulgated by the Supreme Court justify its conclusion? And do those same policy reasons indicate non-recoverability in non-commercial product cases?

Before looking at these matters, it is worth noting the treatment of property damage/economic loss of the type discussed here, in federal legislative proposals on product liability. Current proposals for federal legislation which would

---

[38] *Ibid.* at 928.
[39] *Ibid.* at 929.
[40] See Berman and Greiner, *The Nature and Functions of Law (The Foundation Press Inc.*, 4th ed., 1980), p. 587.

provide a uniform product-liability regime, do not cover loss or damage caused to a product itself.[41] As has been noticed, the trend in state courts is towards recovery of product damage caused or posed by dangerous defects and so the federal proposals involve an important retrenchment. In most of the states which have legislated on product liability, property damage is recoverable and there is no specific exclusion of damage to the product itself.

Conclusion

The matter of recoverable damage raises some intriguing questions, not least about the respective roles of contract and tort/delict. At common law, the principles applicable to personal injury, property damage, and consequential loss are relatively clear. These become progressively more uncertain as one looks first at the costs of removing the danger, and then at damage to the defective product itself. That there has been insufficient ventilation of the issues is apparent from the tentative views offered in the cases. The American experience is instructive. Assuming that a line between recoverable and non-recoverable economic loss is desirable we ought, it is suggested, to draw the line using the "danger" test: if the defect poses an imminent threat of damage to person or property, then the cost of removing the danger should be recoverable. Arguably, repair or replacement costs ought also to be recoverable. In some cases it will be possible to characterise damage within a defective product as damage to other property. If no such imminent threat is posed, or merely qualitative deterioration in the product results, recovery should be left to contract remedies.

Some would argue that the 1987 Act is overly conservative in its treatment of this area, but it would have been very surprising for strict liability to be imposed for losses in respect of which recovery at common law is rather uncertain. The further argument that the Act fails to implement the Directive is based on the idea that the Directive itself is clear on the issue; unhappily, this is not the case and again the conservatism shown by Parliament is understandable. If the "danger" criterion suggested above obtains a sufficient pedigree at common law it would be appropriate to consider its inclusion in a strict liability regime. Such a change would further the policy aims of strict liability.

---

[41] See, *e.g.* S. 666, 100th Cong., 1st Sess. at 102(a)(9) (1987).

A more conservative stance could have been taken, for example by adopting the recommendation of the Law Commission that property damage should be outwith recovery. Insurance arguments are relevant here, but no more so than as regards recovery in negligence generally. If the encouragement of product safety is a key aim of the new rules, then a division between personal and property safety is arbitrary and undesirable, and the resulting provisions in the Act are welcome.

After considerable litigation, the majority of United States courts had finally reached a consensus as to the appropriate way to deal with recoverable loss questions. The various approaches, synthesised in *Pennsylvania Glass*, displayed a quite subtle treatment of the issues, and the resulting separation of unsafe products from the merely shoddy provided a workable solution. *East River* of course negates this view, and in an overly conservative and profoundly unimaginative decision the Supreme Court refused to accept that a proper role for contract could be preserved without denying all tortious recovery for damage to the product. It is suggested that the analysis used by other courts, for example in *Pennsylvania Glass*, represents a more subtle and just treatment of the issue.

It might be argued that policy reasons, similar to those which moved the European Commission, indicate a distinction between damage to commercial property and damage to personal property. In contrast, it can be pointed out that no such distinction obtains at common law. If the prime policy aim in product liability is the encouragement of the manufacture of safer products, then the distinction between commercial and non-commercial property loses its significance. However, it will require further legislation in this country before strict liability for damage to commercial property is included in the regime of strict liability.

The policy aims which moved the Supreme Court in *East River* primarily concerned the retention of a role for contract law. This is a laudable aim but the court overly emphasised the fear of tort interfering with contract. Product safety ought not to be the subject of contractual bargaining. The appropriate principle is that defects which cause a product to be unsafe as regards person or property, including the product itself, ought to be actionable in tort. There is no compelling reason for limiting such recovery to negligence rather than strict liability, but in the absence of clear common law support for the imposition of liability, the reluctance of the legislators to include it within the new regime is understandable.

Chapter 6

DEVELOPMENT RISKS

The central controversy in the field of product liability, which has dominated discussion of the new regime, is the so-called "development risks" defence. By invoking this defence, the person proceeded against can escape liability for loss caused by a defect in a product if he can prove that the state of scientific and technical knowledge at the relevant time was not such that a producer of products of the same description as the product in question might be expected to have discovered the defect if it had existed in his products while they were under his control.

As was noted earlier, the United Kingdom Government insisted upon inclusion of this defence before accepting the Directive. A minority of other Member States are of the view that no such defence is necessary. Accordingly, Article 15 of the Directive allows Member States to derogate from Article 7(e)—which permits the development risks defence—by extending strict liability to include development risks. The resulting difference between states on this central issue is unfortunate in a measure aimed at harmonisation of product liability laws throughout the Community. Earlier drafts of the Directive, in common with the view taken in the Strasbourg Convention, and the recommendations of the Law Commissions and the Pearson Commission, did not permit this derogation.

Much of the time spent on debating the proposed new strict liability regime concerned development risks. Discussion of the issue was prolonged and at times passionate.[1] The European Commission and the European Parliament were divided on this question, reflecting the views of Member States. Policy considerations which were ventilated in these debates are explored in the course of this Chapter. Put simply, those against the defence argue that its inclusion emasculates strict liability

---

[1] For the Second Reading, see Official Report, Fifth Series, Lords, Vol. 482, cols. 1003, *et seq.*; see also Official Report, Fifth Series, Lords, Vol. 483, cols. 819, *et seq.*, and cols. 784 *et seq.*; and House of Commons, May 5, 1987, Standing Committee D, col. 3 *et seq.* In the U.S., draft proposals for federal product liability legislation would include the defence: see, *e.g.* Model Uniform Product Liability Act, s.106.

and subverts the policy aims underlying the new regime. The opposing view is that without such a defence, potential liability would be indeterminate and could be catastrophic, and that more cogent policy considerations (including the wish not to stifle innovation) outweighed the aims of the purists.

Parliamentary and other discussions of the defence have, however, been hampered by a lack of clarity as to the precise scope of the protection which it affords. In its Explanatory and Consultative Note[2] the United Kingdom Government indicated that in its view it will not be easy for a producer successfully to plead this defence. However, in a highly controversial move, when the Bill was introduced the Government used a form of words in the defence which differed substantially from the wording used in the Directive. During the passage of the Bill, the House of Lords restored the Directive's wording only to have the Government's original wording returned in the Commons. The wording in the Act has angered consumer groups, who have stated that they may take the matter to the European Court to decide whether the Government has fulfilled its obligation faithfully to implement the Directive. Indeed, the European Commission has formally protested to the Government about the change of wording arguing that the form of words used in the Act would "empty the directive of much of its content," and is commencing proceedings at the European level. The Department of Trade and Industry is thought to consider the wording in the Act to be the only plausible meaning of a rather enigmatic provision in the Directive. The nature and consequences of the wording adopted will shortly be considered. This Chapter will also include analysis of American experience on use of the state-of-the-art defence, as well as discussing whether the terms "state of the art" and "development risks" are synonymous. It will be argued that the defence as currently worded has the potential to return the new regime to a position very close to that which existed under the law of negligence, and that when the time comes for the presence of the defence to be reviewed—in 1995—the opportunity should be taken to remove it from the scheme of strict liability.

For the sake of brevity, it will simply be noted that, as shown in Chapter 1, no development risks defence exists to a contract claim. Since undiscoverable defects cannot by their nature be identified by the exercise of all care, let alone

---

[2] Implementation of the EC Directive on Product Liability—An Explanatory and Consultative Note (D.T.I., November 1985), para. 22.

reasonable care, liability in negligence will not arise in respect of loss caused by such defects. There also exists a class of defects which are known to science and thus are discoverable. Clearly, the concept of reasonable care involves considerations of feasibility in such situations: discovery may be scientifically possible, but the means required for discovery may not be consistent with the exercise of merely reasonable care, in which case the manufacturer will not be liable.

North Scottish Helicopters Ltd. v. *United Technologies Corp.*[3] illustrates some of the difficulties which a producer may encounter in seeking to discover potential defects in his product. A helicopter caught fire while being given a ground test, and it was argued on behalf of the pursuers that the fire was caused by a defect in the rotor brake mechanism. This brake mechanism was highly complex, but essentially involved a set of pucks being brought into contact with a rotating disc. It was argued that "puck drag" had occurred by a puck failing to disengage from the rotating disc, causing overheating and eventually the ignition of leaked hydraulic fluid. After a welter of expert evidence was led, resulting in an 80-page judgment, Lord Davidson found both the manufacturers of the helicopter and the designers and manufacturers of the brake unit not liable in negligence. The alleged defect in the brake unit was held not to have been discoverable by its manufacturers who were therefore not negligent in failing to guard against or eliminate the danger. Four earlier incidents involving helicopter fires could reasonably be regarded as having been caused by human error so that none of these incidents ought to have alerted the manufacturers of the helicopter to the possibility of a defect in the rotor brake system.

Of wider interest, however, are Lord Davidson's comments on the difficulties facing the pursuer on the discoverability issue:

"As the proof progressed it became clear that the pursuers' experts laboured under serious disadvantages. Although they had considerable engineering ability, none of them had the detailed knowledge and familiarity with the subject that the defenders' various engineering witnesses could command. In addition, the defenders had ample opportunity to

---

[3] The decision on the negligence aspect of the case is, at the time of writing, unreported, but the author has kindly been supplied with a transcript of Lord Davidson's judgment by the solicitor instructed by the successful first defenders.

carry out tests on s76 helicopters and other equipment. The pursuers' experts had no comparable facilities."[4]

His Lordship also considered it to be unfortunate that the pursuers and their experts had little if any knowledge of the detailed exposition to be developed by the experts of the defenders.

The extent to which these difficulties have been alleviated by the new regime is open to some doubt and if, as is likely, an alternative ground of negligence and strict liability is argued in future cases like the above, this will result in even lengthier litigation.

DEVELOPMENT RISKS, STATE OF THE ART AND THE TIME FACTOR IN ESTABLISHING DEFECTIVENESS

Prior to any discussion of how the new legislation has implemented the Directive's provisions on development risks, it is worth seeking to achieve some clarity as to the meanings of the terms "development risks" and "state of the art," and also to understand the relationship between these terms and the time factor in the definition of defect. It is clear that there is some disagreement about the use of terminology in the current context. For many years, the defence now known as development risks was described as the state-of-the-art defence, and a number of commentators used the terms interchangeably. Neither term has a meaning which is self-evident from the words used. Clearly, development risks does not mean the risk that the later development of safer products shows the product in question to have been defective when put into circulation; the definition of defective allows the time factor to be taken into consideration and such a product would not be defective simply by reason of safer products having later been developed. Also, state of the art does not simply mean the current state of industry practice—to argue that the producer carried out the same tests as his fellow producers is not of itself a defence in negligence let alone in strict liability.

Both terms have often been used to mean the same thing: that given the existing state of scientific and technical knowledge the defect was not reasonably discoverable. If it is thought that any need will be served by distinguishing between the two terms

---

[4] *Ibid.* transcript at 56.

then the following distinction may be of help: the term state of the art could be used to connote a product which is not defective when judged against the prevailing safety standards at the time when it was put into circulation; in contrast, the term development risks is used in situations in which the product *is* defective when put into circulation, but the manufacturer has the defence that existing knowledge made the defect not reasonably discoverable.[5] Thus, state of the art arguments relate to the question of defectiveness, while development risks issues arise later, as a defence to a finding of defectiveness. Assume, for example, that it becomes standard practice at some future time for all lawnmowers to have automatic cut-out switches when the cable is damaged. A lawnmower manufactured at the present time would not be considered to be defective simply because it did not have the safety device—it complied with the state of the art, in terms of reasonably expected safety, at the time of being put into circulation. If, on the other hand, a drug is found to cause cancer then it may be found to be defective and it will have been so from the time of being put into circulation. In such a case, the producer will often seek to invoke the development risks defence.

It may be that there is no pressing need to distinguish between state of the art and development risks. However, the above dichotomy may be helpful in indicating that the question of feasible additional safety features in manufactured products is not a development risks question; it is one of defectiveness. Development risks are about reasonable discoverability, and the issue ought not to arise in argument about additional safety features; it does not relate to the preclusion of known hazards but to the question of whether unknown hazards ought to have been discovered. This is, it is suggested, a matter of great importance in understanding how the defence ought to function.

DEVELOPMENT RISKS UNDER THE
CONSUMER PROTECTION ACT 1987

In its Explanatory and Consultative Note on Implementation of the EC Directive on Product Liability, the Government made

---

[5] See Taschner, "European Initiatives: The European Communities, conference paper, SPTL Colloquium on Product Liability," 1984, at p. 12. For a discussion on the meaning of "scientific and technical knowledge" see Newdick, "The Development Risk Defence of the Consumer Protection Act 1987" (1988) 47 C.L.J. 455.

plain its intention not to take advantage of the derogation, which the Directive permits, from inclusion of the development risks defence:

> "A true development risk is rare and yet the availability of the defence has been one of the most controversial issues raised by the Directive. Some have argued that the inclusion of such a defence would leave a significant gap in the liability system, through which victims of unforeseeable disasters would remain uncompensated and which would bring back many of the complexities and legal arguments that the introduction of strict liability is supposed to avoid. Manufacturers, on the other hand, have argued that it would be wrong in principle, and disastrous in practice, for businesses to be held liable for defects that they could not possibly have foreseen. They believe that the absence of this defence would raise insurance costs and inhibit innovation, especially in high risk industries. Many useful new products, which might entail a development risk, would not be put on the market, and consumers as well as business would lose out."[6]

Thus the Government was persuaded that the policy reasons for inclusion outweighed the argument against. More controversy followed, however, when the Government unveiled the wording of the defence in the Bill. There appeared to be material differences between the Bill and the Directive which, as was noticed earlier, upset the consumer lobby and the European Commission.

Section 4(1)(e) of the Act allows the person proceeded against a defence if he can show:

> "that the state of scientific and technical knowledge at the relevant time was not such that a producer of products of the same description as the product in question might be expected to have discovered the defect if it had existed in his products while they were under his control;"

As can be seen from a comparison between the Act's wording and that used in the Directive, the major changes are the substitution of "might be expected" for "enable," and the introduction of the phrase "a producer of products of the same description as the product in question."

[6] Para. 21.

It is reasonably clear that a defence based upon a state of knowledge which enables discovery of a defect is less protective of manufacturers than one based upon a state of knowledge in which discovery might be expected. It could be argued that the Directive focuses upon a state of knowledge, while the Act lays stress upon the conduct of producers. However, in the Government's view there is no material difference between the wording adopted and that in the Directive,[7] but those lobbying on behalf of industry took the view that the Government's version did indeed make it easier for a producer to mount the defence. It is clear that even under the wording in the Directive a producer was not deemed able to be aware of every flash of inspiration possible about the safety of his product. Indeed, even where scientific knowledge had entered the public domain—for example by publication in a scientific journal—the producer could arguably still have invoked the defence if the journal was sufficiently obscure or unavailable to "enable" discovery of the defect. But, the words "might be expected" import a reasonableness test, smacking strongly of that used in negligence.

It could also be argued that the wording in the Act, although intended to create an objective test, introduces an element of subjectivity into the defence by referring to producers of products of the same description as the product in question. This might be taken by a court to involve the state of mind of the average producer of the particular type of product. For example, if the average producer of a particular type of product is a small-scale business, with limited resources for testing, then a producer of such products would not be expected to carry out extensive inquiries into product safety. The wording adopted focuses unwelcome attention on the research facilities and other resources of the average producer. Even if the average producer is purely notional, some decision about his size and resources seems necessary in order to determine what he might be expected to have discovered.

A further difficulty is that there may well be no actual "producer of products as the same description as the product in question." This will often be the case where new products are involved. The Act is not clear as to how such a situation is to be treated. Even if a notional producer is invented, it will be difficult to determine what he might be expected to have discovered about the new product.

[7] Official Reports, Fifth Series, Lords, Vol. 483, col. 785.

It is to be hoped that in construing the wording of the defence in the United Kingdom courts will look for what a notional reasonable producer would have done, rather than what the average producer of that type of product would have done. The worry is that this apparent incursion of subjectivity into the defence will result in the defence being much more widely relied upon than the Directive intended. The United Kingdom courts must also bear in mind, in interpreting the Act, section 1(1):

> "This Part shall have effect for the purpose of making such provision as is necessary in order to comply with the product liability Directive and shall be construed accordingly."

This novel sub-section may allow a court to impose the provision in the Directive, assuming this was found meaningful, in preference to the provision in the Act. It is suggested that a United Kingdom court would be unlikely to take this step unless it was prepared to find s.4(1)(e) itself to be ambiguous.

There is then some scope for the defence to be interpreted in a lenient manner, but the Government has expressed the view that the intention is that the defence will be of limited application. Having rather ironically stated that the defence is "stringently defined in the Directive," the Explanatory and Consultative Note goes on:

> "It is understood that the defence should be interpreted as meaning that the producer will not be liable if he proves that, given the state of scientific and technical knowledge at the time the product was put into circulation, no producer of a product of that kind could have been expected to have discovered the existence of the defect. The burden of proof will fall squarely on the producer to show that the defect could not reasonably be expected to have been discovered. It will not necessarily be enough to show that he has done as many tests as his competitor, nor that he did all the tests required of him by a government regulation setting a minimum standard. It will therefore not be easy for a producer successfully to plead this defence . . . "[8]

"Relevant time" has the meaning accorded to it by section 4(2) and will usually mean the time of supply by the producer, own-brander or importer. It must also be noticed that the

---

[8] Para. 22.

development risks defence, like the other defences in the Act, applies in favour of "the person proceeded against" who may not, of course, always be the producer.

The defence of development risks has always been taken to be of particular importance in high risk industries in which innovation is often the price of success. In the pharmaceuticals, aerospace, chemical and agri-chemical sectors there is some relief not only that the defence has been included, but also that the wording used by the Government has prevailed. If the defence is given a lenient interpretation, then a producer who shows that he has taken the steps which an average or reasonable producer ought to have taken will avoid liability. This is simply a return to a negligence standard of liability, with the burden of proof reversed (since the producer must establish the defence); rather than ask the plaintiff to prove fault, as negligence law does, the new rules will be read as asking the producer to disprove fault. If, on the other hand, the defence is interpreted strictly, to apply as it should to truly undiscoverable defects, then the new regime of liability will fail to achieve an important objective: simplifying the trial process. In every case in which, for example, a drug produces unforeseen side-effects we can expect the producer to establish that he did the usual tests, and then to proceed to a lengthy and expensive trial, involving a parade of expert witnesses, of the discoverability issue. A plaintiff wishing to embark on an action against such a producer will be faced with the major disincentive of very large costs if the action fails.

Although Thalidomide ought not to be taken as a model example of the use of the development risks defence[9] since the danger of the product was, it could be argued, reasonably discoverable, tragedies caused by chemicals and drugs seem bound to continue. Many argue that the risk of harm being caused by undiscoverable defects should be borne by the producer, and spread throughout the consumers of his product by being reflected in the price. The decision to include a development risks defence means that the risk of harm caused by defects which were not reasonably discoverable falls solely upon the victim. Policy reasons for the adoption of the defence will be more fully canvassed later, after consideration of the substantial experience built up by American courts in dealing with the matter.

[9] See Taschner, *op. cit.*, at 7.

THE AMERICAN EXPERIENCE

The Americans do not use the term "development risks" as it is used in this discussion; rather, "state of the art" is the accepted label. One of the leading commentators, Dean Wade, speaks of state of the art as a "chameleon-like term" and states that its use ought to be abandoned since "its meanings are so diverse and so often confused."[10] Twerski says that the term "came to mean all things to all people."[11] This lack of clarity bedevils any attempt at a concise analysis.

A further difficulty is the popularity in products cases of plaintiffs basing their claims on the ground of failure to warn. Since this will involve considerations of foreseeability and knowledge, state of the art questions loom large.

There are three main applications of the term state of the art: first, a manufacturer can assert that he complied with prevailing industry practice and standards; secondly, state of the art evidence can be led in order to show feasibility, or lack of feasibility, of a safer design; lastly, the term can be used to mean scientific undiscoverability of the defect. Following discussion of these, the major, issues, some comment will be offered on the use of state of the art evidence in warning cases, and then in cases involving allegedly unavoidable dangers.

Compliance with industry standards

Evidence that the safety of a particular product matches that practised by the industry in general will of course be a common feature in negligence cases, and may indeed raise a presumption that due care has been exercised. In *Day* v. *Barber-Colman Co.*,[12] a sliding door fell upon and injured a man who was installing it, and he sued the manufacturer in negligence. This was the first case in which the term state of the art was used. The plaintiff argued that a safety device could and should have been fitted to the door. State of the art evidence was led by the defendant, establishing that the product complied with a standardised design which was in common use in the industry at the relevant time. The court stated:

---

[10] Wade, "The Effect in Products Liability of Knowledge Unavailable Prior to Marketing" 58 N.Y.U.L. Rev. 734 (1983) at 751.
[11] Twerski, "A Moderate and Restrained Federal Product Liability Bill: Targeting the Crisis Areas for Resolution" (1985) 18 Univ. of Mich. Jnl. of L. Reform 575.
[12] 10 Ill. App.2d. 494, 135 N.E. 2d. 231 (App.Ct. 1956).

"It is not of itself negligence to use a particular design or method in the manufacture or handling of a product... which is reasonably safe and in customary use in the industry, although other possible designs... might be conceived which would be safer... "[13]

Proof of compliance with accepted practices will not, of course, be conclusive:

"The fact that the custom of manufacturers generally was followed is evidence of due care, but it does not establish its exercise as a matter of law. Obviously, a manufacturer cannot, by concurring in a careless or dangerous method of manufacture, establish their own standard of care."[14]

In another negligence case, Judge Learned Hand articulated the principle thus:

"Indeed in most cases reasonable prudence is in fact common prudence; but strictly it is never its measure; a whole calling may have unduly lagged in the adoption of new and available devices.... Courts must in the end say what is required; there are precautions so imperative that even their universal disregard will not justify their omission."[15]

As in negligence cases, proof of compliance with industry practice will not be conclusive in a strict liability suit. For example, in *Gelsumino* v. *E.W. Bliss and Co.*,[16] the plaintiff was injured when operating a punch press, having slipped and inadvertently touched a floor pedal which set the machine in motion while his hand was under it. Rejecting evidence which sought to establish that the design accorded to industry practice, the court stated that strict liability could not be avoided

"by attempting to show merely that they had done what the rest of the industry had done to make their products safe."[17]

---

[13] *Ibid.* at 508 (Ill. App.). For a discussion on compliance with industry standards in a negligence context in the U.K., see *Brown* v. *Rolls Royce* [1960] 1 W.L.R. 210; but *cf. Stokes* v. *G.K.N. (Bolts and Nuts) Ltd.* [1968] 1 W.L.R. 1776. On reliance by a manufacturer upon a reputable industrial supplier, see *Winward* v. *T.V.R. Engineering Ltd.* [1986] B.T.L.C. 366 (C.A.).

[14] Symposium, "The State of the Art Defense in Strict Products Liability" 57 Marquette L.Rev. 649 (1974), at 651.

[15] *The T.J. Hooper* 60 F.2d. 737 (2d. Cir. 1932) at 740.

[16] 10 Ill. App. 3d. 604, 295 N.E. 2d. 110 (1973).

[17] *Ibid.* at 608 and 113.

Thus, it followed that

> "the state of the art defence is irrelevant to the two strict liability counts.... Conformity to the state of the art is not a defence to a claim involving an unreasonably dangerous product."[18]

While all state jurisdictions accept that simple compliance with industry practice is not conclusive and hence is not a defence to a strict liability action, some are prepared to treat compliance as setting up a presumption of non-defectiveness in negligence and in strict liability actions.[19] Some states permit a similar presumption where the product complies with governmental or legislative regulatory standards. The existence of such a presumption, although rebuttable, weighs heavily against the plaintiff.[20]

Most courts are prepared to admit evidence of industry practice as part of the enquiry into the question of defectiveness. For example, in *Reed* v. *Tiffen Motor Homes Inc.*[21] it was stated that:

> "We find that the state of the art and trade customs are relevant in helping the jury make a determination of whether the product is unreasonably dangerous when used in a manner expected by the ordinary consumer in the community. While only one element in that determination, it is a necessary aid to assist the trier of fact in determining the reasonableness of the manufacturer's design."[22]

Similar reasoning prevailed in *Robinson* v. *Audi NSU Auto Union Atkiengesellschaft and Volkswagen of America Inc.*,[23] where the plaintiffs were severely burned following a rear end collision involving their Audi automobile. They alleged that the car was defective and unreasonably dangerous because the fuel tank was so positioned as to easily be punctured by the contents of the trunk when impacted from behind. In this appeal, the plaintiffs argued that considerations of customary designs were largely irrelevant to strict liability. However, the plaintiffs had themselves

---

[18] *Ibid.*
[19] See discussion in Twerski, *op. cit.*, at 46.
[20] See, *e.g.* Col.Rev.Stat. s.13–21–403 (2) (Supp. 1980); Tenn. Code Ann. s.29–28–104 (1980); Utah Code Ann. s.78–15–6(3) (1977).
[21] 697 F.2d. 1192 (1983).
[22] *Ibid.* at 1198.
[23] 739 F.2d. 1481 (1984).

"introduced numerous exhibits depicting alternative fuel tank designs in use on other cars."[24]

The court agreed with the view expressed in *Cantu* v. *John Deer Co.*,[25] that where the plaintiff with his evidence makes state of the art an issue, the defendant is entitled to respond, and went on to assert that he could use state of the art evidence to attempt to establish the expectations of a reasonable consumer.

In a minority of jurisdictions, including Illinois, Pennsylvania and California, there is some authority for the proposition that state of the art evidence of the type discussed in this section is generally inadmissible. *Horn* v. *General Motors Corp.*[26] furnishes an illustration. Mrs. Horn was involved in a car accident. While struggling to avoid the collision, she drew her hand across the steering column, dislodging a cap which fitted over the horn mechanism. Three sharp prongs were thereby exposed. As the car crashed she was thrown forward, striking her face against the exposed prongs. The court found the car to be defective, and not only held that state of the art was not a defence, but also rejected as inadmissible evidence of industry practice.

Feasibility of safer design

Almost any type of product could have been made to be more safe. Few courts are prepared to hold that a manufacturer must guarantee the absolute safety of his product, and so proof of the fact that a safer design was possible will not alone indicate a finding of defectiveness. However, many courts admit of what they often describe as state of the art evidence in support, or in rebuttal, of the argument that it was technologically or economically feasible for the producer to have made a safer product.[27]

Many of the cases which have involved state of the art evidence have arisen in the context of feasibility of a safer design. These commonly involve claims that safety features were absent from and reasonably ought to have been incorporated in manufactured products. As such, this major class of cases should be distinguished from the situation in which a defect is argued to have been scientifically undiscoverable, where the defendant will argue either that a known risk in a product could

---

[24] *Ibid.* at 1488.
[25] 603 P.2d. 839 (Wash.App. 1979).
[26] 17 Cal.3d. 359, 551 P.2d. 398, 131 Cal.Rptr. 78 (1976).
[27] See Twerski, *op. cit.*, at 593.

not have been discovered or eliminated, or that the risk was unknown and unknowable. Scientifically undiscoverable defects are covered in the next section.

In negligence cases, United States courts have employed concepts familiar to those of English law in seeking to establish what would have been reasonable care in the circumstances. Many have taken it to be implicit in the use of the adjective "reasonable" that risks must be weighed against benefits. In this balancing process, factors other than safety in the absolute sense become important. Thus, the feasibility of an alternative safer design will commonly be an issue. In implied warranty actions, evidence concerning the feasibility, or lack of feasibility, of greater safety will of course be irrelevant.

Where a product case is tried under a strict liability theory, the question of feasible design alternatives is very often a crucial element in the decision.[28] Most jurisdictions in the United States employ the criteria provided in section 402A of the Restatement (Second) of Torts in order to determine defectiveness: thus, a product must be "in a defective condition unreasonably dangerous to the user or consumer." Comment i to section 402A goes on to state that;

"The article sold must be dangerous to an extent beyond that which would be contemplated by the ordinary consumer who purchases, with the ordinary knowledge common to the community as to its characteristics."

However, the section makes it clear that the exercise of all possible care will not preclude a finding of defectiveness:

"The rule stated in Subsection (1) applies although (a) the seller has exercised all possible care in the preparation and sale of his product"

(a) *The consumer expectation test.* Use of a consumer expectation such as that posited by Comment i to section 402A quite clearly raises a number of issues regarding the state of the art. For example, it may be argued that a consumer apprised of ordinary knowledge acquired from the use of products could not expect an as yet untried design. Consumers, whether particularly or generally, may have no expectations regarding the dangerous characteristics of a product or of design alternatives. In addition, the consumer expectation test may be something of

---

[28] Some courts depart from this position: see, *e.g.* O'Brien v. Muskin Corp., n. 45 below.

a trap for consumers—state of the art evidence which establishes that a product is similar in design to others of the same type could be used to show that, since a number of other products were designed in the same way, the consumer should have realised the danger.

Olson v. *Arctic Enterprises Inc.*,[29] neatly illustrates the relationship between state of the art and consumer expectations. Olson alleged that he had been injured as a result of a design defect in a snowmobile made by the defendant company. Evidence was led by the defendants to establish that other snowmobiles were of similar design. It was held that the vehicle, although capable of causing harm, was not defective since it did not present a danger which would not be anticipated by the ordinary consumer.

Similarly, in *Reed*, above, the court referred to Comment i to section 402A and stated:

"While the practice of considering the ordinary consumer's expectation has met with criticism . . . it is the law in South Carolina . . . Further the South Carolina court has explicitly set forth the requirement that a product must be unreasonably dangerous to a consumer with the ordinary knowledge of the community and has held products not to be unreasonably dangerous if the design failed to provide a safety feature outside what the consumer might expect."[30]

In *Robinson*, above, state of the art evidence was similarly allowed in order to establish the expectations of a reasonable consumer. *Bruce* v. *Martin-Marietta Corp.*[31] further illustrates the point:

"There is 'general' agreement that to prove liability under s.402A the plaintiff must show that the product was dangerous beyond the expectation of the ordinary consumer. The state of the art evidence helps to determine the expectation of the ordinary consumer. A consumer would not expect a Model T to have the safety features which are incorporated in automobiles made today. The same expectation applies to airplanes. [The] plaintiffs have not shown that the ordinary consumer would expect a plane made in 1952 to have the safety features of one made in 1970."[32]

---

[29] 349 F.Supp. 761 (D.N.D. 1972).
[30] n. 21 above, at 1197.
[31] 544 F.2d. 442 (10th Cir. 1976).
[32] *Ibid.* at 447.

So, where a consumer expectation test is employed, state of the art evidence can be a decisive factor. But the use of consumer expectations in this way is open to a number of objections. In particular, it could be argued that where a danger is patent or obvious a consumer can expect no more than the standard of safety offered by the product. This patent danger rule is an important objection to the consumer expectation test. A further difficulty is that the average consumer may have no real idea about the safety or dangerousness of the product being used. It seems highly speculative to attempt to gauge the expectations of an ordinary consumer as regards the safety of, for example, the aeroplane in *Martin*, above. Another major difficulty about the consumer expectation test is the confusion regarding whether the test is subjective or objective. As noted earlier, in his dissenting judgment in *Lester* v. *Magic Chef Inc.*,[33] Justice Praeger stated that the consumer expectation test is not an objective test, and went on to say that it was bound to produce inconsistent verdicts in comparable cases.

Accordingly, the consumer expectation test makes it difficult for state of the art evidence regarding feasible design alternatives to be convincing.

(b) *The risk-utility test*. Despite the severe judgmental difficulties which are inherent in a risk-utility decisional model, the technique is widely used. Where it is used, state of the art evidence about the feasibility of design alternatives is a central feature of the balancing process.

Perhaps the most common decisional model is that proposed by Dean Wade.[34] The components of his risk-utility analysis are:

(1) The usefulness and desirability of the product—its utility to the user and to the public as a whole.
(2) The safety aspects of the product—the likelihood that it will cause injury, and the probable seriousness of that injury.
(3) The availability of a substitute product which would meet the same need and not be unsafe.
(4) The manufacturer's ability to eliminate the unsafe character of the product without impairing usefulness or making it too expensive to maintain its utility.
(5) The user's ability to avoid danger by the exercise of care in the use of the product.

[33] Kan., 641 P.2d. 353 (1982).
[34] See the discussion in Chap. 2.

(6) The user's anticipated awareness of the dangers inherent in the product and their avoidability, because of general public knowledge of the obvious condition of the product, or of the existence of suitable warnings or instructions.

(7) The feasibility, on the part of the manufacturer, of spreading the loss by setting the price of the product or carrying liability insurance.

Elements (3) and (4) in the above list most clearly involve considerations of state of the art as used in the current context. Thus, in *Reed*,[35] above, it was said that:

"In design cases South Carolina has held that while any product can be made more safe, the fact that it is not does not automatically make the product unreasonably dangerous."[36]

The court then cited with approval dicta from an earlier case:

"In the final analysis, we have another of the law's balancing acts and numerous factors must be considered, including the usefulness and desirability of the product, the cost involved for added safety, the likelihood and potential seriousness of injury, and the obviousness of danger."[37]

State of the art evidence is only one element in the determination of whether a product is unreasonably dangerous, but

"is a necessary aid to assist the trier of fact in determining the reasonableness of the manufacturer's design."[38]

Certain states take a more restrictive view and demand that the plaintiff prove, and be supported in this by the jury, that a safer, feasible design alternative was available. Thus, in *Lolie* v. *Ohio Brass Co.*,[39] it was held that a design defect strict liability action placed upon the plaintiff the burden of adducing:

"proof that, *inter alia*, (1) the product as designed is incapable of preventing the injury complained of; (2) there existed an alternative design that would have prevented the

---

[35] n. 21 above.
[36] *Ibid.* at 1198.
[37] *Clayton* v. *General Motors Corp. S.C.* 286 S.E. 2d. 129, at 132. (1982).
[38] *Reed*, above, n. 21, at 1198.
[39] 502 F.2d. 741 (7th Cir. 1974).

injury; and (3) in terms of cost, practicality and technological possibility, the alternative design was feasible."[40]

Attempting to show that, on balance, an alternative design is safer and feasible can of course present a great challenge to the plaintiff. For example, in *Korli* v. *Ford*,[41] evidence showed that had the product, a motor vehicle, been equipped with front-hinged rather than rear-hinged doors, then in the circumstances of the case it would have been more safe. However, this was not enough to characterise the product as defective since front-hinged doors were proved by the defendants to be more dangerous in other situations. Similarly in *Olson*,[42] above, the snowmobile case, it was argued that, had rubber tracks been used on the vehicle, less damage would have been done to the injured plaintiff. However, this evidence was counteracted by expert testimony to the effect that such a track was more susceptible to breakage, which would render the vehicle less safe in other situations, for example by stranding the user in a wilderness. Again, in *Wilson* v. *Piper Aircraft Corp.*,[43] the plaintiff alleged that an aeroplane engine was defective in that, since a carburettor rather than a fuel injector was used, fuel system icing was possible. The court rejected this view. Although use of a fuel injector would have decreased the chance of icing it would have rendered the aeroplane less safe in other respects and would adversely have affected utility and price.

Many courts have insisted upon the plaintiff adducing evidence of feasible alternatives,[44] but this is of course too extreme a position, since a product may simply be unreasonably dangerous and have no alternative design. This was the view adopted in *O'Brien* v. *Muskin Corp.*,[45] where the plaintiff suffered head injuries when he dived into an above-ground swimming pool. The pool was lined with vinyl, and the plaintiff alleged that the vinyl was so slippery as to cause his out-thrust arms to separate and thus to cause his head to strike the bottom. No evidence showing the feasibility of an alternative design was presented by the plaintiff. Nevertheless, the New

---

[40] *Ibid.* at 744.
[41] 69 Cal.App.3d. 115, 137 Cal.Rptr. 828 (1977).
[42] Above, n. 29.
[43] 282 Ore. 61, 577 P.2d. 1322 (1978).
[44] See discussion in O'Donnell, "Design Litigation and the State of the Art: Terminology, Practice and Reform" (1978) 11 Ak.L.Rev. 627.
[45] 94 N.J. 169, 463 A.2d. 298 (1983).

Jersey Supreme Court held that even in the absence of an alternative method of making bottoms for above-ground swimming pools, the jury might find that the risks posed by the product outweighed its utility. However, on the facts the plaintiff's comparative negligence operated to bar recovery.

O'Brien has been criticised as going too far,[46] but the principle which it asserts is eminently reasonable. If those who criticise it think that a court ought not to be able to declare a product to be defective simply because no safer alternative can be found, they are leaving the way open for the production of dangerous items which could never be found to be defective.

One real difficulty which faces courts which employ a state of the art defence based upon consideration of feasible design alternatives is the lack of clarity in the meaning of feasibility. Feasibility may be thought to take into account more than simply the technological possibility of implementing the safer design, and may thus be taken to include considerations of cost, marketability, and the need for the safer design to fit easily into a mass production method.[47] But this is too wide a definition of feasibility and use of it effectively re-opens the whole question of defect. Even on the narrower meaning of feasibility—the technological possibility of implementing the safer design— difficulties arise. It may be argued, for example, that the relevant scientific principles simply are unknown, or it may be contended that even though the principles are known the method of implementation of the principles in re-designing the instant product is not known. There are bound to be difficulties of proof in establishing the time at which application of the principles became known, raising important issues about the availability of knowledge which has been generated by, for example, some scientist at a foreign university, but which is not readily available.

Thus, in cases involving feasibility of safer design alternatives, there will often be a need to establish the boundaries of available knowledge. An important issue here is the determination of the appropriate time at which defectiveness is to be adjudged.[48] At what stage is the feasibility of an alternative

---

[46] See, *e.g.* Twerski, *op. cit.*, at 587 *et seq.*

[47] See Robb, "A Practical Approach to the Use of State-of-the-Art Evidence in Strict Products Liability Cases" (1982) 77 N.W.U.L. Rev. 1, at 5.

[48] See Wade, "The Passage of Time: The Implications for Product Liability. On the Effect in Product Liability of Knowledge Unavailable Prior to Marketing" (1983) 58 N.Y.U.L. Rev. 734; see also, Keeton, "Product Liability and the Meaning of Defect" (1973) 5 St. Mary's L.J. 30.

design to be measured—time of trial or time of distribution of the product, or some other time? It is now clear that the majority of jurisdictions accept time of distribution as the appropriate time.[49] This appears to derive from the very meaning of feasibility, which smacks of "contemporary perceptions and priorities."[50] These courts have rejected, often in colourful terms, the argument that with hindsight the product could have been made more safe. Echoing the view expressed in *Bruce* v. *Martin-Marietta Corp.*,[51] that

> "A consumer would not expect a model T to have the safety features which are incorporated in automobiles today"

the New Orleans federal district court has noted that the law does not expect Saturday manufacturers to have the insight available to Monday morning quarterbacks.[52]

Undiscoverable risks and unknown risks

It was noted earlier that questions of feasibility of safer designs arise, in particular, in cases where manufactured products of a non-chemical nature are challenged as defective. Ordinarily, the question is whether a safer material could have been used, or a safety feature incorporated in the product, or a safer situation of design features used. Questions of undiscoverability of a risk, or the unknowability of a risk more commonly arise where substances such as chemical or pharmaceutical products are involved.

Let us first of all seek to define the relevant terminology. Some risks are known to be potentially present but are undiscoverable. The term undiscoverable here connotes a risk that is known, or suspected, to be present in the product, but, effectively, both the presence of the danger in particular samples of the product and the means of elimination of the danger are undiscoverable. Thus, arguments about undiscoverability tend to be raised in manufacturing defect cases: there is a flaw in a particular sample or individual product, but the bulk is not affected. It is a trite observation that in warranty undiscoverability is no defence, while even in negligence the presence of a manufacturing defect raises a strong inference of

---

[49] Wade, *op. cit.* cases cited at n. 85.
[50] *Ibid.*
[51] 544 F.2d. 442 (10th Cir. 1976).
[52] *Dean* v. *General Motors Corp.* 301 F.Supp. 187 at 192 (E.D. La. 1969).

culpability, and so it would be expected that in strict liability there would be little room for the undiscoverability usage of the state of the art defence.

Where by quality control or other testing techniques discovery of the danger was possible, arguments about undiscoverability will largely be untenable. But a manufacturer may argue that he cannot be expected to test every product, or that testing involves destruction of the product, and so, that even with the best quality control procedures, existence of the flawed product was undetectable. Similarly, it may be argued that there was no known means of testing for the type of defect present in flawed items. For example, in *Cunningham* v. *MacNeal Memorial Hospital*,[53] the plaintiff had contracted serum hepatitis from a blood transfusion. It was argued for the hospital and accepted by the court that a small number of blood transfusion patients would contract hepatitis because at the time of transfusion and at the time of trial there was no known means of identifying the presence of the virus. No way of eliminating the risk was known. The Illinois Supreme Court held the blood to be impure and found for the plaintiff, stating in a much quoted part of the judgment:

> "To allow a defense to strict liability on the ground that there is no way, either practical or theoretical, for a defendant to ascertain the presence of impurities in his product would be to emasculate the doctrine [of strict liability] and in a very real sense would signal a retreat to a negligence theory."[54]

This decision is out of step with a number of others in which courts have taken the view that contaminated blood is unavoidably unsafe, and hence afforded the exemption from strict liability which Comment k to section 402A gives to such products.[55] Also, the effect of the decision was, on grounds of public policy, immediately reversed by statute in Illinois,[56] a practice adopted as regards blood products by many other states. The mechanism by which states deny recovery under a strict liability theory is either expressly to exclude blood transfusion from strict liability, or to provide that transfusion is a service rather than a sale of a product, thus taking the supply

---

[53] 47 Ill.2d. 443, 266 N.E.2d. 897 (1970).
[54] At 453, and 902.
[55] See *Hines* v. *St. Joseph's Hospital* 86 N.M. 763, 527 P.2d. 1075 (1974).
[56] Ill. Ann. Stat. ch. 111 1/2 s.5101–5103 (1985).

outside any strict liability regime based upon section 402A, which requires a sale for the imposition of strict liability.

Accordingly, the fact pattern of *Cunningham* will not now in most states give rise to liability, and indeed patients who have contracted AIDS from blood or blood products have been denied recovery under a strict liability theory.[57] Nonetheless, the *Cunningham* decision is of interest since it illustrates the presence of known but undiscoverable dangers. Similar dangers exist in pork products in which trichinae are present, causing trichinosis. Only the most microscopic examination of the carcass can detect the presence of the danger,[58] and in some such cases liability has been denied on undiscoverability grounds.[59] The major difficulty with the denial of recovery in these circumstances is in distinguishing other instances in which manufacturers may assert undiscoverability, such as where testing would destroy the product, or where a foreign body—such as a snail—finds its way into a manufactured product.[60] The better view, it is suggested, is to impose strict liability for all such manufacturing defects and to exclude by statute only those products which public policy demands should be outwith strict liability.

Undiscoverability, in the discussion above, relates to known, or suspected, product dangers. A separate class of cases have involved unknown and unknowable dangers. Clearly, semantic difficulties bedevil this whole area. As Wade has observed:

> "If something has now become known does that not mean that it was discoverable at the earlier time? Questions of this sort tempt one to cut the Gordian knot in frustration and to say that anything now known was knowable at the earlier time."[61]

A number of decisions support the proposition that unknow-

---

[57] See Greif, "Hospital and Blood Bank Liability to Patients Who Contract AIDS Through Blood Transfusions" 23 San Diego L.Rev. 875 (1986).

[58] See *Cheli* v. *Cudahy Bros.* Co. 267 Mich. 690 (1934) at 693.

[59] See discussion in Spradley, "Defensive Use of State of the Art Evidence in Strict Products Liability" 67 Minn. L.Rev. 343 at 385 (1982).

[60] *Ibid.* The contamination of eggs by salmonella would be a good example of a situation where testing would destroy the product. Of course, the eggs would require to have undergone an industrial process before being covered by the Consumer Protection Act 1987. Battery farming is probably not an industrial process.

[61] Wade, *op. cit.*, at 750.

ability of the risk is irrelevant in a strict liability claim.[62] In these cases, presence of the risk has of course become known—hence the claim in the first place—and the court effectively takes the view that the manufacturer should be imputed with knowledge of the dangerous character of the product as known at the time of trial. This could be described as the "doctrinal elegance" view—the central point in strict liability is the objective matter of whether the product is defective, the fact that the manufacturer was unaware of the existence of the defect being irrelevant to the inquiry. Strict liability is about the condition of products not about the conduct or knowledge of manufacturer, although even here considerations of the reasonableness of the manufacturer's conduct can play a part. On this reasoning, Dean Keeton suggests that a product be found to be unreasonably dangerous

> " . . . if and only if a reasonable man, with knowledge of the condition of the product and an appreciation of all the risks as found to exist at the time of trial, would not now market the product at all, or would do so pursuant to a different set of warnings or instructions as to use."[63]

The producer in such cases is imputed to have known that which at the time of distribution was outwith the realm of scientifically available knowledge.

Beshada v. *Johns-Manville Products Corp.*,[64] discussed earlier, is the leading modern example of this kind of attitude. Some 51 plaintiffs argued that the manufacturers and sellers of asbestos ought to incur strict liability for failure to warn of the defects inherent in the product. The defendants contended that the scientific and medical community did not know that insulation products containing asbestos posed a threat of causing asbestos-related disease. It was argued that as knowledge of this danger was not established until the 1960s the defendants had no duty to warn prior to that time. The New Jersey Supreme Court assumed as correct the defendants' claim that the dangers were unknowable. Under reference to *Freund* v. *Cellofilm Properties*[65] and *Cepeda* v. *Cumberland Engineering Co.*,[66] the

---

[62] *Beshada* v. *Johns-Manville Products Corp.* 90 N.J. 191, 447 A.2d 539 (1982) is the leading example of this view.

[63] Keeton, "Product Liability and the Meaning of Defect" 5 St. Mary's L.J. 30 at 37–38.

[64] See n. 62 above.

[65] 87 N.J. 229 (1981).

[66] 76 N.J. 152, 386 A.2d. 816 (1978).

court reasoned that in a failure to warn case the product was defective if its risks had not been reduced to the greatest possible extent. Adopting a doctrinally pure approach to strict liability, the court took the view that the limits of scientific discoverability did not affect the question of defectiveness.

It was accepted by the court that decisions such as *Freund* above had failed fully to resolve the matter of relevant time at which knowledge was to be imputed to the manufacturer—time of trial or time of manufacture. Strict liability, in the court's view, demanded that the knowledge of the product's dangers as known as the time of trial be imputed to the defendant. Much emphasis was laid on the policy aims of strict liability, and the distinction between a strict liability theory and a negligence theory.

In some other state jurisdictions, similar reasoning to that employed in *Beshada* has been used to support a finding of liability. For example, in *Elmore* v. *Owens-Illinois*[67] the Supreme Court of Missouri held that state of the art evidence to the effect that the defendants could not have known of the dangers presented by their product was irrelevant in a strict liability claim. In Missouri, the test for defectiveness is the consumer expectation test drawn from section 402A. Applying this test, and focusing on the policy goals of strict liability, scientific unknowability was held by the court to be no defence.

Developments in New Jersey subsequent to *Beshada* have, however, weakened the authority of that decision. In particular, in *Feldman* v. *Lederle Laboratories*,[68] another strict liability failure to warn case, noted earlier, the court stated:

> "If Beshada were deemed to hold generally or in all cases ... that in a warning context knowledge of the unknowable is irrelevant in determining the applicability of strict liability we would not agree."[69]

The opinion goes on to cite a number of academic articles critical of *Beshada*, and restricts the case "to the circumstances giving rise to its holding."[70] In *Feldman*, the court relied upon *Freund*, above, to the effect that reasonableness of the manufacturer's conduct was relevant in a strict liability claim of this type, and that the state of available knowledge was a consideration in determining reasonableness of conduct. The

---

[67] 673 S.W.2d. 434 (Mo. 1984) (*en banc*).
[68] 97 N.J. 429, 479 A.2d. 374 (1984).
[69] *Ibid.* at 455 and 387.
[70] *Ibid.*

manufacturer was held to the standard of an expert and was thus deemed to know all dangerous propensities of the product which were reasonably knowable. The imputation of this knowledge distinguished strict liability from negligence. In addition, the *Feldman* court placed the burden of proving the lack of available knowledge on the manufacturer.

As was noted in the earlier discussion of the warnings issue, it is by no means clear what the effect of the *Beshada-Feldman* dichotomy is, even in New Jersey. It may be that *Beshada* is restricted to asbestos products and *Feldman* is restricted to pharmaceuticals. Also, *Feldman* appears to authorise the view that proof by the manufacturer of unknowability of the defect is a complete defence in a failure to warn claim, in contrast to *O'Brien*, above, which uses lack of feasibility of a safer design as one factor in the risk-utility analysis.

Beshada's doctrinal elegance approach is attractive, although the extent to which the decision furthers the policy aims of strict liability can be questioned. It may also be argued that the doctrine of strict liability has no "profound and sacrosanct theoretical basis"[71] and that elegance of construction should not defeat pragmatic considerations.[72]

Pragmatism has influenced courts such as that in *Feldman* to allow evidence that the defect was scientifically unknowable to exculpate the manufacturer. In taking this line, some courts have relied upon Dean Wade's view, contrasting with that of Keeton, quoted above, that for the purposes of strict liability the defendant be imputed with knowledge only of defects that were scientifically knowable at the time of distribution.[73]

Before exploring the policy arguments underpinning the *Beshada-Feldman* dichotomy, and pertinent to all uses of state of the art evidence, some brief comment must be given about such evidence in the context of the distinctions between manufacturing defects, design defects and failure to warn. Also, United States courts generally treat as a separate category "unavoidably unsafe" products and this separate treatment merits some consideration.

---

[71] O'Donnell, *op. cit.*, at 643.
[72] *Ibid.* at 644, the author states, "what, after all, are the courts telling us when they announce . . . that the state of the art is not relevant—that manufacturers must do something which is not possible yet—or useful—or worth the cost?"
[73] Above, n. 48

Manufacturing defects, design defects, and failure to warn

American product liability law, as was made clear earlier, classifies product defects as fitting into one of the following three types: (a) manufacturing defects, where some failure in quality control or in the manufacturing process has caused the flaw in the product. Here, the product fails to match the standard of the other products of the same type produced by the manufacturer; (b) design defects, where some design deficiency such as the absence of a safety feature or the improper siting of a part of the product is present; (c) failure to warn, where the deficiency alleged is an inadequacy in or absence of a proper warning.

Failure to warn cases are often described as similar if not identical to design defect cases, in the sense that the warning is but one feature of the product's overall design. However, as was noted earlier, many plaintiffs are keen to litigate on warning rather than general design grounds, and there was an explosion of warnings cases during the 1970s.

Of the uses of the term state of the art in relation to the types of product defect just stated, the following general guidelines can be identified. Where there is a manufacturing defect, the main use of state of the art evidence is to argue that the defect was scientifically undiscoverable. The potential for the presence of the manufacturing defect is known, but the means of detecting or eliminating the defect are not known. As suggested above, it is only where public policy dictates that liability ought not to be imposed—such as, arguably, the heptatitis in blood cases—that an exception should be allowed from the rule of strict liability for manufacturing defects, although an appropriately worded warning would elide liability.

Where the defect is one of design, state of the art evidence will often be led in order to establish or disprove the feasibility of an alternative design. Knowledge issues commonly will not arise in these cases, since often the dispute will concern use of particular materials, the presence or adequacy of safety features, or positioning of parts of the product. But there may well be cases involving feasibility in which knowledge issues are raised, for example where the possible application of a particular technique was not scientifically known at the relevant time or where the product behaves in a wholly unforeseen way. Here a test of what knowledge was scientifically available will help solve the question of defect. Such cases will involve known risks; it is the means of reducing or avoiding the risk which is argued to be unknowable. A consumer expectation test alone, or a risk utility test alone, or a test drawing on each of these, will be used to determine the question of defectiveness.

State of the art evidence as used in manufacturing and design defect cases thus becomes part of the very inquiry into defectiveness; it is relevant in helping to determine consumer expectations and it is an important element in risk utility analysis. It is of central importance to notice that state of the art evidence of this type will not generally involve unknown and unknowable risks which, it will later be argued, is the true province of the development risk defence in our new regime.

Where the theory upon which the plaintiff's argument is based is failure to warn, state of the art evidence can play a rather different role to that discussed above. In cases where there is an allegation of an inadequate warning or a lack of warning against *known* dangers there is no real difference from the role played above. Here the use of state of the art evidence is very similar to that in design defect litigation. Warnings are viewed as one part of the product's overall design, and evidence of industry custom or feasibility of alternatives is fed into a risk-utility or consumer expectation test for defect. Where, however, there is a failure to warn case involving unknown and unknowable dangers the majority of states adopt a view similar to that in *Feldman* to the effect that proof of the unknowability of the danger at the time of distribution will be wholly exculpatory of the defendant manufacturer. As noted, a minority, represented by decisions such as *Beshada*, are prepared to impose liability for failure to warn of unknowable dangers.

It is important to note that the cases discussed above, in which unknown and unknowable dangers have been presented by products, have involved chemical products such as asbestos or pharmaceuticals. It may be observed that these products form the major, if not the only, class of products involving unknown and unknowable risks. This is the true field of development risk liability.

Unavoidably unsafe products

A discussion of state of the art evidence in United States cases would be incomplete without reference to that category of product which is labelled "unavoidably unsafe." Comment k to section 402A provides:

"There are some products which, in the present state of human knowledge, are quite incapable of being made safe for their intended and ordinary use. These are especially common in the field of drugs. An outstanding example is the vaccine for the Pasteur treatment of rabies, which not uncommonly leads to very serious and damaging consequences when it is injected. Since the disease itself invariably leads to a dreadful death, both the marketing and the use of the vaccine are fully justified, notwithstanding the unavoidable high degree of risk which they involve. Such a product properly prepared, and accom-panied by proper directions and warning, is not defective, nor is it unreasonably dangerous. The same is true of many other drugs, vaccines, and the like, many of which for this very reason cannot be legally sold except to physicians, or under the prescription of a physician. It is also true in particular of many new or experimental drugs as to which, because of lack of time and opportunity for sufficient medical experience, there can be no assurance of safety, or perhaps even of purity of ingredients, but such experience as there is justifies the marketing and use of the drug notwithstanding a medically recognizable risk. The seller of such products, again with the qualification that they are properly prepared and marketed, and proper warning is given, where the situation calls for it, is not to be held to strict liability for unfortunate consequences attending their use, merely because he has undertaken to supply the public with an apparently useful and desirable product, attended with a known but apparently reasonable risk."

There have been many cases in which the exoneration from liability which Comment k gives has been sought by manufacturers,[74] but space permits only a very brief discussion.

The question of whether a product is unavoidably unsafe depends, for the purposes of Comment k, on two separate factors: first, the risk must be unavoidable under the present state of human knowledge; and, secondly, such experience as there is must justify the marketing and use of the product. Each of these components demands use of state-of-the-art evidence as to the unavoidability of the danger.

Clearly, the exemption given by Comment k will often be sought by the manufacturers of pharmaceutical products. *Basko*

[74-75] See Spradley, *op. cit.* See also, Page, Generic Product Risks: The Case Against Comment k and for Strict Tort Liability, 58 N.Y.U.L. Rev. 853 (1983).

v. *Sterling Drug, Inc.*[76] is frequently cited in illustration of such use of Comment k. The plaintiff took three different drugs in treatment of a skin disease. As a reaction to the presence of chloroquinine in two of the drugs, which he had been taking for some years, the plaintiff suffered an impair-ment of vision resulting in near blindness. Denying strict liability, the court held that the product was unavoidably unsafe within the meaning of Comment k. The comment speaks of the presence of a proper warning, and this was taken by the court in *Basko* to import a negligence standard as regards unavoidably unsafe products: if the danger is detect-able by the exercise of due care then a warning is necessary.[77]

The negligence standard of liability which would apply were Comment k to exclude prescription drugs from strict liability, was argued to be the appropriate standard in *Feldman* v. *Lederle Laboratories.*[78] However, the court took the view, which it is suggested is apparent from the tenor of the Comment itself, that not all prescription drugs are unavoidably unsafe for the purposes of Comment k:

"Comment k immunizes from strict liability the manufac-turers of some products, including certain drugs, that are unavoidably unsafe. However, we see no reason to hold as a matter of law and policy that all prescription drugs that are unsafe are unavoidably so. Drugs, like any other products, may contain defects that could have been avoided by better manufacturing or design. Whether a drug is unavoidably unsafe should be decided on a case by case basis; we perceive no justification for giving all prescription drug manufacturers a blanket immunity from strict liability manufacturing and design defect claims under Comment k.

Moreover, even if a prescription drug were unavoidably unsafe, the Comment k immunity would not eliminate strict liability for failure to provide a proper warning.... Irrespective of whether a court or a jury decides that the drug falls within the special category of Comment k, that finding may not absolve the manufacturer of its failure to warn the physician or the consumer of the condition within

---

[76] 416 F.2d. 417 (2d.Cir. 1969).
[77] See also *Christhofferson* v. *Kaiser Foundation Hosps.* 15 Cal.App.3d. 75 (1972).
[78] n. 68 above.

the manufacturer's actual or constructive knowledge affecting the safety, fitness or suitability of the drug."[79]

Accordingly, pharmaceuticals may contain defects which should have been eliminated or properly warned against and strict liability will often be appropriate. The question as to whether a drug is unavoidably unsafe will therefore be decided on a case-by-case basis. Cases like *Feldman* indicate a rather limited role for the category of unavoidably unsafe products in United States product liability litigation.

Finally, it is of central importance to observe that comment k simply makes it clear that on a risk-utility balance the products to which it applies are not defective or unreasonably dangerous; the comment does not introduce a defence to a finding of defectiveness, it holds that, in appropriate circumstances, and for a limited class of products, benefits outweigh risks. This may well be the case where, for example, there is an adverse reaction to a drug by a small percentage of users. Such a situation may involve the question of defectiveness, rather than, or in addition to, development risks. The wording of the development risks defence in the Consumer Protection Act 1987 might allow the defence to be argued in United Kingdom cases where prior detection and warning of the group affected could not be expected of the manufacturer.

State of the art/development risks—the policy choices

What lessons can our regime of strict liability draw from this American experience of the use of state of the art evidence? Immediately, it should be observed that two of the major uses of this evidence in the United States—establishing industry practices, and establishing feasibility or the lack of feasibility of an alternative design—ought to be relevant in our regime in the determination of defect, rather than as a defence to a finding of defect. In other words, the simple distinction set out earlier in this Chapter between known dangers and unknown dangers is the key to discovering what assistance can be obtained from the United States cases. If the danger is known, then evidence about the current state of scientific knowledge will be relevant to a determination of whether detection of the presence of the risk in a particular batch, or a method of elimination of the risk, is within possibility. These cases will not involve the development risks defence, since the evidence will concern defectiveness

[79] *Ibid.* at 447 and 383.

in the first place. Here there is a known danger, and an adequate warning will often preclude a finding of defectiveness.

State of the art of the type just discussed is therefore about known risks, while development risk concerns risks which are unknown and which could not have been known. Of the types of state of the art evidence discussed above, the last category—cases such as *Feldman* and *Beshada*—will be those which involve the defence. This does not necessarily mean that it is only chemical products such as pharmaceuticals which allow use of the defence, although these will certainly be the main instances of its use.

The overriding difficulty, it is suggested, is that, as currently worded, our development risks defence will permit manufacturers to bring evidence of industry practice and feasibility as a defence to a finding of defectiveness. In other words, the use of such evidence fails at the "defect" stage, but is then used to show what a manufacturer of products of the same description might be expected to have discovered. The United Kingdom courts may well find it impossible to restrict the defence to dangers which were unknown and which could not have been known. Before offering some concluding comment on the use of the defence under the 1987 Act, it is worth exploring the policy reasons underpinning the imposition of liability for unknown and unknowable dangers, followed by the policy arguments which led the United Kingdom Parliament to accept the defence as worded.

Beshada:—policy reasons for imposing strict liability for unknowable dangers

The court in *Beshada* offered a number of policy reasons in support of its decision to impose strict liability even where the danger was unknown and unknowable. First, risk spreading was seen as one of the most important arguments for imposing strict liability. Manufacturers and distributors are in the best position, reasoned the court, to bear the costs of injuries caused by defective products, by insuring against liability and reflecting the costs in the price. At the centre of strict liability, according to the court, lies the basic normative premise that manufacturers rather than victims ought to bear the cost of injuries. This argument ought not to be accepted uncritically, and in the case itself a number of cogent points were made in an attempt to rebut it. In particular, it was contended that imposition of liability for unknowable hazards cannot further the goal of risk spreading since, by definition, such hazards are not predicted and so the price will not have been adjusted so as to reflect the costs of injury. If the price was later adjusted to compensate for the unanticipated risk, later users would pay the increased price caused by compensating earlier victims. The court accepted that there was some truth in this argument, but said of its own finding that "it is not a bad result."[80] On balance, it is suggested that the court is correct. The risk certainly is spread, even if only through future users rather than those, including the victim, who used earlier.

In further support of its finding the *Beshada* court cited the policy aim of accident avoidance:

> "By imposing on manufacturers the costs of failure to discover hazards, we create an incentive for them to invest more actively in safety research."[81]

Undoubtedly, the threat of liability for undiscovered defects will cause producers to seek out potential liability-triggering dangers, but it is arguable that this incentive does not arise when the defect was unknowable as well as unknown. It could also be argued that a traditional state of the art rule consisting of an obligation to stay abreast of the current state of knowledge provides a sufficient incentive to test products.[82] Some would even say that the imposition of liability for unknowable risks creates a positive disincentive to carry out safety research—if you are to be liable for all risks whether or not you could have discovered them, why seek to discover any risks? This view may possess some superficial cogency, but looked at more closely it is a counsel of despair; any manufacturer who takes this line will be fortunate to survive.

The third policy matter of importance to the decision in *Beshada* was simplification of the fact-finding process:

> "The analysis thus far has assumed that it is possible to define what constitutes 'undiscoverable' knowledge and that it will be reasonably possible to determine what knowledge was technologically discoverable at a given time. In fact, both assumptions are highly questionable. The vast confusion that is virtually certain to arise from any attempt to

---

[80] n. 62 above, at 206 and 547.
[81] *Ibid.* at 207 and 548.
[82] See Love, "New Jersey Advances the State of the Art in Products Liability" 15 Conn. L.Rev. 661 (1983) at 680.

deal in a trial setting with the concept of scientific knowability constitutes a strong reason for avoiding the concept altogether by striking the state-of-the-art defense.

Scientific knowability, as we understand it, refers not to what in fact was known at any time, but to what could have been known at the time. In other words, even if no scientist had actually formed the belief that asbestos was dangerous, the hazards would be deemed 'knowable' if a scientist could have formed that belief by applying research or performing tests that were available at the time. Proof of what could have been known will inevitably be complicated, costly, confusing and time-consuming. Each side will have to produce experts in the history of science and technology to speculate as to what knowledge was feasible in a given year......we should resist legal rules that will so greatly add to the costs both sides incur in trying a case."[83]

These are powerful words. Questions of available scientific knowledge, difficult at any time, are greatly complicated by the need to establish the state of such knowledge at some past date. However, these arguments were not found to be persuasive by the same court in *Feldman*, although in that case no real attempt was made to rebut the policy arguments advanced in *Beshada*. Instead, reference was made to the many commentators who had criticised the *Beshada* decision.[84]

Some of these commentators have cited the apparent illogicality of *Beshada* in seeming to require a warning of that which could not have been known, and some also criticise the decision as imposing absolute liability. Each is wrong: the apparent illogicality stems from the need for a strict liability theory to focus upon the product rather than the conduct of the manufacturer; and absolute liability is not imposed—the manufacturer is liable only for unreasonable dangers. Other arguments against the *Beshada* holding include that it is unfair to the manufacturer, that accurate risk-spreading is not possible, that no real incentive to carry out more safety research is given, and that the trial process will not radically be simplified. On

---

[83] Above n. 62, at 207–208 and 548.
[84] See, *e.g.*: Page, *op. cit.*; Schwartz, "The Post-Sale Duty to Warn: Two Unfortunate Forks in the Road to a Reasonable Doctrine" 58 N.Y.U.L.Rev. 892 (1983); Wade, *op. cit.*; Comment, "Requiring Omniscience: The Duty to Warn of Scientifically Undiscoverable Product Defects" 71 Geo. L.J. 1635 (1983); Comment, *Beshada* v. *Johns-Manville Products Corp.*: "Adding Uncertainty to Injury" 35 Rutgers L.Rev. 982.

balance, however, it is suggested that the *Beshada* policy grounds outweigh the counter arguments. The only, and major, difficulty is the availability of insurance cover against unknowable risks and there is a lack of clear information about the ability of insurers to provide cover for such risks. That some asbestos manufacturers, including the defendants in *Beshada*, filed for bankruptcy under Chapter 11 of the federal bankruptcy code as an attempt to stem the flow of legal actions against them, may be an indication of the difficulties, in the United States at least, of obtaining insurance cover.

POLICY ISSUES AND DEVELOPMENT RISKS IN THE UNITED KINGDOM

The question of whether the United Kingdom ought to adopt the defence of development risks, or derogate from that part of the Directive, attracted passionate argument during the progress of the legislation through Parliament.[85] As noted above, the wording in the Act was the original wording of the Bill as introduced in the House of Lords. That wording, different from the Directive, was described by the Minister as a clarification of the wording of the Directive. In the House of Lords, the wording of the Directive was inserted in place of the Government's version, but at the Committee stage in the Commons after only a brief discussion and no vote (which it seems clear the Government would have won in any event) the government version was re-instated. Fears expressed by industry dominated the brief discussion of the defence, and the imminence of the dissolution of Parliament for the pending general election truncated debate and forced a reluctant House of Lords to accept the Commons version lest the whole measure be lost.

Policy arguments for and against the defence were similar to those mooted in the United States, and can broadly be grouped under the following heads:

Innovation

It was argued that the defence was a vital part of the Bill. Omission of the defence would inhibit British industry from producing new and innovative products. Manufacturers who have to face unquantifiable liabilities from unforeseen risks will

---

[85] See, *e.g.* Official Report, Fifth Series, Lords, Vol. 483, cols. 819–846; Official Report, Fifth Series, Lords, Vol. 483, cols. 1017 *et seq.*

be unwilling to invest in research and development for the future. Most other Member States, it was argued, would be including the defence. Only Belgium, France and Luxembourg would dispense entirely with the defence, and Germany would dispense with it only for pharmaceuticals. Without this defence, Britain would be at a disadvantage as against most of Europe. Lord Denning, originally against the defence, changed his mind after reading about the development of an AIDS drug, and was concerned that without the defence such developments would be inhibited. Also, it was contended that much innovation comes from small companies, which financially are less well placed to obtain the necessary insurance cover. It was even hinted that jobs could be lost if development of new products were to be inhibited.

Against these points, it was noted that innovation does not appear to have been stifled in countries which do not permit the defence, such as the United States, or France, or as regards pharmaceuticals, in Germany. Furthermore, if some states permit the defence and others do not, those which include it, such as the United Kingdom, may become the testing ground for untried products.

Insurance

Availability of insurance, perhaps the central point for debate, again divided the policy makers. On the one hand, it was stated that premiums would be prohibitively high were the defence excluded. A briefing paper from the Association of British Insurers was relied upon to assert that in most instances absence of the defence would not be a problem, but with a very few industries, which have a heavy development risk, such as pharmaceuticals and aerospace, the difference could be critical and the amount of capacity would be reduced. The trend in the United States towards exclusion of liability for risks that could not have been known was pointed out, as were the financial ceilings upon total liability and special insurance arrangements used in Germany to provide cover for the pharmaceutical industry.

On the other hand, it was argued that in countries where the defence is not available, adequate insurance arrangements have been made. Further, our producers have had to obtain insurance cover, and will now need more cover, for export to those countries. This does not appear to have caused undue difficulty for the insurers. There are no serious differences in insurance costs between such countries and ourselves. As a compromise, it was suggested that the development risks defence be permitted only for high-risk sectors and not across the board.

Risk-spreading

It was strongly urged that the manufacturer is in a better position than the victim to meet the costs of injury. Insurance costs would effectively be met by all purchasers of the product. This, it was argued, was preferable to concentration of the risk on the unfortunates who suffer harm from product defects.

> "It is a question of whether individuals who suffer grievous hardship and illness and who undergo terrible suffering shall have to bear their suffering alone and uncompensated, or whether the rest of us, who buy the same products, should not contribute."[86]

Others argue that, since insurance will be expensive if obtainable at all, risk-spreading will be difficult. Again, where a danger previously unknown becomes known, it is only future consumers who will have the cost spread amongst them.

Trial process

Those who oppose the defence contend that its presence can only complicate and thus lengthen the trial of product liability cases. For the manufacturer to make out the defence, it was argued, he would need a number of expensive experts as witnesses to the state of knowledge at the relevant time. In a matter as difficult as the state of scientific and technical knowledge at a particular time, conflicting views from plaintiff and defence experts can be expected. Any person seeking to raise an action and concerned that a development risks defence will be used against him, may well be dissuaded by the costs resulting from a failure from pursuing his action.

CONCLUSION

Development risk, a central and delicate aspect of the new regime, has been included as a defence in the 1987 Act. But the wording of section 4(1)(e) impedes what ought to be the true application of the defence—to unknown dangers which could

---

[86] *Ibid.* Vol. 483, col. 845, *per* Baroness Burton of Coventry.

not have been known. That the EC Commission felt obliged to quarrel in such strong terms with the wording in the Act is therefore no surprise.

The two points which are at issue regarding development risks are: ought there to be a defence of development risks in the first place? and, if so, what form ought the defence to take? As shown in the above discussion, the policy arguments have been quite fully canvassed, particularly in *Beshada* and in the parliamentary debates. It is interesting to notice here the Government's own policy aims for the regime of strict liability. The Government stated itself to have been much influenced by the reasoning of the Pearson Commission, which cited the following practical and policy reasons for strict liability:

(a) All consumers should have the same protection as that enjoyed by the direct purchaser.

(b) The producer reaps benefits if the product is a success; he should also accept losses if the product fails and injures people (the doctrine of implied warranty).

(c) Strict liability would encourage higher safety standards.

(d) The producer is in the best position to arrange insurance cover, and can pass the extra cost to the consumer through the price mechanism.

(e) The strong European trend towards strict liability should not be ignored.[87]

It is difficult to see how the inclusion of a development risks defence furthers any of these aims; indeed, each could be taken to support the exclusion of the defence. However, the minister explained that more pressing policy reasons prompted the inclusion of the defence:

"We base our case for the retention of the development risks defence on three fundamental reasons. The first reason is that it is an integral part of the directive and an important part of the harmonisation that the directive seeks to achieve . . . . . . one of the factors that it is important to bear in mind in considering questions such as competitive disadvantage is the context in which we are discussing these matters. The Bill, implementing the directive, is intended to introduce harmonisation. The purpose of the directive is to harmonise the law among member states of the European Community. That is important to bear in mind.

[87] "Implementation of EC Directive on Product Liability—An Explanatory and Consultative Note" D.T.I., November 1985, para. 7.

Secondly, we believe that not to have such a defence would stifle innovation. Thirdly,...not to have the defence would undoubtedly lead to serious problems with insurance.

Each of these reasons by itself would be highly persuasive. Taken together, we think—although I appreciate that genuinely held views may differ—that they amount to an unanswerable case."[88]

Expressing the desire to help victims of product defects in the emotional language used by some contributors to the debate does not help to produce the clarity of thought required for the consideration of the issues involved. But, even discounting for the emotive reactions, the *Beshada* reasoning is powerful. Only the clearest indication that the insurance industry cannot cope, or that the expense of coping would so increase the costs of products as to create serious worries of inflation, ought to rebut that powerful reasoning. Unfortunately, the debates have been lamentably under-informed on the insurance issues. Raising the spectre of a United States-style insurance crisis is disingenuous; it is common knowledge that features of their legal system which we do not possess, such as contingency fees, juries deciding on damages awards, and punitive damages in product cases, fuel the explosion of already over-inflated awards of damages. A much more sophisticated inquiry into the ability of the industry to cover the risk is urgently needed. Why is it that cover is provided in other regimes which have no development risks defence, and how do our producers who export to such countries obtain adequate insurance?

Even if a need for a development risks defence was clearly made out, it could not, it is suggested, justify the version of the defence which has found its way into the legislation. Development risks, as has frequently been asserted above, truly concern dangers which were not known and which could not have been known. This plainly was the sense of the Directive. The wording chosen will permit producers to adduce evidence of the state of the art as regards industry custom and feasibility of alternative designs, even for products which have been found to be defective. As stated above, these issues are part of the question of defectiveness and ought not to be admitted in defence of a finding of defectiveness. The formula of what producers of products of the same description as the product in question might be expected to have discovered makes it very difficult for

[88] House of Commons, Standing Committee D, May 5, 1987, col. 30.

United Kingdom courts to restrict development risks to its true scope.

The need for the defence is to be reviewed by the EC Commission in 1995. Unless the defence can be shown to have protected manufacturers against overwhelming liability, as is unlikely to be the case, then the opportunity should be taken to evict from the sphere of strict liability what is effectively a trespasser from the world of negligence. Only then will the policy aims underlying the new regime fully be realised.

Chapter 7

OTHER DEFENCES, PRESCRIPTION AND LIMITATION

Two remaining matters require discussion in order to complete this examination of the main aspects of product liability law. In addition to the development risks defence, the Consumer Protection Act 1987 permits a number of other defences, including that of contributory negligence; also, the Act introduces a new scheme of prescription and limitation of liability. These matters are examined in this chapter. Following the familiar structure, the principles of United States product liability law in both of these areas will be considered, again with a view to drawing lessons from that experience.

The major task regarding defences is to analyse the use of contributory negligence in the context of strict liability for product defects, a defence which will often be invoked where a defective product has been misused.[1] Before discussing this matter, the other defences provided in the Act will be considered. It goes without saying that this discussion is of *defences* arising when a product has been found to be defective. It will be recalled that certain criteria have to be established before a product is found to be defective. For example, the plaintiff may have to argue that no adequate warning was given, or that the use to which the product was put was a reasonably expected use, or that the product was defective even when judged by the standards prevailing at the time when it was put into circulation. Evidence led by manufacturers in rebuttal of a plaintiff's claims on such points does not constitute a defence to a finding of defectiveness; rather, it relates to the question of defect in the first place.

DEFENCES UNDER THE 1987 ACT

Section 4 provides a list of defences which can be used by the "person proceeded against" in response to a claim under the Act. Of course, as the Act makes clear, the burden of establishing these defences lies with the defendant. These defences will now be examined in turn, with the exception of

---

[1] See the discussion in Chap. 4, above.

the development risks defence made available by section 4(1)(*e*), which has already been discussed.

Section 4(1)(a)

"that the defect is attributable to compliance with any requirement imposed by or under any enactment or with any Community obligation";

Little need be said about this defence. The language of the provision makes it plain that only compliance with an enactment will suffice: compliance with a voluntary code of practice or relevant British standard is therefore not enough. Presumably, the term enactment means statutory provisions or delegated legislation of the United Kingdom Parliament, so that, for example, a manufacturer whose products are defective in order to comply with a German regulation cannot invoke the defence in respect of products distributed in the United Kingdom.

It must also be emphasised that simple compliance with, for example, statutory safety regulations does not preclude a finding of defect. As the subsection makes clear, the defect must be "attributable" to compliance with the enactment or Community obligation: in other words, the product had to be defective in order to comply with the provision in question.

In its Explanatory and Consultative note, the Government expressed the following view as to the meaning of the provision:

"It should be stressed that mere compliance with a regulation will not necessarily discharge a producer from liability; he would have to show that the defect was the *inevitable* result of compliance, *i.e.* that it was impossible for the product to have been produced in accordance with the regulations without causing the product to be defective."[2]

This is a very unlikely eventuality and accordingly the defence is of minimal value to many potential defenders. As is absolutely plain, most enactments regarding products are designed specifically to impose greater safety standards, rather than to result in the production of dangerous goods. It is hoped that there do not exist many enactments which require the production of defective products.[3] However, there certainly will

---

[2] Implementation of the EC Directive on Product Liability—An Explanatory and Consultative Note, D.T.I., para. 56.

[3] See Lord Griffiths, Developments in the Law of Product Liability, (Holdsworth Club, Univ. of Birmingham, 1987) p. 14.

be instances where the defence will be invoked. For example, safety footwear regulations in a particular Member State may state that the soles be made from a specific material so as to make them non-slip; if this material is non-insulating, it would arguably render the footwear defective for other purposes, such as use in electrical work.

Section 4(1)(b)

> "that the person proceeded against did not at any time supply the product to another";

This provision implements another defence given in the Directive—that the person proceeded against did not put the product into circulation. The major difference between the Act and the Directive on this matter is that "supply" is used in place of the phrase, "put into circulation." The reason given for the terminology used is that "supply" is the more precise term.[4] "Supply" is defined in section 46, to include a wide range of activities, including in particular:

> "(a) selling, hiring out or lending the goods;
> (b) entering into a hire-purchase agreement to furnish the goods;
> (c) the performance of any contract for work and materials to furnish the goods;
> (d) providing the goods in exchange for any consideration (including trading stamps) other than money;
> (e) providing the goods in or in connection with the performance of any statutory function; or
> (f) giving the goods as a prize or otherwise making a gift of the goods";

A number of product-related claims will be capable of being met with this defence. For example, where a factory produces a toxic waste which is then dumped or emitted into the atmosphere, there will have been no supply within the definition in the Act. Where an employee suffers injury while, for example, handling a defective product being produced by his employer, the defence in section 4(1)(b) will often allow the employer to avoid liability since no supply has occurred. However, it is possible that while engaged in the production of the main product an employee is injured by a defective component part, which had been supplied to the producer of the

[4] Official Report, Fifth Series, Lords, Vol. 483, col. 807.

main product by another. Here the component would have been supplied for the purposes of liability under the Act, and an action would lie against the producer of the component. It ought to be recalled that many cases of product-related injury in the workplace will be brought under the Employer's Liability (Defective Equipment) Act 1969, which facilitates an action against the employer in respect of defective equipment used at work. But where the product is not within the definition of "equipment" in the 1969 Act recourse is likely, in appropriate cases, such as injury caused by a component, to the Consumer Protection Act 1987.

According to the Government in its explanatory report, the defence will also exempt from the scheme of liability medicinal materials used in trials before marketing.[5] Finally, the defence would also apply where, for example, the wrong producer is sued, and also where goods have been stolen from the producer before being put into circulation, for here again there is no supply of the goods in terms of section 46.

However, the wording in the Act is not free of difficulty. For example, it has been suggested that goods which are transferred subject to a *Romalpa* clause would not be regarded as having been sold, although a court may take the view that they have been loaned so as to bring the transfer within the meaning of supply in section 46.[6]

Section 4(1)(c)

> "that the following conditions are satisfied, that is to say—
> (i) that the only supply of the product to another by the person proceeded against was otherwise than in the course of a business of that person's; and
> (ii) that section 2(2) above does not apply to that person, or applies to him by virtue only of things done otherwise than with a view to profit";

This subsection implements Article 7(e) of the Directive, which affords as a defence to the producer:

> "that the product was neither manufactured by him for sale or any form of distribution for economic purposes nor

---

[5] Implementation of the EC Directive on Product Liability—An Explanatory and Consultative Note, D.T.I., Nov. 1985, para. 56(a).
[6] Miller, *Product Liability and Safety Encyclopaedia*, III at 175. (Butterworths looseleaf).

manufactured or distributed by him in the course of his business."

Accordingly, the provision in the Act requires both elements to be satisfied: it only exempts products which were supplied other than in the course of a business *and*, where the supplier is the producer, own-brander or importer into the EEC, supplied other than with a view to profit. Thus, a person who sells his lawnmower to his neighbour can use this defence to avoid potential liability under the Act as a supplier, since the goods were supplied other than in the course of a business and he is not the producer, own-brander or importer. Similarly, if he gives (rather than sells) his neighbour a bottle of home-made wine, which proves to be defective, liability under the Act can be avoided.

Section 4(1)(d)

"that the defect did not exist in the product at the relevant time";

Section 4(2) defines "relevant time." In respect of electricity, "relevant time" means the time at which it was generated, being a time before it was transmitted or distributed. For products other than electricity, the meaning of "relevant time" differs according to whether or not the person proceeded against is a person to whom section 2(2) applies—the producer, own-brander or importer into the EEC. Where he is, the relevant time is the time when he supplied the product to another. Where he is not, the relevant time is the time when the product was last supplied by a producer, an own-brander or an importer into the EEC.

The broad effect of the definition of "relevant time" is that the producer, own-brander or importer is not liable for products which were not defective when he put them into circulation. Obviously, this provision will not allow manufacturers to evade liability for latent defects since the product is defective, even if not apparently so, at the time of supply. It is not a defence in these circumstances that the defect was not known: the defence only arises if the defect did not exist. Where, however, the product becomes defective for a reason other than the design or production process of its producer, such as the sale of foodstuff which was not defective when supplied but which became defective through having been kept too long prior to sale, the defence will be open to the producer. So, if warnings, instructions, safety features on containers or packaging and the like, are removed by a third party, protection from liability may be available. Likewise, mishandling, poor fitting, servicing or adjusting, may render an otherwise safe product defective. In all of these cases, the Act effectively excludes liability where there is no causal connection between the defect and the design or production process.

When litigated, this provision is likely to raise some challenging questions. For example, it will often be very difficult for a manufacturer to establish from the remains of a defective product that it was not defective when it left his hands. In some cases, it will not be enough for the manufacturer to say that wear and tear caused the defect. While there are some products which become dangerous through ordinary use but which provided an acceptable level of safety when first supplied, there are many others which would not be expected to become unsafe after a period of ordinary use. Take, for example, the hypothetical producers of two types of electric cable for use on domestic appliances. The first cable cracks and eventually exposes live wires after say nine years of ordinary use. It is arguable that here the product was not defective when supplied. Assume that the second cable cracks after one year of ordinary use, perhaps because less expensive insulating material was used: it must of course be open to a court to find that the second cable was defective and to deny the defence in section 4(1)(d).

A further difficulty with the definition of "relevant time" arises from its application where the person proceeded against is not the producer, own-brander or importer. Here, the relevant time is the time when the product was last supplied by the producer, own-brander or importer. This would appear to have the rather unfortunate consequence that, where the product becomes defective because of some act by the retail supplier, for example, removal of a warning,[7] no liability will attach under the Act. The producer, own-brander or importer will not be liable since the product was not defective when supplied by him, and for exactly the same reason the retail supplier will be able to use the defence under section 4(1)(d). So, if a retailer keeps, say, a tin of prawns until they decay and become dangerous and then sells them, a customer injured thereby has no claim against the retailer under the 1987 Act. Of course, if it is the buyer of

[7] See Harvey, *Law of Consumer Protection and Fair Trading*, (Butterworths, 3rd ed., 1987) p. 151.

the product from the retailer who suffers the loss, a fairly straightforward claim under section 14 of the Sale of Goods Act 1979 will lie. Even where a non-purchaser is the victim, the retailer's conduct ought to be quite readily actionable in tort.

It seems bizarre to permit a defence for the retailer where his own conduct clearly is culpable. However, the policy justification for the defence may be that the pre-existing protections noted above are adequate and that the purpose of the 1987 Act is to make the retailer liable only for products which were defective when they left the hands of the producer, own-brander or importer. In this way, the liability of the retailer is subsidiary to that of the others. Also, to use some other "relevant time" for the retailer—such as the time of supply by him—could involve the retailer in liability for defects which are wholly outwith his control but which happen to arise after supply by the producer, own-brander or importer.

Section 4(1)(f)

"that the defect—
(i) constituted a defect in a product ('the subsequent product') in which the product in question had been comprised; and
(ii) was wholly attributable to the design of the subsequent product or to compliance by the producer of the product in question with instructions given by the producer of the subsequent product."

In its Explanatory and Consultative Note, the Government explains the defence as follows:

"In other words, suppliers of components made to the specification of the manufacturer of the final product will not be liable if the defect in the component was the *inevitable* result of compliance with the specification or of the design of the final product over which the component supplier has no control (though the final product manufacturer *would* be liable in these circumstances)."[8]

The broad import of the provision is quite clear: that, where a component is made to the order of a manufacturer of the finished product, and it is then used by him for a purpose for which it was not designed, the component producer is not liable. But, it might be thought that the defence is capable of being

[8] At para. 56(*d*).

asserted by a component supplier to the effect that the producer's design or specification meant that the product had to be defective, and that this was known to the component producer. However, it is more likely that the courts will interpret the words of the provision so as to limit use of the defence to circumstances in which the component itself is *not* defective, but becomes defective because of its use in the subsequent product.

Nonetheless, the protection afforded by the defence is likely to be viewed as of significance by many producers of components, for it is common practice for the specification of components to be less than the highest safety standard of the producer. However, there is a strong argument that such protection is superfluous and so that the defence is unnecessary. A component part which becomes defective only when used in the main product would, it is suggested, not itself fail the test of defect in section 3. As indicated above, what the Act may have done is to allow the defence to be argued by the component producer even where his product, considered independently, does not meet legitimate expectations of safety.

VOLENTI NON FIT INJURIA AND CONTRIBUTORY NEGLIGENCE

Volenti

Of the four major contributors to the debate on the move to strict liability, only the Law Commissions specifically recommended that claims based on the new strict liability should be subject to the defence of "assumption of risk."[9] It was felt that this defence was particularly appropriate to drugs with side effects:

"It is well known that many drugs relieve pain or illness but may directly or indirectly bring on other unpleasant and sometimes damaging results. There is a risk with most drugs and it may be appropriate that the patient should be told the risk so that he knows what to expect. Sometimes he will be willing to take the risk, sometimes not. It would, in our opinion, be wrong to allow him to claim compensation in respect of a risk that he willingly assumed. The same comment applies to wilful misuse by the person injured of the product in question. For example, there should, in our view, be no right of compensation for the person who

[9] Cmnd. 6831 (1977), para. 125(*n*).

deliberately ignores whatever instructions or warnings are given as to the proper use of the product."[10]

It will be noticed that no explicit provision in the Act deals with *volenti non fit injuria*. One reason for this is that *volenti* is most apposite in duty of care situations, and of course, strict liability under the Act is not a duty situation in the accepted sense. The application of the rule that no injury is done to one who consents, is generally taken to mean that the plaintiff has agreed, expressly or impliedly, to exempt the defendant from the duty of care which otherwise he would have owed. Mere knowledge by the plaintiff of the risk does not of itself amount to consent, although it can evidence consent.[11] Thus, it is difficult to use the concept of *volenti* in order to establish agreement to the waiver of a strict liability obligation. It is more likely, however, that *volenti* is not required since the definition of defect and the doctrine of contributory negligence afford sufficient protection to the defendant.

Certainly, the examples quoted above from the Law Commissions can, in any event, be accommodated elsewhere in the regime of strict liability. There are instances of people assuming a known risk, such as using a drug and ignoring a warning. A recent and interesting example of this involves the drug used to treat acne, Accutane, which if taken by pregnant women can cause birth defects. Despite clear warnings carried by the product:

"Severe human birth defects are known to occur in women taking Accutane during pregnancy."

along with a recommendation of use of an effective contraceptive, many pregnant women have used the drug, and a number of children have been affected.

Conduct of this type by the plaintiff can fit into three possible categories. First, where the harm is partly caused by the actions of the victim, the defence of contributory negligence may be available, that defence being capable of partial or full exclusion of liability. Secondly, the new rules continue to insist upon proof of a causal link between defect and harm; where the harm is not caused by the defect in the product but solely by the actions of the user, then no causal link will be established, because of the *novus actus interveniens*, and the harm will not therefore be actionable. Thirdly, the assumption of a risk will

[10] *Ibid.* para. 106.
[11] See, *e.g. Smith* v. *Charles Baker* [1891] A.C. 325.

commonly preclude a finding that the product was defective and hence will be pertinent to the matter of defect rather than to a defence to a finding of defect. For example, misuse of a product or the ignoring of warnings or instructions, as in the example above, will often result in no finding of defectiveness upon which to found a claim under the Act. Where a drug has a known side effect, but the beneficial properties of the drug are held to outweigh the risks of the harmful effects—where, in other words, benefits exceed costs—the product ought to be found not to be defective. Conversely, where a product carries a warning as to its risks, that product may still be found to be defective despite the warning.[12] Accordingly, there will be little room for a plea of *volenti* in most cases under the new rules.

Contributory negligence

As a matter of doctrinal elegance, it could be argued that fault on the part of a user of a product should be irrelevant in a system of liability in which fault by the manufacturer apparently is irrelevant. Contributory negligence can be said to involve two concepts—causation and blameworthiness—and it is arguable that the latter has no place in a strict liability system. However, those contributing to the debate on the proposals for a move to strict liability were of the view that the defence of contributory negligence was necessary. Accordingly, the 1987 Act, in section 6(4), states:

"Where any damage is caused partly by a defect in a product and partly by the fault of the person suffering the damage, the Law Reform (Contributory Negligence) Act 1945 and section 5 of the Fatal Accidents Act 1976 (contributory negligence) shall have effect as if the defect were the fault of every person liable by virtue of this Part for the damage caused by the defect."

Contributory negligence in the context of product liability is already well documented under existing negligence rules[13] and it is likely that its main uses under the Act will be in similar situations. Thus, misuse of a defective product and use of patently dangerous products are expected to continue to provide the chief illustrations of the defence. In many cases, product misuse will result in a finding that the product was not defective

---

[12] See *O'Brien* v. *Muskin Corp.* 94 N.J. 169, 463 A.2d. 298 (1983), discussed in Chap. 7 above.

[13] See Miller and Lovell, *Product Liability* (Butterworths, 1977) pp. 293–296.

in the first place. However, it will be recalled from the discussion earlier that some forms of misuse may fit into the category of reasonably expected uses, and also that the manufacturer cannot easily avail himself of the plea that his product was so obviously dangerous that it should have not been used as it was by the plaintiff. In such circumstances, the product may well be found to be defective, and the plaintiff's conduct may not even be enough to raise the defence of contributory negligence.

It is unlikely that courts in the United Kingdom will encounter much difficulty in apportioning responsibility by comparing the fault of the plaintiff with the strict liability of the defendant. However, it is suggested that the blameworthiness of the plaintiff ought to be of less importance than the causal weight of his conduct.

ASSUMPTION OF RISK, CONTRIBUTORY NEGLIGENCE AND COMPARATIVE FAULT IN THE UNITED STATES

In the majority of states which have adopted section 402A of the Restatement (Second) of Torts, similar defences to those listed above would be available, although for some courts non-defectiveness at the time of supply does not necessarily preclude liability.

In relation to contributory negligence and assumption of risk, a range of approaches is discernible in state legislatures and courts. Indeed, one judge has described the doctrine of assumption of risk as an "enigma wrapped in a mystery."[14] Given the varied and developing nature of this area, the forthcoming discussion does not seek to explain all variations in the treatment of these matters in the United States.

Historically, contributory negligence and assumption of risk each operated to bar recovery by the plaintiff.[15] On the adoption by many states of section 402A's scheme of strict product liability, United States courts and state legislatures embarked upon a period of rapid change in their treatment of these defences. Comment n of section 402A states:

> "Contributory negligence of the plaintiff is not a defence when such negligence consists merely in a failure to discover the defect in the product, or to guard against the

---

[14] *Blackburn* v. *Dorta* 340 So.2d. 287 (1977), *per* Sundberg J.
[15] See Wade, "Comparative Negligence—Its Development in the United States and Its Present Status in Louisiana" 40 La.L.Rev. 299 (1980).

possibility of its existence. On the other hand the form of contributory negligence which consists in voluntarily and unreasonably proceeding to encounter a known danger, and commonly passes under the name of assumption of risk, is a defence under this Section as in other cases of strict liability. If the consumer discovers the defect and is aware of the danger, and nevertheless proceeds unreasonably to make use of the product and is injured by it, he is barred from recovery."

Thus, adoption of section 402A resulted in the abolition of contributory negligence as a defence to a strict product liability action.[16] This trend, however, was short-lived in that many states proceeded to adopt some form of comparative fault. The doctrine of comparative fault, which in some states is the result of legislation and in others of judicial decision,[17] commonly operates in one of two ways. In some jurisdictions so-called "pure" comparative fault is employed. This works in a similar fashion to our version of contributory negligence, in that negligence on the part of the plaintiff can reduce his award of damages by the percentage contribution of his fault, even where that contribution is higher than that of the defendant. Other jurisdictions use a modified comparative fault system, by which only contributory negligence which is less, or not greater than, that of the defendant, does not wholly bar recovery.[18]

Although more than half of the states in the United States have statutory product liability laws, only in a small minority of these measures is there specific treatment of comparative fault.[19] However, in all but a small minority of states, a system of comparative fault has been adopted, with a rough split of 50/50 between adoption by legislation and adoption by judicial decision.[20] Of those which have adopted comparative fault, the

---

[16] See Trine, "Product Liability—Meeting the Defenses," Trial, Nov. 1985, 24. See also: McNamara, "Use of Comparative Fault in Strict Products Liability: *Bell* v. *Jet Wheel Blast, Division of Ervin Industries*, 31 Loy.L.Rev. 1014 (1986)"; Revitt, "Strict Liability and Comparative Fault: What Standard Should Apply?" Ill.Bar.Jnl. Dec. 1986, 218; Garrison, "Merger of Comparative Fault and Strict Products Liability in Missouri," 54 U.M.K.C.L.Rev. 243 (1986).

[17] See Trine, *op. cit.*

[18] See Phillips, "The Status of Products Liability Law in the United States of America, Conference Paper presented to S.P.T.L. Colloquium," Sept. 1984, at 10.

[19] See Cronan, Proposed Federal Product Liability Act, 29 *Trial Lawyers Guide* 498 at 500 *et. seq.* (1986).

[20] Twerski, "A Moderate and Restrained Federal Product Liability Bill: Targeting the Crisis Areas for Resolution," 18 Univ. of Mich.J. of L.Ref. 575 (1985) at 622.

majority have used a system of modified comparative fault in preference to the pure approach. Sixteen or so states use pure comparative fault, the rest split approximately into equal camps allowing fault which first, is "not as great as," and secondly "not greater than," that of the defendant to permit recovery.[21] In the jurisdictions using modified comparative fault, fault on the plaintiff's part of more than the permitted amount triggers the common law complete defence of contributory negligence.[22] The overwhelming trend in those four-fifths or so of the states which use comparative fault is to apply it to strict product liability claims.[23] However, in many of these jurisdictions certain types of conduct by the plaintiff will not operate as fault on his part. For example, failure to discover the defect and similar types of "passive negligence" have been excluded, as has been workplace injury caused by a defective product where the injured person has no real choice but to use the product.[24]

Recent decisions illustrative of some of the various approaches taken by states include that of the Illinois Supreme Court in *Simpson* v. *General Motors Corp.*[25] The plaintiff, on behalf of the deceased Leland Simpson who had been killed when the earth-moving vehicle which he was operating rolled over on an icy hill, argued that the vehicle was unreasonably dangerous. It was contended by the plaintiff that a roll-over protection device or structure ought to have been incorporated in the product's design. The defendant company, which had designed and manufactured the vehicle, led evidence to the effect that Mr. Simpson had been aware of the absence of protection against damage caused by the vehicle rolling over. This knowledge, it was argued, ought to allow the defences of assumption of risk and contributory negligence. Finding for the plaintiff, it was held by the court at first instance that assumption of risk was a defence, but that contributory negligence was not. Five per cent. of the cause of the accident was attributed to assumption of the risk by the deceased, and the rest of the cause was attributed to the manufacturer. On appeal, the defendant argued that assumption of risk ought to be a complete defence and that contributory negligence ought to operate in mitigation of recovery. The appellate court, and then the state Supreme Court, affirmed the decision at first instance.

[21] *Ibid.* at 623.
[22] *Ibid.* at 623–624.
[23] Phillips, *op. cit.*, at 10.
[24] See Trine, *op. cit.*, at 26.
[25] 108 Ill.2d. 146, 483 N.E. 2d. 1 (1985).

Motivated chiefly by considerations of consumer protection, the Supreme Court affirmed dicta in an earlier decision[26] to the effect that only unforeseeable misuse of the product or assumption of the risk ought to be permitted as damage-reducing factors. Simple lack of due care would not mitigate the award of damages.

Arizona achieves the same result, but by legislation rather than judicial decision: contributory negligence is not a defence and assumption of risk mitigates rather than negates an award.[27]

Such a view is at odds with that adopted by many other courts, which permit reduction for the portion of the injury attributable to the fault of the consumer. A number of state courts (including those in Minnesota, Texas and Washington) take the view that assumption of risk, misuse and contributory negligence are all damage-reducing factors. *Daly* v. *General Motors Corp.*[28] is often cited as an illustration of the prevailing view that the plaintiff's fault operates in reduction of recovery. Here, the widow of a man who was killed when he was thrown from his car following its collision with a guard rail, brought a strict product liability claim against the manufacturer of the car. It was argued that a door latch on the car had a design defect which had caused the door to open following collision. Evidence that the driver had failed to exercise due care for his own safety, including allegations that he had been drinking and had failed to use safety devices[29] was led to establish contributory negligence. Holding that the conduct of the user could operate to reduce the recoverable amount of damages, the California Supreme Court took the view that its decision did not undermine the purpose of strict liability, since the plaintiff's recovery

> "is restricted only to the extent that his own lack of reasonable care contributed to his injury."[30]

Of course the difference between those jurisdictions which allow contributory negligence and those which require assumption of risk or misuse can be quite significant given the restrictive definition of assumption of risk which is generally adopted. In order to avail himself of this latter defence the defendant must show that the consumer was aware of the

---

[26] *Williams* v. *Brown Manuf. Co.* 45 Ill.2d. 418, 261 N.E.2d. 305 (1970).
[27] Ariz.Rev.Stats.Ann. para. 12–2501.
[28] 20 Cal.3d. 725, 575 P.2d. 1162 (1978).
[29] See Revitt, *op. cit.*, at 219.
[30] 20 Cal.3d. 725 at 737.

defective nature of the product, that he understood and appreciated its unreasonably dangerous condition, and that he disregarded the danger and proceeded voluntarily to use the product.[31] In a number of cases which have permitted use of contributory negligence the conduct of the user which resulted in the reduction of his award of damages would not, of course, satisfy the stricter assumption of risk criteria.

Duncan v. *Cessna Aircraft Co.*,[32] a decision of the Supreme Court of Texas, illustrates a balanced approach, in which a plaintiff's negligence which is less than assumption of risk but which goes further than mere failure to discover a defect operates in mitigation of the award. Given that the fault or conduct of the defendant was not at issue in a strict liability suit, the court styled its approach as based upon "comparative causation" and reasoned that this would

> "allow comparison of plaintiff's conduct, whether it is characterised as assumption of risk, misuse, or failure to mitigate or avoid damages, with the conduct or product of a defendant, whether the suit . . . [involves] theories of strict products liability, breach of warranty, or negligence."[33]

Misuse or alteration of a product, which results in injury to the user, can conceptually be located at two places in the theoretical framework of strict product liability. First, if the misuse or alteration is extreme, it will commonly be found that there was no defect in the product and hence no basis for liability. Alternatively, where the product is defective, misuse or alteration can be accommodated within the comparative fault doctrine as assumption of risk or contributory negligence. There seems to be no need for a separate category of misuse in jurisdictions which adopt comparative fault to include contributory negligence since it is already accommodated by that concept. If a jurisdiction uses section 402A without a comparative fault doctrine, and we have noticed that few states take this approach, misuse of the defective product will be irrelevant if it does not raise the plaintiff's conduct to assumption of risk. Of course, even under a comparative fault framework, the defendant can still lead evidence that the plaintiff's conduct in misusing or altering the product was so

---

[31] See *Williams* v. *Brown Manuf. Co.*, n. 26 above.
[32] 665 S.W.2d. 414 (Tex. 1984).
[33] *Ibid.* at 428.

extreme as to be the sole cause of injury and that the product itself was not defective.

Proposed federal product liability legislation seeks to impose some order upon the disparate approaches taken by states to cases in which the injured person is at least partly the author of his own misfortune. Senate Bill 100, for example, would impose a system of "pure" comparative fault, described as "comparative responsibility," in which a reduction in recoverable damages is the result of a jury finding that the injured party's own fault or responsibility contributed towards his loss.[34] "Comparative responsibility," as regards the plaintiff's conduct, would include: misuse of a product; alteration or modification of a product in a manner not consistent with the reasonably anticipated conduct of a user; and contributory negligence or assumption of risk.[35] Such conduct by the plaintiff will not be a complete bar to recovery, unless he is 100 per cent. responsible, but will go to reduction of the award. This of course cuts across the pattern of approaches in individual states.

Some courts and commentators assert that comparative fault can have no place in a regime of strict liability, because of the doctrinal differences between negligence and strict tort. Thus, it has been said that,

> "Fault and non-fault (strict liability) are by nature inconsistent.[36]

and that,

> "Application of comparative negligence to strict liability does present one serious difficulty. This is the lack of a basis for comparison."[37]

This was the view taken by the dissenting minority in *Daly* v. *General Motors Corp.*, above, who argued that conceptually, negligence ought not to be an issue in a strict liability claim, and that the intrusion of negligence would undermine the very purpose of strict product liability. The defect in the product was felt to be of so much more significance than the conduct of the plaintiff as to remove the latter from the scope of the inquiry.

---

[34] See discussion in Cronan, *op. cit.*, at 499.
[35] *Ibid.*
[36] Fischer, "Products Liability—Applicability of Comparative Negligence" 43 Mo.L.Rev. 431 (1978) at 433.
[37] Levine, *Strict Products Liability and Comparative Negligence: The Collision of Fault and No-Fault* 14 San Diego L.Rev. 337 (1977) at 356.

Against this "doctrinal elegance" view, it was argued that strict product liability has no sacrosanct theoretical basis, and that considerations of fairness and equity justified a reduction in the award. This view recognises that negligence concepts often intrude into ostensibly strict product liability. When one considers the risk-spreading rationale behind strict liability under which the risk of harm is borne by all consumers of the manufacturer's product, it is unfair to expect those very consumers to pay, in the cost of the product, for harms which are the fault of the injured user and not caused by the defective product. The American experience, disparate though it is, shows that notions of fault on the part of the user can be accommodated within a regime of strict product liability. Again, what this shows is the difficulty in wholly excluding concepts such as fault or responsibility from a strict liability regime. Arguably, the prime policy aim—accident prevention—will best be achieved by imposing upon a manufacturer liability for harm *caused* by his products. When the cause of harm is the plaintiff's own conduct, no apparent conceptual difficulty can overcome the fundamental fairness of permitting a reduction for comparative fault. It is suggested therefore, that the approach in cases such as *Duncan*, above, and indeed its stress on causation rather than blameworthiness, makes contributory negligence more acceptable in a strict liability regime. The proposed federal statute also strikes a workable balance, if used as part of a strict liability regime. However, it must be recognised that the need to prove fault on the part of the plaintiff will necessarily increase the complexity and hence the time of the trial process.

PRESCRIPTION AND LIMITATION

In implementation of Articles 10 and 11 of the Directive, section 6(6) of the Act provides that Schedule 1 to the Act shall have effect for the purpose of amending the Limitation Act 1980 and the Prescription and Limitation (Scotland) Act 1973 in their applications to actions under Part I of the 1987 Act. The schedule introduces the special scheme of a three-year limitation of actions and a 10-year "long stop" on liability under the Act.

In England, Schedule 1 inserts after section 11 of the Limitation Act 1980, a new section 11A which provides that actions under Part I of the 1987 Act,

> "shall not be brought after the expiration of the period of three years from whichever is the later of—

(a) the date on which the cause of action accrued; and
(b) the date of knowledge of the injured person or, in the case
of loss of or damage to property, the date of knowledge of the
plaintiff or (if earlier) of any person in whom his cause of action
was previously vested."

References to a person's date of knowledge are references to the
date on which he first had knowledge of the following facts:

"(a) such facts about the damage caused by the defect as would
      lead a reasonable person who had suffered such damage
      to consider it sufficiently serious to justify his instituting
      proceedings for damages against a defendant who did not
      dispute liability and was able to satisfy a judgment; and
(b)   that the damage was wholly or partly attributable to the
      facts and circumstances alleged to constitute the defect;
      and
(c)   the identity of the defendant;"[38]

Knowledge of whether, as a matter of law, the product was
defective, or, in the case of damage to property, knowledge of a
date when the person had no right of action, is disregarded.[39]
The usual amendments to the running of the period where the
injured person dies before the expiry of the triennium, extension of
the limitation period in case of disability, postponement of limitation period in case of fraud, concealment or mistake, and discre-
tionary exclusion of the time limit, apply to actions under Part I of
the 1987 Act.[40]
These provisions in the Act are non-controversial, and the new
scheme of limitation fits quite neatly with the pre-existing regime.
The new section 11A also provides that actions under Part I of the
1987 Act

"shall not be brought after the expiration of the period of ten
years from the relevant time, within the meaning of section 4 of
the said Act of 1987; and this subsection shall operate to extinguish a right of action and shall do so whether or not that right of
action had accrued, or time under the following provisions of
this Act had begun to run, at the end of the said period of ten
years."[41]

---

[38] Limitation Act 1980, s.14(1A), as inserted by Sched. 1 para. 3, Consumer Protection Act 1987.
[39] *Ibid.*
[40] Limitation Act 1980, P.II as amended by Sched. 3 para. 5, Consumer Protection
Act 1987.
[41] s.11A(3).

It will be recalled that the meaning of "relevant time" differs according to whether the person proceeded against is within the class of persons covered by section 2(2), that is, producer, own-brander (within the meaning in section 2(2)) or importer into the EEC. Also, where the product is electricity, "relevant time" has a specific meaning.

The net effect of the provision is to extinguish a right of action under Part I 10 years after the product was put into circulation.

In Scotland, the new scheme of prescription and limitation was achieved by amending, again largely by the insertion of new provisions, the Prescription and Limitation (Scotland) Act 1973. A new Part IIA is inserted into the statute, dealing first in section 22A with the 10-years' prescription of obligations, and later with the three-year limitation rules.

In each case the pre-existing rules as to interruption of the time period for limitation remain.[42]

It is an unfortunate consequence of the implementation of the Directive, which in many respects harmonises the law on product liability within Member States, that in the important area of limitation and prescription some disharmony is occasioned within domestic systems. This is of particular concern in Scotland, where the new provisions sit rather uneasily within an otherwise relatively simple and uniform set of rules. It might be contended that European harmony, as we proceed towards the target of a truly Common Market in 1992, is of greater importance than internal uniformity. Indeed, the time limits in the product liability rules have already had a significant impact upon legal policy in England in that the Advisory Committee to the Lord Chancellor, when looking at proposals to reduce the limitation period to two or even one year, took the view that to have three years for product liability and less for other personal injury cases, would be undesirable.[43] Another argument commonly put in favour of harmonisation of time limits, and indeed harmonisation generally, is that it reduces "forum-shopping" between jurisdictions. This point was found to be unconvincing by the Scottish Law Commission,[44] which noted that the primary reason for 'forum shopping" was the differing levels of damages awarded in particular jurisdictions.

[42] See Art. 10 of the EEC Directive (85/374/EEC).
[43] See Lord Griffiths, *op. cit.*, n. 3 above, at 16–17.
[44] Cmnd. 6831 (1977), para. 147.

The 10-year "cut-off" period raises wider and more controversial issues. Given the relative life spans of products in general, 10 years appears to be a reasonable window of exposure to potential liability. But any cut-off period has an element of arbitrariness. Different types of product have many different lengths of expected non-dangerous life; there are many products which persons generally could not reasonably expect to last for 10 years, but equally there are others, such as aircraft, for which such expectations are reasonable. Also, it would appear to be anomalous that in a regime of strict product liability, liability does not subsist for as long as the product is defective.[45] Further, the absence of a similar cut off for retailers in respect of their liabilities under the Sale of Goods Act 1979 has not proved to be overly burdensome.[46] It may also be thought iniquitous that an injured person could be barred by the cut-off period even before the three-year limitation period has started to run. There are certainly some product-caused injuries (for example, asbestos-related diseases, or the cancers caused by diethylstilbestrol) which do not manifest themselves for a considerable period after use of the product. As Lord Denning said in the context of the pre-existing rules on limitation:

> "No one supposes that Parliament intended to bar a man by a time-limit before he is injured at all . . . a man may lose his right of action before he has got it. Which is absurd."[47]

It is a further difficulty that different cut-off periods can be applied within the same product, as where various components were supplied at different times, and the product itself supplied later again. Take, for example, a car with a defective component part. Assume that the component was supplied just over 10 years prior to injury, and that the car was supplied just under 10 years from that date. An action against the producer of the component is time-barred, but action against the car manufacturer is not.[48]

Cogent arguments can be mustered on the other side of the debate.[49] Strict liability, it could be argued, ought not to rest for

---

[45] *Ibid.* at para. 154.

[46] *Ibid.* at para. 155.

[47] *Watson* v. *Fram Reinforced Concrete Co. (Scotland) Ltd. and Winget Ltd.* 1960 S.C.(H.L.) 92 at 115.

[48] The car manufacturer's claim against the producer of the component for contribution or indemnity is of course unaffected by the 1987 Act.

[49] See discussion in the Law Commissions' Report, Cmnd. 6831 (1977), paras. 151–160.

an indefinite period upon the producer. A cut-off period would aid the minimisation of insurance costs, itself of benefit to consumers of the product in question. At the practical level, it also creates a point in time at which, for the purposes of liability under the new Act at least, the very full records, which will now require to be kept by the product producer, may cease to be kept. Proof of defectiveness, or indeed non-defectiveness, at a date of circulation some years gone, is difficult, and a cut off is of value in that regard.

There are, it is conceded, some good practical reasons for having a cut-off period. But this part of the new regime ought not to be looked at as a discrete element: it is part of a wider scheme in which the producer already has the benefit of other rules as to time, and in particular, the producer has a development risks defence which protects him against unreasonable exposure to liability. The cut-off provisions would, it is suggested, have been rather more attractive in a system of strict liability which did not permit the defence of development risks.

Statutes of Limitation and Statutes of Repose in United States Product Liability Law

State jurisdictions in the United States have adopted a variety of measures on prescription and limitation of actions. In general, the distinction between a statute of limitation and a statute of repose[50] is equivalent to that in our system between the limitation period and the cut-off period.

There are differences in state approaches to the matter of accrual of a cause of action. The spectrum of possible starting dates for the commencement of the limitation period includes: date of sale; date of injury; date of actual or reasonably possible discovery by the plaintiff of his injury; date of actual or reasonably possible discovery of the causal connection between the defective product and the harm suffered; date of actual or reasonably possible discovery of the identity of the potential defendant. As an alternative to choosing one point on this spectrum as the starting date, a system could adopt a rule based on a combination of these dates, and, as has been noted, that is the path taken in the new regime in Europe ushered in by the Directive.

---

[50] There is a wide variety of Statutes of Repose and some five different uses of the term: see McGovern, *The Variety, Policy and Constitutionality of Product Liability Statutes of Repose* 30 Am.U.L.Rev. 579 (1981).

As a general rule, American courts adopt date of injury as the starting point.[51] Thus, in *Romano* v. *Westinghouse Elec. Co.*,[52] for example, where a house was damaged by a fire caused by an explosion in a television set, the limitation period began to run from the time of the explosion.[53] Some courts even contemplate the notion that the time can run from a point earlier than the occurrence of harm: in *Maly* v. *Magnavox Co.*,[54] for example, facts similar to the above case prompted the court to find that the action accrued when the harm was suffered, unless it could be established that the plaintiff knew of the defect at an earlier date.[55]

Other courts have been prepared to adopt the next position in the spectrum, the clock ticking from the point in time at which the plaintiff's injury was capable of discovery. This exception is most commonly availed in cases where injury is manifested only at a date long removed from its initial incidence. Asbestos litigation is the common example of the use of this criterion.[56] However, even in asbestosis claims, some courts have held that the period commenced when the injury was suffered.[57] Other courts reach the next point in the spectrum, holding, for example, that in a case where injury was caused by an intra-uterine device, the cause of action accrued from the point at which the plaintiff reasonably ought to have discovered that the device had been the cause of her injury.[58] Only in a small minority of states is the next point reached, delaying the running of time until discovery of the identity of the potential defendant.[59]

Thus, there is no uniformity in the approaches of the various state courts. The rather harsh "date of injury" rule is still commonly adhered to, but there is evidence of something of a trend for courts to ameliorate the effects of this rule in cases where injury is gradual or is manifested only at a significantly later date. It can be seen that the provisions of the 1987 Act are

---

[51] Reynolds, *Statute of Limitations Problems in Products Liability Cases— Exercises in Privity, Symmetry and Repose*, 38 Okla.L.Rev. 667 (1985) at 671.

[52] 336 A.2d. 555 (R.I. 1975).

[53] See the discussion in Reynolds, *op. cit.*, at 671.

[54] 460 F.Supp. 47 (N.D.Miss. 1978).

[55] See Reynolds *op. cit.*, at 677.

[56] See, *e.g. Clutter* v. *Johns-Manville Sales Corp.* 646 F.2d. 1151 (6th Cir. 1981).

[57] *Large* v. *Bucyrus-Erie Co.* 524 F.Supp. 285 (E.D.Va. 1981).

[58] *Ballew* v. *A.H. Robins Co.* 688 F.2d. 1325 (11th Cir. 1982), discussed in Reynolds, *op. cit.*, at 673.

[59] *Ibid.*

rather more generous to the plaintiff than is the American system, since in the former the running of time does not commence until knowledge of the damage, that it was caused by the defect, and the identity of the defendant.

Statutes of repose, imposing a long stop on exposure to potential liability, had been in use in some states even prior to the adoption of a strict product liability, but became more fashionable following upon the analysis of product liability problems in the United States by the Interagency Task Force. The broad aim of these statutes is,

> "to reverse perceived increases in product liability litigation and to lower products liability insurance costs."[60]

Cut-off times vary, some states choosing, for example, eight years from date of sale (e.g. Oregon), others 10 years (e.g. Tennessee) others 12 years (e.g. Illinois). Six years is the shortest and 12 the longest.[61] As an alternative to date of sale as the starting point some jurisdictions adopt date of manufacture.[62] As in the regime created by the EEC Directive, the running of the cut-off period may not be interrupted by events, such as insanity of the plaintiff, which serve to suspend the limitation period.[63] In some states, rather than give a complete cut off, the legislation creates a rebuttable presumption that after a set period the product is non-defective.[64]

Plaintiffs who perceive injustice in the working of the statute of repose have challenged statutes on the ground of constitutionality.[65] In particular, it has been asserted that repose legislation violates the Due Process clause or the Equal Protection clause of the constitution, or that it precludes unrestricted access to courts. Such authority as there is, particularly from Florida, Illinois and Indiana, suggests a general unwillingness of courts to find violation of the constitution.[66] For example, in *Pitts* v. *Unarco Industries Inc.*[67]

---

[60] See Rosen, "1984 Annual Survey of American Law, Products Liability—State of the Art Defense and Statutes of Repose" (Dec. 1985), 825.

[61] See Schwartz, "New Products, Old Products, Evolving Law, Retroactive Law," 58 N.Y.U.L. Rev. 796 (1983) at 843.

[62] Rosen, *op. cit.*, p. 834.

[63] See, *e.g.* DeLay v. *Marathon LeTourneau Sales & Serv. Co.* 48 Or.App. 811, 618 P.2d. 11 (1980).

[64] See Schwartz, *op. cit.*, at 848.

[65] See Rosen, *op. cit.*, p. 836.

[66] See Reynolds, *op. cit.*, at 692–693.

[67] 712 F.2d. 276 (7th Cir. 1983).

the Court of Appeals for the Seventh Circuit rejected the plaintiff's arguments against the trial court's application of Indiana's 10-year statute of repose to an asbestosis claim.[68] However, rejection of constitutional arguments has not been the uniform response of United States courts, and in *Heath* v. *Sears, Roebuck & Co.*,[69] for example, the Supreme Court of New Hampshire upheld the contention of violation of the constitution, particularly on the ground that products liability plaintiffs were unreasonably being discriminated against.[70]

Policy arguments similar to those canvassed earlier have been ventilated in the United States debates on the merit of repose statutes.[71] One argument has been that cut-off limits are needed so as to prevent products supplied some time ago being judged by current safety standards.[72] Whatever strength this argument may possess in a United States context, where product safety can be judged on a retroactive basis,[73] it bears no relevance to the United Kingdom regime, since it is absolutely clear that products are to be judged by safety standards prevailing at the time of supply.[74]

The elimination of difficulties caused to manufacturers in maintaining and finding evidence about their products is also cited in support of repose legislation.[75] Again this argument is not wholly convincing. Records covering the repose period, commonly 10 years,[76] still must be kept, and presumably records for longer periods will routinely be kept in case of negligence or warranty claims. Given the ease which technology has brought to information storage, the record-keeping argument founders.

Of more cogency is the costs argument. Insurance costs are cut because there is no need to speculate about long-term risks. Put simply, it is argued that manufacturers can save on insurance and will also be confronted with less claims. The costs thus saved are passed on indirectly to the consumer since no rise in product prices to cover what would have been the increased costs actually takes place. It has even been argued that there is

---

[68] See also, *Scalf* v. *Berkel Inc.* 448 N.E.2d. 1201 (1983).

[69] 123 N.H. 512, 464 A.2d. 288 (1983).

[70] See discussion in Rosen, *op. cit.*, pp. 836 *et. seq.*

[71] *Ibid.* pp. 834–835.

[72] *Ibid.* See also, McGovern, *op. cit.*, at 589.

[73] See Schwartz, *op. cit.*

[74] See the discussion in Chap. 2, above.

[75] See Rosen, *op. cit.*, p. 834.

[76] This is the period applicable in Europe under the Directive and is a common length for U.S. statutes of repose: see Schwartz, *op. cit.*, at 842–843.

a saving for society in general since less litigation creates less pressure on the courts,[77] but this is a difficult point to take seriously.

As in all of its manifestations in debates about product liability, the significance of legal rules to insurance costs has not been the subject of sufficiently rigorous analysis. Even the major study of the American product liability insurance crisis undertaken by the Interagency Task Force drew inconclusive results as to the role of particular aspects of the law in fuelling the crisis.[78] It has been argued that insurance costs in areas other than product liability also increased during the critical period, and that this period has in any event come to an end, the insurance industry having come to terms with the liability explosion of the last two decades.[79]

One piece of evidence which would be of value in assessing the merit of the insurance argument is the extent to which old products are the subject of litigation, the average awards of damages for such claims, and the relative insurance costs. The available evidence on these matters suggests that the insurance argument is not wholly persuasive. One survey states that only 2.7 per cent. of the products which were the subject of product liability claims were supplied more than six years before the injury.[80] Conflicting evidence was gathered by the Interagency Task Force[81]: in a survey of appeal cases in eight state jurisdictions, covering the period 1965–1978, the findings were as follows: the average product was made in 1963; 10 per cent. of the products were produced in 1955 or before, four per cent. were produced in 1950 or before; in nearly 10 per cent. of cases 10 years or more had passed between supply of the product and the occurrence of injury; in the majority of cases, injury occurred within two years of purchase.[82] This research, drawing as it does only upon appellate decisions, and relating, in some of its findings, to date of trial rather than date of injury, is not sufficiently scientific as a basis for policy. Other, apparently more reliable[83] data shows that only 2.8 per cent. of all injuries

---

[77] See McGovern, *op. cit.*, at 594.
[78] 3 Interagency Task Force on Product Liability, U.S. Dept. of Commerce, Final Report of the Legal Study 1–36 (1977).
[79] Rosen, *op. cit.*, p. 835.
[80] "Massery, Date-of-Sale Statutes of Limitation—A New Immunity for Product Suppliers" [1977] Ins.L.J. 535.
[81] Report, n. 78 above, at 75.
[82] See discussion in Schwartz, *op. cit.*, at 813 *et. seq.*
[83] *Ibid.* at 813.

which resulted in claims, and which gave rise to 6.6 per cent. of total compensation paid, were caused by products which were at least 10 years old.[84]

An alternative approach to the cut-off problem, canvassed in versions of the proposed federal legislation,[85] is to assign a useful life to particular products and then to time-bar claims in respect of injuries suffered after the expiry of the useful life. This suggestion is so fraught with practical difficulties as to render its adoption unlikely.

CONCLUSION

The existence of a long stop of 10 years in the Consumer Protection Act 1987 is broadly in keeping with the approach of United States jurisdictions. A number of practical and policy considerations support this position. However, it must be recalled that United States product liability law, taken together with peculiarities of the United States legal system, is significantly more burdensome upon the manufacturer than the new scheme of liability in the United Kingdom. In the absence of sufficiently convincing evidence that there will be a serious increase in costs for manufacturers or their insurers, it is difficult to counter the argument that liability should run for as long as the product is defective. Given the known latency of many product risks, it is fundamentally unjust to bar a claim on an arbitrary cut-off test, perhaps before the cause of action has even accrued.

---

[84] See Martin, "A Statute of Repose for Product Liability Claims" 50 Fordham L.Rev. 745 (1982), referred to by Schwartz, *op. cit.*, at 847.
[85] See Reynolds, *op. cit.*, at 695.

Chapter 8

CONCLUSION

Cogent policy reasons justified the introduction of a scheme of strict liability for product defects. However, the regime contained in Part I of the Consumer Protection Act 1987 falls some way short of providing a true system of strict liability. The new rules carry so much uncertainty and in important respects bear so many similarities to the law of negligence that some doubt can be cast upon the usefulness of the legislation.

It was always clear that the introduction of a statutory scheme covering a major area such as product liability would necessarily involve the exclusion of certain persons from the scope of reparation. The drawing of the required boundaries is done by a new set of concepts, in particular, "defect," "product," "damage" and the development risks defence. Each of these concepts carries with it uncertainties and ambiguities which are capable of being resolved only after litigation. Perhaps the least clear of these concepts is the elusive notion of "defect." The Act gives no readily ascertainable objective standard against which products can be measured. A major policy aim of the reformers was the encouragement of higher safety standards, but a manufacturer must have a clear understanding of the type of deficiency which could expose him to litigation. The lack of clarity evident in the Act's definition will minimise its hortatory function.

Replacing the doctrine of reasonable care with a criterion which focuses upon the product introduces so many variables into the inquiry that the ability of courts rationally to adjudicate upon product design can be called into question. Seeking refuge from the ad hoc nature of a simple consumer expectation test, many American courts, urged on by academic commentators, have devised often quite complex risk-benefit indicators—so-called "decisional models." It is not to be expected that courts in the United Kingdom will follow this example. However, some flesh requires to be put on to the rather bare criterion in the Act, at least in order that legal advisers can advise their clients with some degree of certainty. Some form of risk-benefit model may achieve this aim.

As far as the concept of "product" and the chain of liability is concerned, the scheme in the Act strikes a fair balance. The

213

economic efficiencies which could have been achieved by a pure form of channelling of liability have rightly been sacrificed in order to afford proper protection to injured persons. Again however, the new concept creates some shadows of ambiguity, for example as regards the treatment of information products.

Important questions will also arise in regard to the use of warnings and instructions attached to products. The Act is likely to create an increase in the use of such information, but it is doubtful whether the criteria for strict liability in warnings cases has advanced much beyond that of the law of negligence. If in 1995 the development risks defence is removed from the regime of liability, then courts in the United Kingdom may be faced with the apparent illogicality of finding that a manufacturer is liable in respect of an undiscoverable defect which he therefore could not have warned against.

The Act is quite definite on the matter of recoverable loss, although as the general American experience demonstrates there is significant room for improvement upon the rather unsubtle approach typified by decisions such as the *East River*[1] case. The prospect of widespread recovery of damages for pure economic loss has receded from the horizon of potential developments in the common law of negligence, and in commercial cases, this can be justified. However, there is again room for development in the context of pure economic loss suffered by consumers.

In general the defences available under the Act are reasonable, with some minor difficulties of interpretation, and with the exception of development risks.

These criticisms would perhaps have been rather insubstantial on their own and the uncertainties inherent in the new scheme would have been tolerable in a properly constructed regime of strict liability. The new rules, while in places opaque and requiring of judicial interpretation, would have comprised a worthwhile step forward for the law. These new concepts should eventually, in some cases after litigation, provide more certainty than the open-textured language of the common law. With certainty will come shorter judgments, speedier justice and less expensive litigation. However, at least in the early life of the new rules these objectives may be frustrated since it is to be thought that many plaintiffs will proceed as in the United States on alternative negligence and strict liability grounds. The

---

[1] *East River Steamship Corp.* v. *Transamerica Delaval Inc.* 106 S.Ct. 2295 (1986). Discussed fully in Chap. 5, above.

real problem is that the new scheme is imbalanced because of the inclusion of a development risks defence.

There remains some underlying uncertainty about just how marginal or otherwise the changes wrought in the law of reparation by the shift to the new regime will prove to be. For defects caused by the manufacturing process there will, arguably, be no real change—such defects should trigger liability under negligence as well as under the new rules. Similarly, for defects which could not feasibly have been discovered the development risks defence returns us to a position close to that in the law of negligence. However, in the key area of design defects, the major impact of the changes brought about by the Act may be felt. The new rules will provide the courts with more opportunities to stigmatise a design as defective than under the law of negligence. If the courts take these opportunities, the new rules could have a significant impact.

There is much wrong with the United Kingdom system of compensating those who suffer loss. If one area of the law of tort is to be hived off and reformed, such as has taken place with product liability, then the reforms must, to be justifiable, have real significance. So many inadequacies remain in the legislation and in the common law that the voices of those seeking a more radical approach to compensation will not, even in the field of product liability, be stifled.

As originally mooted, with no development risks defence, the scheme of strict liability represented a balanced whole, albeit with some inherent uncertainties. That balance has been upset by the inclusion of a development risks defence, which goes even further than permitted by the Directive. If given a lenient interpretation, this defence could make the step forward achieved by the Act so minimal as to be of doubtful worth. Arguably, an equally effective and much less problematic shift in favour of the victims of defective products could have been achieved by reversing the burden of proof so that the producer would have to establish that he had taken reasonable care.[2]

However, the presence of the development risks defence is to be reviewed in 1995. In the present writer's view, it is only if this review results in removal of the defence that the new legislation will have been truly worthwhile. Even then, however, as the foregoing discussion has endeavoured to show, there is

---

[2] For the Law Commissions' views on this matter, see Cmnd. 6831 (1977), paras. 34–37.

significant room for improvement both in the legislation and in the common law.

Meanwhile, in the United States, intensive lobbying[3] goes on in an attempt to secure the passing of federal legislation which may return the liability standard to that of negligence. The United States system certainly has its problems, although these are not the making of the substantive law. In Europe, the "lowest-common-denominator" approach to change has triumphed. All that was needed was for one Member State to insist upon the inclusion of the development risks defence and most of the others were virtually forced to adopt a similar position lest manufacturing interests in their own countries be placed at a disadvantage. In this way, the well-balanced proposals of the major contributors to the debate on reform of the law were seriously diluted, and principle gave way to pragmatism.

[3] For an interesting account of some of the claims made on behalf of the manufacturers' lobby, see Twerski, "A Moderate and Restrained Federal Product Liability Bill: Targeting the Crisis Areas for Resolution" 18 Univ. of Mich.J. of L.Ref. 575 (1985). For the first time in the history of federal attempts at reform, a Uniform Product Safety Bill obtained, on June 14, 1988, the approval of the House of Representatives' Energy and Commerce Committee: *The Financial Times* August 25, 1988. However, there is still a long way to go before such legislation is passed, and there is no pressing reason to suggest that this attempt will fare better than the various others which in recent years have foundered.

INDEX